Christ, our righteousness

Titles in this series:

1 *Possessed by God*, David Peterson
2 *God's Unfaithful Wife*, Raymond C. Ortland Jr
3 *Jesus and the Logic of History*, Paul W. Barnett
4 *Hear, My Son*, Daniel J. Estes
5 *Original Sin*, Henri Blocher
6 *Now Choose Life*, J. Gary Millar
7 *Neither Poverty nor Riches*, Craig L. Blomberg
8 *Slave of Christ*, Murray J. Harris
9 *Christ, our Righteousness*, Mark A. Seifrid
10 *Five Festal Garments*, Barry G. Webb
11 *Salvation to the Ends of the Earth*, Andreas J. Köstenberger
   and Peter T. O'Brien

NEW STUDIES IN BIBLICAL THEOLOGY 9

Series editor: D. A. Carson

Christ, our righteousness

PAUL'S THEOLOGY OF JUSTIFICATION

Mark A. Seifrid

APOLLOS

INTERVARSITY PRESS
DOWNERS GROVE, ILLINOIS 60515

APOLLOS (an imprint of Inter-Varsity Press),
38 De Montfort Street, Leicester LE1 7GP, England
World Wide Web: www.ivpbooks.com
Email: ivp@uccf.org.uk

INTERVARSITY PRESS
PO Box 1400, Downers Grove, Illinois 60515, USA
World Wide Web: www.ivpress.com
Email: mail@ivpress.com

First published 2000
Reprinted 2000, 2003

British Library Cataloguing in Publication Data
A catalogue record for this book is available from the British Library.

UK ISBN 0–85111–470–9

Library of Congress Cataloging-in-Publication Data
This data has been requested.

US ISBN 0–8308–2609–2

Set in Times New Roman
Typeset in Great Britain
Printed in Great Britain by Creative Print and Design (Wales), Ebbw Vale

Therefore the Christ who is grasped by faith
and who lives in the heart
is the true Christian righteousness,
on account of which God counts us righteous
and grants us eternal life.

Martin Luther, on Galatians 2:16,
in Luther's Works, ed. J. Pelikan (vols. 1–30) and H. Lehmann (vols. 31–55),
vol. 26, *Lectures on Galatians 1535, chapters 1–4*,
trans. J. Pelikan (St Louis: Concordia, 1963)

Contents

Series preface   11

1. **The conversion of Paul as the justification of the**
   ungodly   13
   The pre-Christian Paul and the nation of Israel   17
      Paul and ethnicity   19
      Paul and the exile   21
   Paul's conversion   25
      Paul's pursuit of the law   25
      Paul's persecution of the church   28
      Paul's conversion according to Acts   30
   Conclusion   32

2. **The righteousness of God: the message of Romans**   35
   The revelation of the 'righteousness of God'   36
      Faith and the revelation of God's righteousness   37
      The 'righteousness of God' in biblical usage   38
      The 'righteousness of God revealed in the
      gospel   45
   The justification of God and the ungodly   47
      The righteousness of God's wrath against
         idolatry (Rom. 1:18–32)   48
      The impartiality of divine judgment
         (Rom. 2:1–16)   51
      The possession of the law as no advantage
         (Rom. 2:17–29)   54
      The advantage of the Jew in the oracles of
         God (Rom. 3:1–18)   56
      The law of God and the righteousness of God
         (Rom. 3:19–20)   60
      The righteousness of God in Christ
         (Rom. 3:21–26)   63
   Justification and hope (Rom. 3:27 – 8:39)   67

3. **Beyond Romans: justification by faith in the letters of Paul**   67
    The Thessalonian correspondence   77
    Galatians   79
    The Corinthian correspondence   83
    Philippians   88
    Justification in the later letters of Paul   90

4. **The righteousness of God and the law of God**   95
    Paul's legal terms   95
        'Law' and related terms   96
        'Letter' in Paul's usage   98
        The 'works of the law'   99
    The law as witness to the righteousness of
    God in Christ   105
        Selected passages from Galatians
            Galatians 2:15–21   106
            Galatians 3:1 – 4:7   107
            Galatians 4:21–31   109
            2 Corinthians 3:1–18   109
            Romans 7:1 – 8:11   114
            Romans 9:30 – 10:13   119
        Summary   123

5. **The justification of the ungodly and the obedience of faith**   129
    Faith as God's work through the gospel   130
    Faith as obedience to the gospel   133
    The faith of Christ   139
    Faith and justification   147
    Justification by faith and judgment according
    to works   147

6. **The justification of ungodly Israel and the nations**   151
    Israel as the creation of God's promise
        (Rom. 9:1–13)   152
    God's righteousness and Israel's rejection
        (Rom. 9:14 – 10:21)   154
    The triumph of God in Israel's redemption
        (Rom. 11:1–36)   158
    Israel's exile in Romans 9 – 11   168

7. **Justification in Paul, the New Testament witness**
   and beyond   171
        Justification as verdict and vindication   171
        Justification in the witness of the New Testament   177
        Faith, works, and justification according to James   179
        Justification and Protestant–Roman Catholic
        dialogues   183
        Christian preaching of the gospel   185

Bibliography   187
Index of authors   199
Index of subjects   201
Index of Bible references   207
Index of ancient writings   221

Series preface

New Studies in Biblical Theology is a series of monographs that address key issues in the discipline of biblical theology. Contributions to the series focus on one or more of three areas: 1. the nature and status of biblical theology, including its relations with other disciplines (e.g., historical theology, exegesis, systematic theology, historical criticism, narrative theology); 2. the articulation and exposition of the structure of thought of a particular biblical writer or corpus; and 3. the delineation of a biblical theme across all or part of the biblical corpora.

Above all, these monographs are creative attempts to help thinking Christians understand their Bibles better. The series aims simultaneously to instruct and to edify, to interact with the current literature, and to point the way ahead. In God's universe, mind and heart should not be divorced: in this series we will try not to separate what God has joined together. While the notes interact with the best of the scholarly literature, the text is uncluttered with untransliterated Greek and Hebrew, and tries to avoid too much technical jargon. The volumes are written within the framework of confessional evangelicalism, but there is always an attempt at thoughtful engagement with the sweep of the relevant literature.

Dr Mark Seifrid is no novice with respect to justification in the thinking of the apostle Paul. Quite apart from the 1992 publication of his doctoral dissertation, *Justification by Faith: The Origin and Development of a Central Pauline Theme* (Leiden: Brill), he has continued his work on this theme in constant study that has generated a series of careful essays. He is persuaded, rightly, that while the 'new perspective on Paul' has made some gains and overturned some errors, its diverse forms converge in several ill-judged errors that touch something central in Christian thought: how men and women may be right with God. Dr Seifrid not only expounds the place of justification in Paul's thought, but shows how the apostle fits into his own historical context, and how his writings on this theme fit into the Christian canon. For Dr Seifrid understands that the issues turn not only on minute exegesis, but on exegesis that is grounded in central biblical themes and terminology. But he is no slave to mere traditionalism. He does not hesitate to amend more traditional formulations that he judges inadequate. Everywhere in this volume there is a careful listening to texts.

Dr Seifrid would be the first to acknowledge that in some ways this is an introductory essay, a survey of the whole. Detailed exegesis and reflection belong to other volumes. But it is this holistic vision that makes this book so powerful. One may disagree here and there with minor exegetical points, while coming away with a much better grasp of what is at stake. We perceive in the welter of contemporary discussion on justification that there are some fundamental truths, truths bound up with the honour and glory of God, that must not be ignored or minimized. This book has a prophetic quality, and my earnest hope is that Dr Seifrid will not prove to be without honour in his own country.

D. A. Carson
Trinity Evangelical Divinity School

Chapter One

The conversion of Paul as the justification of the ungodly

According to his own testimony, Paul's coming to faith in Christ involved the surrender of the heritage and piety which he once treasured:

> If anyone else supposes that they might boast in the flesh, I far more: circumcised the eighth day, of the nation of Israel, of the tribe of Benjamin, a Hebrew of Hebrews, according to the law, a Pharisee, according to zeal, a persecutor of the church, according to the righteousness which is in the law, blameless (Phil. 3:4b–6).

We may therefore properly describe his encounter with the risen Christ as his 'conversion'. He clearly did not cease to be a Jew, to love his kinspeople, and to cherish the hope of their salvation (see e.g. Rom. 9:1–5; 11:1–2). Nor did he abandon his high view of the law – indeed, its holiness most probably rose in his estimation (Rom. 7:12). He did, however, decisively reject the ideals which had shaped and guided his life up to that point. That which had been his pride and honour became for him mere 'dung', in view of 'that surpassing thing of knowing Christ Jesus my Lord' (Phil. 3:8). He does not mince words concerning the revaluation of his values. If we are to interpret Paul and his gospel of God's justifying work in Christ, we must gain some understanding of the Judaism which he knew, and with which he broke. Quite naturally, therefore, Paul's conversion has been and undoubtedly shall continue to be the subject of scholarly interest.[1] Here we can give only a brief overview of this topic as a sort of prologue to our investigation of the message of justification in his letters.

---

[1] On this topic see, inter alia, Kim 1982; Hengel 1991; Seifrid 1992a: 136–181; Avemarie 1996a; Hengel & Schwemer 1997: 91–101; Longenecker 1997.

Over the past twenty years or so, a significant change has taken place in the way most scholars assess first-century Judaism. From the beginnings of critical biblical study until well into the twentieth century, Protestant scholarship often was guided by a misleading image of Paul and his Jewish contemporaries.[2] Frequently, it was supposed that they regarded eternal life as based upon a weighing and recompense of deeds, and consequently could never be assured of acquiring sufficient 'merit' to relieve the burden of sin. In coming to faith in Christ Paul found relief for his guilty conscience, or so it was thought. Although various studies of early Judaism challenged this view, it was a provocative article on Paul which especially caught the attention of more recent scholarship, and marked the changing perspective which was to emerge in years to come. The author of that article, Krister Stendahl, claimed that there is no evidence in Paul's letters that he ever suffered from an 'introspective conscience', burdened by the pangs of guilt. This image, he argued, is largely a projection of western culture.[3] Following Stendahl's article, E. P. Sanders' (1977) comparison of Paul's thought with the understanding of salvation found in a broad range of early Jewish materials appeared.[4] With this study a 'new perspective on Paul' emerged among biblical scholars (Dunn 1983: 95–122).

In place of the older misconceptions, Sanders found in early Jewish thought a 'pattern of religion', which he summarized as follows:

(1) God has chosen Israel and (2) given the law. The law implies both (3) God's promise to maintain the election and (4) the requirement to obey. (5) God rewards obedience and punishes transgression. (6) The law provides for means of atonement,

---

[2] See the history of research in Avemarie 1996a.

[3] Stendahl 1963. Often this older image of Paul is attributed to Luther, a comparison which fits neither Paul nor Luther. It is overlooked that Luther knew a lenient penitential tradition as well as a strict one. Although he was given assurance that God's anger against sin was satisfied with a 'mere sigh' of repentance, he simply could not persuade himself that such comfort was valid: 'For I used to ask myself, "Who knows whether such consolations are to be believed?"' (WA 40.II.411.14, cited and translated by Steinmetz 1995: 8). Having found the answer to his questions in the word of promise fulfilled in Christ, it was the 'cheap grace' of the sale of indulgences which stirred him out of his more or less personal concerns into public action (see Brecht 1985: 183–202). Luther did not regard the conscience which torments itself with guilt as something positive, but as a tool of the devil. It is the last resort of the fallen human being in which we seek to escape God. On Luther's anguished conscience, see Steinmetz 1995: 1–11 and Rupp 1953: 102–120.

[4] See also Sanders 1982; 1983; 1991 and 1992.

and atonement results in (7) maintenance or re-establishment of the covenantal relationship. (8) All those who are maintained in the covenant by obedience, atonement and God's mercy belong to the group which will be saved. An important interpretation of the first and last points is that election and ultimately salvation are considered to be by God's mercy rather than human achievement (Sanders 1977: 422).

This 'covenantal nomism' was characteristic of Paul and most Jews of his day. In place of the priority given to judgment and recompense in older Protestant scholarship, Sanders lays emphasis upon God's election of Israel. One was 'in the covenant', i.e. elected to salvation, unless by a heinous transgression (without repentance) one chose to remove oneself from it (1977: 136–137). All one needed to do to enjoy forgiveness was to 'intend' to remain within the covenant which God had established with his people (1977: 182).

As Philippians 3:4–6 indicates, there is something that rings true in this criticism of the older portrait of Paul. When Paul speaks of his past life in Judaism, he speaks of that of which he was proud and in which he regarded himself as successful. There is no good indication in Paul's letters that he once was burdened with a sense of guilt. Not even Romans 7 reveals much in this regard, since in this chapter Paul does not describe his psychological state, but his condition as seen from the perspective of faith.

It must be said, however, that Sanders' own work is subject to one of the criticisms that he directed against the older treatments of early Judaism. Just as earlier Protestant works interpreted the rabbinic materials solely in terms of their expressions of expectation of recompense at the final judgment, Sanders reconstructs the early Jewish understanding of salvation through the lens of God's election of Israel.[5] In a very thorough and careful study, Friedrich Avemarie

---

[5] 'Rabbinic' Judaism refers to the Judaism which developed in the second century AD, and was represented especially by the Mishna, Tosephta and narrative writings (*haggadoth*), and the (later) forms of the Talmud. Traditions which appear in these materials, and authorities which they cite, extend back into the second century BC, and in some measure represent the Judaism which Paul knew. Other materials, such as the so-called 'apocrypha' and pseudepigrapha of the Old Testament (transmitted primarily through Christians), which were actually composed in the first century or earlier, provide a more direct image of the agitation and diversity within Judaism of this period. Here we may also think of Jewish contemporaries such as Philo and Josephus. To these we must also add the writings which have been discovered at Qumran for a proper understanding of early Judaism.

(1996a) has shown that rabbinic Judaism tolerated a certain tension between affirmations of Israel's unconditioned election and God's demand for righteous conduct.[6] Although Sanders' paradigm for understanding early Judaism enjoys broader support in the materials than the older view, it is also quite clear that the rabbis also could speak of salvation as being contingent upon obedience. In fact, they could even speak of the salvation of Gentiles (those outside 'the covenant') on the basis of good deeds.[7] Rather than striving to produce a system in which all apparent contradictions were eliminated, the rabbis viewed salvation from at least two independent perspectives.[8] In other words, in the rabbinic materials, 'covenantalism' stands alongside 'nomism' without the overarching synthesis which Sanders has proposed.

When we shift our attention to the pseudepigrapha and the Qumran writings, which provide a more vivid and direct picture of first-century Judaism, it becomes clear that first-century Jews could indeed regard salvation as contingent upon obedience.[9] Of course, this belief does not at all mean that they felt uncertain about their salvation. Indeed, the evidence from Paul's letters suggests just the opposite. Israel's possession of the law and conformity to its demands set it apart from

---

[6] See also Avemarie 1996b and 1999.

[7] See Avemarie 1996a: 575–584; 1999: 108–126: Israel's salvation at Sinai depended on its obedience, as did its future deliverance from hell (Midr. Deut. 33:2; *Lev. Rab.* 1:11). Likewise, the salvation of certain individuals is said to result from their obedience (*y. Pe'a* 1:1). The reward for keeping the law is eternal life (*'Abot R. Natan* B 10). Righteous Gentiles may inherit the world to come (*t. Sanh.* 13:2; *b. 'Abod. Zar.* 10b). Avemarie (1996b) has further shown that while Sanders associates Israel's election with the Sinai covenant, in the rabbinic materials it is connected to the promises to the fathers.

[8] Correspondingly, while the rabbis at times speak of God's gracious forgiveness of Israel or of sinners within it, they also provide a variety of grounds for this divine action: notions of the sacrificial system might be operative, or the Israelites might atone for one another, or God acts on behalf of his name or promises (see *Lev. Rab.* 27:3; 30:12, to which Dr Avemarie called my attention).

[9] A number of factors may account for the differences between these writings and the rabbinic materials. Rabbinic Judaism represents a consolidation of Jewish thought over a long period, following two wars with Rome, and the destruction of the temple. It was therefore inherently broader and more inclusive in outlook, less directed to specific situations, and more oriented toward ongoing Jewish life in the wake of these events. The pseudepigraphal writings and those from Qumran were intended to preserve and extend particular forms of piety in competition with other groups which made up the variety of Jewish life prior to the first Jewish revolt. Generally they have a polemical edge, and not infrequently draw boundaries which exclude other Jews from salvation. Cf. Seifrid 1992a: 78–135.

the nations as God's chosen people.[10] And within Israel, there were those like Paul who excelled in their understanding and practice of the law, and therefore stood out as particularly pious members of the nation.[11]

Philippians 3:4–6 again shows that Paul's view of his standing before God was shaped both by Israel's election and by his own obedience to the law. Although we shall have more to say about this matter in the course of this study, we may suggest here that Paul's conversion involved two dimensions. On the one hand, he came to understand that God's judgment rests upon the entire human race, including Israel itself. In his own terms, he would say that he came to see that God has subjected all human beings to the power of sin (e.g. Rom. 3:9; see Laato 1995). No longer did mere membership in the nation of Israel hold the promise of salvation for him. The promises given to Israel had been fulfilled in the risen Christ, and were to be possessed by faith. No longer did he regard conformity to the law as attainable by his efforts. Right and true though that demand is, Paul recognized that he was unable to fulfil it. He was a prisoner to 'the law of sin' in his 'members' (Rom. 7:23). Concomitantly, the mercy of God thereby became the mercy of *God* for Paul, that is, the free act of the Creator, dependent on neither the national heritage nor the piety of its recipients. 'He did not spare his own Son, but gave him up for us all' (Rom. 8:32). Once, for Paul, as for his contemporaries, Israel's election and the demand of the law stood side by side in unresolved tension. Now he found their resolution, not in some synthesis or new idea, but in an event: the incarnation, crucifixion and resurrection of the Son of God. In Christ the demand of the law and the fulfilment of promise meet.

The pre-Christian Paul and the nation of Israel

The wide acceptance of Sanders' interpretation of Paul and early Judaism has led many to look for new ways to understand Paul's conversion and subsequent theology.[12] Two current approaches attempt

---

[10] See e.g. Rom. 2:17–19; 9:30 – 10:4; Gal. 2:11–21.

[11] In addition to Phil. 3:4–6, see Gal. 1:14.

[12] Sanders himself was content to describe Paul's conversion as an inexplicable break with his past. In his view, we can know only that Paul had a revelation in which he came to believe that Christ is the Saviour of Jew and Gentile alike (1977: 441–442; 1982: 432–433; 1983: 208). Yet most scholars have been dissatisfied with this appeal to ignorance. Paul's continued regard for the law of Moses, his affirmation of the election of Israel, and his arguments from the Hebrew Scriptures call for some explanation of his

to explain Paul by focusing upon his beliefs regarding the nation of Israel apart from questions of his personal piety. From the very start, we may be suspicious of the exclusion of the latter topic, which runs through early Judaism and Paul's letters. Nevertheless, we must consider the details of these proposals on their own merits. One of these more recent interpretations of Paul argues that his conversion had to do with his rejection of claims to Jewish national privilege. In this reading, Paul was converted from an insistence upon circumcision and other 'works of the law' as boundary markers which signalled Israel's exclusive possession of the promise of salvation. He later took up this teaching in the controversy over Gentile circumcision, arguing that God's grace applies to all nations (see esp. Dunn 1990: 183–241; 1997). Or, in a variation on this theme, Paul is supposed to have understood Christ to replace the law as the boundary marker of a redefined Israel (Donaldson 1997a). Another approach claims that Paul and most Jews of his day regarded themselves as still enduring the experience of the exile to Babylon. According to this paradigm (at least in some of its representations) one need not suppose that Paul was conscious of any personal guilt: the cross supplies the answer to his plight as a member of the nation. This understanding of Paul appears to integrate his post-conversion thought very nicely with the Judaism he once practised. The theology of his letters is a continuation of that for which he had always hoped, to which the new insight is added that the hour of salvation had arrived in Christ.

These new ways of interpreting Paul in terms of 'ethnicity' and 'exile' are not mutually exclusive, of course. One might suppose that the pre-Christian Paul was confident of God's promises to Israel and that at the same time he regarded the nation as currently experiencing the exile. Moreover, as we have suggested, both readings depend on a problematic distinction between Paul's national consciousness and his personal piety (cf. Gal. 1:14; Phil. 3:4–6). In the end, Sanders' theory and these newer 'national' interpretations of Paul's conversion represent complementary caricatures. Whereas Sanders supposes that Paul made a more or less irrational break with his Jewish beliefs, the 'national' portrayals of Paul's conversion seek to establish a continuity that Paul would never have accepted. They overlook Paul's understanding of the new creation which has come about in Christ (2 Cor. 5:16–17). In his view, his conversion was the gift of sight to a blind person, the opening of his eyes to see the glory of Christ (2 Cor.

---

conversion against his Jewish background.

4:1–6). In that vision of Christ, and only there, he saw the truth about himself. His conversion involved a conscious turning away from his past. Yet it cannot be explained in mere intellectual, psychological or ethical terms.[13]

Paul and ethnicity

The claim that Paul's rejection of symbols of ethnic privilege stood at the centre of his conversion and subsequent theology has led to considerable discussion over the meaning of the expression 'the works of the law' in the letters of Paul. Although we shall reserve our discussion of this expression for a later chapter, a number of preliminary comments are appropriate here.

In large measure, the new 'ethnic' reading of 'the works of the law' comes as a reaction to the once influential 'existential' interpretation of Paul. In the mid-twentieth century, the New Testament scholar Rudolf Bultmann interpreted the pursuit of 'works of the law' as a self-striving to gain God's approval. Paul regarded such works as wrong because they represented an assertion of the ego, a failure to trust in God. One wins life not by self-effort, but by yielding oneself to God. There is some truth to this analysis of Paul's thought, but it is only a half-truth. Bultmann and his pupils elevated the formal aspect of faith, utter reliance upon God, to the status of an absolute in their appropriation of Paul's thought (although, we must point out, not always in their description of it).[14] In so doing they turned 'faith' into an insight at which in theory any reflective human being might arrive. The cross thereby becomes a mere symbol for an enduring reality and in principle is dispensable.[15]

The 'new perspective' on Paul sets aside this existential paradigm and argues instead that Paul abandoned a 'nationalistic' pride at his conversion. Although this change in perspective seems dramatic, the portrait of Paul it presents is not essentially different from that of Bultmann. Both readings understand Paul to have arrived at an insight which is essentially accessible to every human being. His coming to faith cannot legitimately be reduced to the embrace of an ethical stance

---

[13] For a brief survey of Christian understanding of conversion in the light of Paul's conversion, see Corley 1997.

[14] See Bultmann 1951: 270–274, 314–324, where the emphasis on the 'existential' aspect of faith is clear.

[15] Here, again, we must acknowledge that Bultmann somewhat inconsistently never regarded it so.

any more than it can be described as the gaining of an existential insight. Did Paul need the 'word of the cross' to tell him that a selfish nationalism was wrong? Could he not gather that much from the Scriptures themselves? Indeed, it is not at all clear that a Jewish nationalism in itself is wrong. Don't the Scriptures speak of the streaming of the nations to Zion (Is. 2:1–4; Mic. 4:1–5)? Why would it have been evil for Paul to embrace an 'ethnocentric' interpretation of the promise of salvation? What was so terribly wrong about seeking to gather the Gentiles into Judaism as his opponents in Galatia did? As we shall see, despite a decisive difference between Paul and his opponents, his gospel 'to the Jew first' is no less nationalistic than was theirs.

Furthermore, Paul does not at all reject the emblems of Jewish identity. He always employs Jewish terminology such as '(the) circumcision', 'those of the circumcision', or 'those of the law' and even 'the person of the works of the law' in a neutral sense, or even positively.[16] He never speaks negatively of circumcision. As an ethnic symbol it is a matter of indifference for him.[17] Nowhere in his letters does he attack Jewish observance of the law, and in fact he indicates that he himself returned to it (1 Cor. 9:20; cf. Acts 18:18; 21:15–26). It is therefore striking that he speaks of 'those who are of the works of the law' as being under 'the curse of the law' (Gal. 3:10). In view of his broader usage, it is altogether unlikely that he has the 'ethnicity' of such works in view.[18] Indeed, despite the inclusion of the Gentiles in God's promise to Abraham, the priority of the 'Jew' is fundamental to his gospel.[19] It is not the particularity of the promise which he combats

---

[16] See Rom. 2:25–28; 4:10–12, 14; 15:8; Gal. 2:16, and the discussion in chapter 4 below.

[17] Gal. 5:6; 6:15; 1 Cor. 7:18–19. Circumcision has prophetic-typological significance for Paul, as a prefigurement of the saving realities of faith and the work of the Spirit, and as such conveys no intrinsic saving advantage (Rom. 4:9–12; 2:25–29; Phil. 3:3; Eph. 2:11–13; Col. 2:11; 3:11). Only when this truth is violated and circumcision becomes a mark of piety does circumcision become a threat to the gospel for Paul (Rom. 2:25–29; 4:9–12; Gal. 5:2–6).

[18] Dunn has come some distance toward recognizing this aspect of Paul's thought, since he is willing to speak of the 'works of the law' as a test case for (Jewish) faithfulness (1990: 244–245; 1997: 151). Yet he still insists upon a disjunction between 'corporate' and 'individual' identity, and therefore downplays the saving significance of that 'faithfulness'. He supposes that the issue lay simply in determining how far the blessing of the covenant extends: Paul opposes practices which separate Jew from Gentile, i.e., faithful from unfaithful (1990: 246; 1997: 151–152). Of course Paul did so, but one has not understood his gospel if one separates its social dimension from its individual dimension.

[19] See the discussion in chapter 6 below of Rom. 11:15, 25–36, which speak of the

in his letters, but the subsuming of the promise to Abraham into the law of Moses: 'if those of the law are heirs, faith is made empty and the promise annulled' (Rom. 4:14).

The real cause for Paul's rejection of the 'works of the law' lies beyond both self-understanding and ethics. As we shall see, faith for Paul is the correlate to Christ's cross and resurrection. It is obedience to the promise of God fulfilled in that event (see e.g. Rom. 4:13–25). One is justified not because of a mere inward disposition, but because of Christ in whom God has atoned for sin and effected a new creation. The content and basis of faith are definitive, and not merely its form. For this reason both the existential and nationalistic readings of Paul fail. On the one hand, his rejection of the 'works of the law' proceeds from a judgment about a state of affairs, not from a 'decision' to which the human being is summoned.[20] On the other hand, faith excludes 'works of the law' not because of an ethical principle such as the evil of nationalism, but because of the cross in which all such 'works' have been judged.[21] Likewise, Paul's conversion was far more than a 'paradigm shift' in which he merely adjusted his prior belief about the prerequisite for sharing in salvation.[22] It is a mistake, then, to suppose that Paul was opposed to 'works of the law' because he saw them as emblems of an exclusive, national hope of salvation. As we shall see, these 'works' bore a 'religio-national' significance for Paul's Jewish contemporaries, and likewise for him prior to his conversion (Rom. 9:30–33). He rejected them because they represented a false claim to righteousness.

Paul and the exile

According to the other current interpretation of Paul, he along with

---

salvation of Israel. His thought on this matter is not essentially different from that of Jesus (e.g. Mark 7:24–30; Matt. 10:5–6; 15:24). Cf. Donaldson 1997b. See also Dunn 1998: 526–529, who himself recognizes that Paul expects the eschatological salvation of Israel.

[20] Furthermore, within the Judaism which Paul knew, self-confidence did not exclude dependence on God's assistance, especially that given through the gift of the law. See Avemarie 1996a: 376–445; Seifrid 1992a.

[21] We may readily see this in Romans, where the contrast between the 'works of the law' and the cross (3:20–26) appears prior to that between the 'works of the law' and faith (3:27–31). In Galatians, too, Paul appeals to the cross as the basis for his rejection of the 'works of the law' (2:15–21; 3:10–14). Cf. Dunn 1992.

[22] Against Donaldson 1997a: 1–49, 185. Paul's new 'conviction' about Christ brought a judgment on himself, his works, his sin. Donaldson's thesis comes out looking more like a change of mind than a change of heart.

much of early Judaism regarded the nation as being in a continuing state of exile, despite the return to the land. The Deuteronomic pattern of events had yet to come to completion: the people awaited the removal of Israel's guilt and the promise of restoration (see esp. Deut. 28 – 30). Faith in Christ resolved Paul's deepest longing. In his encounter with the risen Christ, he came to believe that the exile had ended in the death of the Messiah, who bore the curse of the law for Israel on a Roman cross. Jesus' resurrection signalled the ushering in of the nations to share in the blessings of the covenant (see e.g. Wright 1992: 268–279; Thielman 1994: 46–48).

Despite its apparent novelty and current appeal, this reading of Paul is a mere variation on an older theme. To shift from speaking of the burden of personal guilt to that of the nation represents no real movement away from psychologism. If it is to provide an adequate explanation of Paul's thought, the exilic interpretation must suppose that generally Jews understood the nation to be in exile and that they regarded this condition to be a result of a corporate guilt in which they shared. Paul must have had this sense of malaise prior to his conversion. Afterwards it became the basis of his announcement of the gospel.

The theory implicitly assumes that the human being is capable of self-diagnosis. As with Job's sorry comforters, the problem of sin for Israel can supposedly be read off the outward course of events. In comparison with Paul's thought, this conception of sin is highly superficial, as we shall see in the following chapter. Here it is sufficient to indicate that the exilic interpretation runs into difficulties in Paul's letters themselves. The attraction which Judaism held for Paul's churches in Galatia is very difficult to understand if one assumes that Jews generally were lamenting their condition. The attractiveness of Judaism, and of Jerusalem as its centre, is felt throughout the letter to the Galatians (see Gal. 1:10 – 2:10; 2:11–21; 6:16). Paul's assertion that the heavenly Jerusalem, not the earthly, is the 'mother' of believers presupposes that the earthly city bore considerable influence in the minds of his converts (Gal. 4:21–31). He declares that the earthly Jerusalem 'is enslaved with her children', not because of Roman occupation (of which his converts already would have been aware), but because of its failure to believe the gospel (Gal. 5:25).

It is well beyond the scope of our study to investigate the complicated views of the exile which appear in early Jewish writings. Here we wish only to point out some texts which call into question the claim that many Jews in Paul's day understood Israel to be under the curse of exile.

Often in extrabiblical sources from this period, 'Israel' is divided into the pious and the wicked. Those who adhere to the demands of the law in the present will be prepared for the restoration which is yet to come. The rest will suffer punishment with the enemies of God's people (see Steck 1967: 189–192). The 'sin' of the people is no longer absolute, as the 'exilic' reading of Paul requires.[23] Those who are obedient may await the future with confidence, as for example in the book of Baruch, where the author claims, 'We praise you from our exile because we have turned away from our hearts all the unrighteousness of our fathers who sinned before you' (3:7).[24] This development is of considerable significance, since now the piety of some within the nation is decoupled from its outward condition.

The early Jewish materials often present the exile as having ended in some sense or another, even if they also regard it as continuing or recurring. The book of Judith speaks directly of the end of the exile (4:1–5; 5:17–19). The conclusion of the pseudepigraphal book of Baruch suggests that the return from exile is already in progress (4:36; 5:5–9). The Qumran community regarded itself as the remnant, delivered from the continuing guilt of the nation, even if they entered a new exile in their separation from Jerusalem.[25] The book of Tobit appears to envisage a two-stage conclusion to the exile: by God's mercy some return from the exile and rebuild the temple in an imperfect way; later all return from exile and rebuild Jerusalem in splendour. The exile has ended for some, but the 'times of fulfilment' are yet to come (Tobit 14:1–9).[26] Philo can speak of God himself as 'homeland, kinsfolk and inheritance' and regard the exile as the Jewish colonization of the world, even though he also expects an end of exile.[27] Josephus can treat the exile as having ended after seventy years, only to be followed by subsequent 'exiles', including the one he himself experienced.[28] For his own reasons, he regards exile positively and seems to lack an expectation of a return (Feldman 1997).

---

[23] Here the literature also varies from its biblical antecedents.

[24] See also the Prayer of Azariah 18. Among other early Jewish writings *1 Enoch*, Tobit, the *Psalms of Solomon*, 4 Ezra and the Qumran writings (despite their emphasis on unconditioned grace) display this sort of thinking.

[25] See, e.g., the Cairo Damascus Document 1:1–17; 3:10–21.

[26] Note that only the obedient will be saved; 14:7–9.

[27] See Philo, *Quis Rerum Divinarum Heres* 26–27. Philo's expectation of an end of exile appears in *De Praemiis et Poenis* 162–172.

[28] *Antiquities* 4:314; 10:112–113; 10:247–277; 11:1–4.

Quite understandably, those in the land could regard themselves as not being in exile. The Mishnah contains a saying ascribed to Abtalion, who lived in Jerusalem under Herodian rule in the first century BC. He warns teachers of the law to guard their words so that they may not become guilty of the punishment of exile, and be exiled to the place of 'bad waters', i.e. bad teaching. Despite subjugation to Rome, he obviously did not regard himself to be in exile (*m. 'Aboth* 1:11).[29] The form of the Passover Seder recorded in the Mishnah is significant in this regard, since it may reflect something of the practice and thought of many Jews in this period. A father is to instruct the son concerning the redemption from Egypt from Deuteronomy 26, 'beginning with the disgrace and ending with the glory' (Deut. 26:5–9). No mention is made of the subsequent description of exile and return in Deuteronomy 28 – 32 (*m. Pesạ* 10:4). This perspective is likewise apparent in the words concerning the Passover attributed to Gamaliel (just possibly the first-century Gamaliel I, although more likely his grandson):

> In every generation a person is duty-bound to regard himself as if he has personally gone forth from Egypt … Therefore we are duty-bound to thank, praise, glorify, honor, exalt, extol, and bless him who did for our forefathers and for us all these miracles. He brought us forth from slavery to freedom, anguish to joy, mourning to festival, darkness to great light, subjugation to redemption, so we should say before him, Hallelujah! (*m. Pesạ* 10:5).[30]

The celebration presupposes that contemporary Israel enjoys its initial redemption from Egypt, whatever its trials at the moment.

It is not at all clear, therefore, that there was a widespread sense among Jews of Paul's day that Israel remained in exile in the way that this theory demands.[31] The pervasive sense of national guilt and lament

---

[29] Cf. the saying of Rabbi Nehorai in *m. 'Aboth* 4:18, who speaks positively of 'exile to a place of Torah', cited by Feldman 1997. See further Dunn 1997: 148–149.

[30] I have cited the translation by Neusner 1988. Even Rabbi Aqiba, who is said to include a petition for the rebuilding of Jerusalem and proper worship in the temple, concludes the Seder with the benediction, 'Blessed are you, Lord, who has redeemed Israel!' (*m. Pesạ* 10:6).

[31] Both Wright 1992: 268–279 and Thielman 1994: 48–68 operate with an ill-defined conception of 'exile', in which they suppose that any deficiency in Israel's condition (Diaspora, temple, Roman rule) signalled to all or most Jews that the 'nation' (as a whole!) was still in exile. Even at a glance, it is apparent that early Jewish sources are far more nuanced than this, as is apparent from the few texts cited above.

which it requires is lacking in the sources. Undoubtedly many Jews in Paul's day regarded the exile as in some sense continuing. Yet many Jews also supposed that the exile had in some sense ended or that its effects had been ameliorated, even if it remained. The return to the land, the reconstruction of the temple, and the adjustment by many Jews to life in the Diaspora brought forth varied perspectives on Israel's experience.

There is no evidence that Paul, who returned from the Diaspora to Jerusalem in his youth, and who refers to his former practice of the law as 'blameless', considered himself part of a nation suffering in exile for its guilt. Furthermore, when Paul speaks of Israel's failure in his letters he treats the nation as a whole. We therefore cannot suppose that he regarded part of the nation as being in exile or as thinking itself to be in exile, as the early Jewish sources might allow. The judgment which he formed concerning his people was all-encompassing. It is derived not from an assessment of Israel's outward condition, but from its rejection of Jesus as Messiah. As we shall later see, when Israel's exile appears in Romans 9 – 11, it is in a form nearly the opposite of the 'exilic' interpretation. According to Paul, a new exile has begun in Israel's unbelief which will be ended only at the Messiah's return.

Paul's conversion

In addition to Paul's autobiographical statement in Galatians 1, several of Paul's self-references shed light on his conversion.[32] We must also take into account his statements in Romans 9 – 11 concerning Israel as a whole. Supplementing these, we have Luke's extended narrative of Paul's conversion, which appears three times in the book of Acts (9:1–19; 22:1; 26:1–23).

Paul's pursuit of the law

Paul's account of his coming to faith in Galatians is remarkably succinct. Indeed the moment of 'conversion' does not really appear at all, only his activity before and after his encounter with Christ.[33] He

---

[32] Rom. 7:7–25; 1 Cor. 15:8–10; 2 Cor. 4:1–6; Phil. 3:6; 1 Tim. 1:12–16.

[33] Fredriksen 1986, along with others, has argued that converts demonstrably remember their conversion through the lens of their (changing) experience: Paul's conversion therefore remains basically inaccessible to us. However, she fails to appreciate that Paul does not really give us an account of his *experience* of call or conversion, but only of his accompanying activities. Moreover, it is not at all clear that

introduces his brief statement about his conversion in Galatians 1:13–14 by referring to his persecution of the church, with which he assumes Galatians already are familiar. With some irony he then adds: 'And I was advancing in Judaism beyond many contemporaries in my nation, being exceedingly zealous for my ancestral traditions.'

Here, for the only time in his letters, Paul refers to his former religion as 'Judaism'. Clearly we find here the language of an outsider, who looks back upon his past with detachment. As he writes this letter, his former life had become for him an ethnic and cultural heritage, but not in itself obedience to the living God. In this respect, Paul offers himself as a model for his Galatian readers, who are inclined to adopt circumcision and thereby embrace 'Judaism'.

At the same time, the statement sheds light on Paul's thinking prior to his faith in Christ. His 'zeal' for his 'ancestral traditions' clearly was religious zeal. Conversely, his religious identity was rooted in his ethnic and national heritage. The same sort of thinking is reflected in his rehearsal of his advantages in Philippians 3:4–6, which we cited at the outset of this chapter. It is implicitly present in his characterization of Israel in Romans 9 – 10. Obviously, Paul did not understand his piety in merely private terms, but as part of a people and a tradition. He was, first of all, a member of the people whom God had chosen; secondly, an heir of a particularly faithful heritage within that nation; thirdly, an adherent of a group which strictly observed the law; and finally, personally exemplary in zeal and righteousness.

It is not clear precisely how the tension between 'election' and 'demand' which characterized early Judaism played itself out in Paul's life. We certainly cannot conclude from these statements that Paul thought that membership in Israel or the 'covenant with the fathers' ensured his salvation. As we have noted, the rabbinic materials attest the possibility of this stance, and in the Gospels we find John the Baptist preaching against a crass confidence of this sort.[34] Significantly, however, we never find Paul charging his contemporaries with harbouring the belief that they possessed a guarantee of salvation. When he does call into question a misplaced assurance on the part of Jews, it is the sufficiency of Israel's obedience which he challenges (Rom. 9:30–33). This is the case even when he dismisses the

---

we should dismiss the testimony of Acts, which does provide an external confirmation of Paul's statements.

[34] 'Do not suppose that you can say to yourselves, "We have Abraham as our Father." For I tell you, God is able to raise up children for Abraham from these stones' (Matt. 3:9; Luke 3:9).

assumption that Israel enjoyed a privileged knowledge of God's will through the law. He assumes that his rhetorical Jewish dialogue partner would agree with him that merely knowing God's will is insufficient apart from doing it (Rom. 2:17–29). Therefore Paul's consciousness of his ranking and progress in 'Judaism' (Gal. 1:14) in all likelihood means that he understood his standing with God as based not merely upon his ethnic and familial background, but also upon his own obedience to the law. He was not content to be a properly circumcised Israelite of the tribe of Benjamin. He adhered to the law as a Pharisee with a consciousness that it was an achievement which set him apart from other Jews.

A number of scholars have been quick to argue on the basis of Paul's claim to 'blamelessness with regard to the righteousness of the law' that he enjoyed a 'robust conscience' and did not suffer from guilt prior to his conversion (Phil. 3:6). To interpret Paul in this way, however, represents the same sort of psychologizing involved in the older image of Paul's anguished conscience, only in the reverse direction. We simply do not know how Paul dealt with guilt prior to his conversion. Furthermore, to interpret 'guilt' in subjective terms is to ignore the understanding of sin which appears in Paul's letters. It is not in the first instance a psychological state, but a state of affairs, a power over all human beings.[35] We do not find Paul retrospectively exploring his pre-Christian conscience, because it was irrelevant to him. Where he speaks of his preconversion life, he speaks not of what he thought or felt, but of what he did, particularly his persecution of the people of God.[36] In this he obviously regards himself as having been guilty of a fundamental sin. It is impossible to miss the irony in his final statements in Philippians 3:6. His zeal was such that he was a 'persecutor of the church', to which he adds, 'as to the righteousness which is in the law [I was] blameless'. In looking back upon his preconversion life, he sees that the law was capable of providing a righteousness according to human standards, but not before God and in the heart, where he now knows Christ as Saviour (Phil. 3:7–8).

We must therefore avoid the dead-end of a psychological interpretation of Paul's conversion. Paul himself excludes it when he declares that an act of God put an end to his pursuit of the law. Recalling the pattern of the calling of the prophets, he unmistakably

---

[35] Cf. Rom. 3:9; Gal. 3:22. We shall return to this view repeatedly in our following discussion.

[36] Gal. 1:13; Phil. 3:6; 1 Cor. 15:9.

points to the sovereign working of God as the basis of his coming to faith: 'When it pleased God, who set me apart from my mother's womb and called me by his grace, to reveal his Son to me, I did not immediately consult flesh and blood' (Gal. 1:15–16).[37]

God's choice and calling were unconditioned by Paul's 'progress in Judaism' (verse 14). From birth God had set him apart, like the prophets before him, prior to any works or worthiness on his part.[38] His 'calling' came by the sheer grace of God. His coming to faith was a matter of divine revelation in which Paul himself played no role. It was a 'birth', indeed a premature one (1 Cor. 15:8). This perspective also appears in 2 Corinthians 4:6, where Paul describes his conversion as a creation *ex nihilo*. Just as God by his word alone created light out of darkness, he caused the knowledge of the glory of God in 'the face of Jesus Christ' to shine forth as light from Paul's own heart. Paul may well allude here to the appearance to him of the risen Christ, who is the very image of God (2 Cor. 4:4–6; see Kim 1982). He is certainly not claiming, however, that this 'experience' was his alone as an apostle. The glory of Christ is present within the gospel, which itself is 'light', and is given forth through the apostle himself as a bearer of that Good News (2 Cor. 4:4, 6). This contrast which Paul draws between the absolutes of darkness and light, and his interpretation of his conversion as a new creation, make it clear that he regards this change as purely and utterly an act of God. Paul's heart was the 'darkness' in which the light of the gospel now shines.[39] A psychological preparation for conversion has no place here.

Paul's persecution of the church

As we have noted, in both Galatians 1 and Philippians 3, Paul ironically juxtaposes his persecution of the church with his progress in Judaism. In retrospect, he regards this activity as a great transgression, in which his own ungodliness was exposed.[40]

The objects of Paul's persecution, in all probability, were Jewish believers in Christ, not Gentiles.[41] Although there has been a tendency

[37] See Is. 49:1; Jer. 1:5.
[38] Cf. Rom. 9:11–12; Jer. 1:4–12.
[39] He describes the minds of 'the sons of Israel' similarly in the preceding context. Only when one turns to the Lord (i.e. Christ) is Moses' veil, the hardening of the heart, removed (2 Cor. 3:12–18).
[40] In addition to Gal. 1:13–14 and Phil. 3:6, see 1 Cor. 15:9, 'I do not deserve to be called an apostle, because I persecuted the church of God.' Cf. 1 Tim. 1:13.
[41] A Gentile mission had not developed at the time of Paul's conversion. According to

to suppose that Paul persecuted only one segment of the early believing community (Greek-speaking Jewish believers who were critical of the law) the evidence which can be mustered for this reconstruction from the book of Acts, particularly from Stephen's speech, is rather weak.[42] Paul's own unqualified statements suggest that he persecuted the whole believing community without distinction, as for example, in Galatians 1:23–24, where Paul recounts that the churches of Judea rejoiced to hear that their former persecutor proclaimed the 'faith' he once persecuted. That 'faith' can be nothing other than the message of salvation through repentance and faith in Jesus as risen Messiah and Lord.

It is worth remembering that it was not simply a confession which Paul persecuted, but a confessing community. Their insistence that salvation was to be found through repentance and faith in Jesus alone represented a judgment on their society and a challenge to their contemporaries. This was not merely the case of a group within Judaism which maintained exclusive claims, like the Essenes, who could more or less be tolerated because of their isolation. The earliest believers openly announced that the decisive moment in Israel's history had arrived, that the Messiah had appeared. Obedience to this resurrected Lord, this 'prophet like Moses', could not be postponed (Acts 3:22–26; cf. 2:36; 4:12). Moreover, it was the *crucified* Jesus whom they proclaimed as the risen Messiah, a proclamation which, as Paul's own later statements indicate, was highly offensive (1 Cor. 1:23). The Messiah represented the hope of the nation for deliverance from all her foes, and the embodiment of the well-being of the people. The fate of this one represented the righteousness of the entire nation, its vindication by God over against its enemies. It was therefore unthinkable that God would allow this saviour to be crucified.[43] Indeed, in the minds of most Jews, the Scriptures themselves pronounced a curse on the crucified Jesus: Deuteronomy 21:23, which declares that 'cursed is the one who hangs on a tree', was interpreted in this period as referring to crucifixion.[44] Paul's

---

the account in Acts, which Paul's letters give no reason to doubt, Paul's persecution of believers took place in Jerusalem in the first place. And Paul's report of the churches of Judea indicates that *they* had been the objects of his persecution (Gal. 1:22).

[42] The charges against Stephen, that he spoke against the temple and the law (Acts 6:11, 14), are unsubstantiated in his speech. He only points to the prophetic assertion that God transcends the temple and charges his adversaries with themselves failing to keep the law (Acts 7:48–53). On this topic see Hill 1992.

[43] As, in fact, the Gospels report Peter himself once saying to Jesus (Matt. 16:22).

[44] See especially the Qumran Temple Scroll 64:7–12.

persecution of the church therefore appears as an attempt to suppress the confession of the crucified Jesus as Messiah, a confession which called into question his entire conception of God, of Israel, and of himself.

Paul's conversion according to Acts

While the testimony of Acts offers nothing to change the picture of Paul's conversion we gain from his letters, it adds a new perspective on the event. As in Paul's letters, it appears that he persecuted the entire believing community, not merely one wing of it. He attacked 'the disciples of the Lord', and thought that he had to oppose 'the name, "Jesus of Nazareth" (Acts 9:1; 22:4; 26:9). According to Luke, the young man Saul guarded the robes of the witnesses to Stephen's 'blasphemy', and fully approved of putting him to death (Acts 7:54 – 8:1). Luke thereby implies that Paul was aware of the words of Stephen which brought the Sanhedrin to its action: 'Behold, I see the heavens opened, and the Son of Man standing at the right hand of God!' (7:56). This is the only direct attribution of the title 'Son of Man' to Jesus outside the Gospels. Stephen here announces the exaltation of the suffering and rejected Jesus, whom he names as 'the Righteous One' (verse 52).

Luke provides no explanation for Paul's hostility to Jesus, but his portrait fully corresponds with the conclusion that the idea of a crucified Messiah was blasphemous to him. In the report of Acts, he appears as an unusually well-connected young man, with access to the Sanhedrin and the high-priestly circle.[45] He opposed the faith of the earliest Christians because it pronounced judgment on his world and his position within that world.

According to Luke's report, Saul is blinded by the appearance of the risen Jesus, an event which clearly symbolizes his spiritual state (Acts 9:8–19; 22:11–13). When the glorified Christ addresses him with the question, 'Saul, Saul, why are you persecuting me?', he responds with complete ignorance, 'Who are you, Lord?' He could draw no connection between the exalted figure who appeared, and 'Jesus the Nazarene' whom he opposed. His blindness was an expression of his prior condition, and was removed only through the testimony of the

---

[45] Acts 9:1–2; 22:5; 26:10. Likewise Paul's family seems to have been of high status and to have enjoyed such contact; see Acts 23:12–16. Robert Plummer has called my attention to Paul's unusual connection with the high-priestly circle in Acts.

believing Ananias (9:17; 22:12–16).

Ananias' words to Saul, which are reported in 22:12–16, are in themselves of importance. God appointed Saul to know his will. This reminds us of Paul's own language in Galatians 1:15–16, where he indicates that God revealed Jesus Christ to him when it pleased God himself. Further, Saul was allowed to see 'the Righteous One'. This title, which believers apply to Jesus several times in Acts (3:14; 7:52; 22:14), is drawn from the description of the vindication of the Suffering Servant in Isaiah 53:11:

> The Righteous One, my Servant, shall justify the many.
> And he shall bear their iniquities.

We may readily infer from Luke's presentation of his encounter with Ananias that Paul received instruction in which Jesus' death and resurrection were interpreted in precisely these terms. The crucified and exalted Messiah was the Suffering Servant of Isaiah, whose death was an atonement for sin, effecting justification. In the text of Acts Ananias continues his message to Paul by urging him to be baptized immediately, calling on Jesus' name for the forgiveness of his sins (22:17). It seems likely, therefore, that from his earliest days as a believer, Paul interpreted the cross and resurrection as the justifying work of God. Once his eyes had been opened to the glory of the resurrected Christ, he understood the crucifixion of the Messiah on the basis of the Scriptures, as he was instructed.[46] Paul himself later presupposes that Peter (and other Jewish Christians) understood the cross as the justifying act of God, even if they did not fully grasp the significance of this truth (Gal. 2:15–16).[47]

In Luke's third account of Paul's conversion, an additional statement appears in the words of the risen Jesus: 'Saul, Saul, why are you persecuting me? It is hard for you to kick against the goads' (Acts 26:14). This is a proverbial form, which expresses the futility and self-inflicted harm which come from resisting an overwhelming

---

[46] We need not suppose a conflict here between Ananias' words to Saul, and Paul's claim that he received his gospel through a revelation of the risen Christ (Gal. 1:12). Luke presents Ananias as only confirming and interpreting the revelation which had already taken place. Scripture was understood similarly, as a revelation which required interpretation by divine help.

[47] It is also possible that several concise but powerful statements of Paul regarding the justifying work of Christ reflect the confession of the earliest believers (Rom. 3:21–26; 4:25; 2 Cor. 5:21).

power.[48] In context Paul narrates in considerable detail his harsh treatment of those who confessed the name 'Jesus of Nazareth'. All of it was to no avail in the face of the authority of the risen Lord, whose utterance recalls the advice of Gamaliel, 'If their counsel is of God, you shall not be able to resist them, and you may perhaps be found fighting against God' (Acts 5:39). Correspondingly, in this account Paul describes his emotions as he persecuted the church: 'I was out of my mind with rage at them [the saints], pursuing them up to and into other cities.'

As I have suggested in my translation, the word Luke uses to describe Paul's mental state conveys the idea of insanity. In the narrative Luke artfully uses a related term in Festus' protest against Paul's testimony of conversion: 'You are out of your mind, Paul!', to which Paul replies, 'I am speaking words of truth and sound thinking.' Contrary to what Festus thought, Paul was quite sane; his conversion had brought him to his senses.

Luke is not performing some sort of psychological analysis on Paul in his description of his 'madness' or in his reference to the words of the risen Jesus. Paul's 'madness' arose from his conclusion 'that it was necessary to do many things contrary to the name "Jesus of Nazareth"' (Acts 26:9). Prior to his conversion, Paul fought with heart and soul against the confession of a crucified Messiah. His rage corresponded to his blindness. The grace of God came to him like 'a plumb-line from above' without any preparation on his part, just as Paul himself indicates in his letters.

Conclusion

Both Paul and Luke interpret his conversion as an unconditioned act of God's mercy, to which Paul brought no preparation but his sins. All attempts to find a psychological basis for that conversion shatter against this foundational element of the New Testament witness. Neither anxiety over his guilt nor distress over the condition of his nation prepared him for his encounter with the risen Christ. Conversely, faith in Christ revealed something beyond a mere ethical or existential insight to Paul. His eyes were opened to see the glory of the crucified and risen Christ, who, he says, 'loved me and gave

---

[48] The earliest reference is found in a fragment of a poem by Pindar (in the Maehler edition, 2:94). See also Aeschylus, *Agamemnon* line 1624, Euripides, *Bacchanalia* 795; Aristophanes Gramm., *Historiae animalum epitome* 2.431.3; Aelius Aristides, *Pros Platōna peri rhētorikēs*, line 230.

himself up for me' (Gal. 2:20). In this same faith, the reality of his own sin and guilt was exposed. Neither his good standing as a member of the nation of Israel, nor his energetic pursuit of the law, could change who he was: a fallen human being under the power of sin and death. His national origin and personal piety represented mere 'flesh', fallen and rebellious humanity. In retrospect, he came to regard his former pursuit of the law as a partial obedience, a cheap substitute for the absolute demand of love toward God and neighbour. All his false assumptions about his own standing and that of his nation came under challenge from the community of believers who bore witness to the crucified Jesus as the risen Messiah. In his persecution of this 'church of God', Paul's ungodliness was exposed in its ugliest form. Yet precisely in the midst of this transgression God chose to reveal his Son to Paul. Then he learned that the Righteous One, who in his death bore the sins of many, justifies the ungodly.

Chapter Two

The righteousness of God: the message of Romans

Between Paul's conversion and his letter to Rome stand fourteen years of apostolic witness and labour, in which according to his own reckoning he had brought to completion the proclamation of the gospel among the Gentiles in the eastern Mediterranean: 'From Jerusalem as far as Illyricum, I have fulfilled the gospel of Christ.' Undoubtedly his understanding of the gospel deepened in these years, especially in the severe difficulties he endured. Yet it does not appear that he developed or changed his theological commitments. He himself displays no awareness that his message changed substantially in the course of his service. The letters which he composed in this period of his ministry, despite their varying formulations, display a common understanding of the message of salvation. There is something to be gained, therefore, by examining Paul's mature exposition of his gospel in Romans. Here one is able to see something of the dimensions of 'justification' in Paul's thought, its depth and richness. Naturally, it is important to take care that we do not read Romans into Paul's other letters, each of which has its own occasion and purpose. It is equally important, however, to avoid the temptation of current scholarship to atomize his letters. As he wrote his letter to Rome, Paul looked back upon his ministry in the eastern Mediterranean as a single, completed task. We shall use it as our starting-point for exploring Paul's theology of justification, and shall return to it to examine the place of Israel in Paul's gospel.

While there has been considerable debate concerning Paul's reason for writing to Rome, the most satisfying conclusion remains that the letter introduces Paul's gospel to a primarily Gentile church which he had not planted. Other aims which have been suggested for Romans either fail to convince, or are best viewed as aspects of this larger purpose.[1] Above all else, Paul's statements in the opening and closing

---

[1] For further discussion see Seifrid 1992a: 182–210.

of the letter signal to us that his aim is to secure a commitment to the gospel he proclaimed in Rome:[2] '[Jesus Christ our Lord], through whom we have received grace and apostleship unto the obedience of faith among all the Gentiles on behalf of his name, among whom you, too, are ones called by Jesus Christ' (Rom. 1:5–6).[3]

Romans is no less occasional than the rest of Paul's letters, but in this case the occasion leads him to a thorough exposition of his gospel. The particular concerns of the house-churches which made up the Roman congregation are not absent from the letter, but they do not take centre stage. That is not to say that Paul here develops a systematic theology. He writes to those who shared Christian beliefs and practices with him, and instructs and communicates rather than presenting ideas in abstraction. Yet his directness of address derives from his gospel, in which humanity is called to account before God, and not simply from the needs of a first-century church. In the gospel, which Paul sets forth in Romans, we see the driving force of his faith, which had brought him to this point in his apostolic mission and which carried him forward.[4]

The revelation of the 'righteousness of God'

In announcing his intent to preach the gospel in the cultured city of Rome and not merely among the 'barbarians' in the provinces, Paul declares: 'I am not ashamed of the gospel, for it is the power of God for salvation for everyone who believes, for the Jew first and also for the Greek, for the righteousness of God is revealed in it from faith unto faith, just as it is written, "The righteous one shall live by faith"' (Rom. 1:16–17).

This announcement obviously represents a summary of the gospel which Paul elaborates in the course of the letter. A great deal depends on how we interpret this brief statement, and 'the righteousness of God' which Paul names as the basis of the 'good news' he proclaimed.

---

[2] See Rom. 1:1–17 and 12:1–3; 15:14–33. On this topic, see Jervis 1991.

[3] See also Rom. 1:14–15; 12:1–3; 15:13–16, 25–27.

[4] We may regard Romans (with Philippians after it) as a transition point or hinge in Paul's ministry. Behind it lies the initial Gentile mission reflected in the earlier letters (the Thessalonian correspondence, Galatians, and the Corinthian correspondence). After it comes the consolidation of largely Gentile churches, which appears in varying ways in the disputed letters (Colossians, Ephesians, and the Pastoral Epistles).

Faith and the revelation of God's righteousness

In seeking to understand Paul, we must first note that he locates 'justification' in an act of revelation: the 'righteousness of God' has been revealed in the gospel (Rom. 1:17). As he later says, it has *now* been manifest apart from the law (3:21). The gospel in which Jesus Christ is proclaimed is a 'mystery' hidden in the past, but now made known (16:25–27). This 'revealed righteousness of God' is therefore not something entirely new. It accords with 'that which has been written' (1:17).[5] 'The law and the Prophets' bear witness to this righteousness (3:21; 16:26). Correspondingly, although Scripture announced God's saving purposes, those purposes remained hidden until the arrival of the gospel. In other words, promise and fulfilment are not joined in a straightforward and transparent manner. Otherwise Paul could not speak of the gospel as the revelation of a *mystery* (16:25–27). The fulfilment of promise transcends and contradicts human expectation: the 'righteousness of God' is revealed 'by faith unto faith'.

In fact, the primary theme of Romans 1:16–17 is the demand for faith, as a glance at these verses shows. It is the exclusive means of salvation, of the revelation of God's righteousness, and of life. As we shall see, Paul regards it as integral to the way in which God justifies the ungodly. He has already described his apostolate as securing the 'obedience of faith among all the Gentiles' (1:5), and will return to this imperative of faith repeatedly in the letter. In this context, he appeals to Scripture to undergird the central role he assigns to faith: 'as it is written, "the righteous one shall live by faith"' (1:17).[6]

Faith is not new, then. The manner in which God justifies remains constant in promise and fulfilment. The text which Paul cites, Habbakuk 2:4, speaks of the one who lives by the 'faithfulness' of the vision of coming salvation, that is, by the promise of God.[7] In

---

[5] On revelation as the interpretation of scriptural mysteries, see Bockmuehl 1990.

[6] It is *in the gospel* that the righteousness of God is revealed. The placement of the prepositional phrases immediately after the verb strongly suggests that they modify it (*dikaiosynē gar theou en autō apokalyptetai ek pisteōs eis pistin*). Paul picks up the initial prepositional phrase *ek pisteōs* in the explanatory and confirming citation from Habbakuk. It is therefore highly unlikely that he refers to the faithfulness of God or Christ in the first prepositional phrase (against, inter alia, Dunn 1988: 1:43–44; Campbell 1994: 277–281). See Schlatter 1935: 39–42.

[7] Although *be'emûnātô* is generally taken to refer to the 'faithfulness of the righteous one', it is most natural to understand it as speaking of the 'faithfulness' of the vision (*hāzôn*) to which the preceding text repeatedly refers. The LXX rendering (*ho de dikaios ek pisteōs mou zēsetai*; 'the righteous one shall live by my faithfulness') reflects the sense of the Hebrew text, since it is God, of course, who brings the vision to reality.

interpreting this Scripture as speaking of the faith of the righteous one, Paul underscores the way in which Habbakuk's vision contains a call to faith. Over against the 'proud one' who relies upon wealth and earthly goods (whose 'spirit is not right within him') stands the 'righteous one' who waits for the salvation promised in the vision (Hab. 2:1–4, 5–20). To this one who believes, and this one alone, God grants 'life'. The prophetic call for faith is the same as the call of the gospel, in which the vision of salvation has come to fulfilment.

In appealing to this Scripture Paul is clarifying the meaning of the 'righteousness of God', which is revealed in the gospel. Implicitly, therefore this 'righteousness of God' is nothing other than the 'life' which is given to the one who believes. Because 'life' and 'righteousness' are contingent upon faith, Paul speaks in a twofold manner of the righteousness of God as revealed 'from faith unto faith'.[8] Faith is both the source and goal of the righteousness of God, the means of 'seeing' it and the demand which it lays upon us. 'Faith' is no mere disposition in this context, but submission to the promise of God fulfilled in the gospel.[9] Just as the work of God in Christ's cross and resurrection is revealed and effective by faith, faith is nothing other than obedience to the proclamation of that cross and resurrection.

The 'righteousness of God' in biblical usage

Paul's expression 'the righteousness of God is revealed' recalls various biblical descriptions of God's saving righteousness, particularly Psalm 98:

> Sing to the Lord a new song, for he has worked wonders,
>> His right hand and his holy arm have worked salvation for him.
> The Lord has made known his salvation;
>> To the eyes of the nations he has *revealed his righteousness*.
> He has remembered his constant love and his faithfulness to the house of Israel;
> All the ends of the earth have seen the salvation of our God.
>> (Ps. 98:1–3).

---

[8] Against Dunn 1988: 1:43–44; cf. Moo 1996: 76.

[9] Later in the letter Paul uses precisely this language to describe faith. See Rom. 6:17; Rom. 10:3. Here he anticipates his discussion of the justifying faith of Abraham into which those who believe the gospel enter.

In this psalm, as in other biblical examples, the 'righteousness of God' clearly signifies an act of God in which his saving righteousness is displayed.[10] The psalmist envisages God intervening on behalf of his people against unnamed enemies before the eyes of all the nations. Salvation comes only on account of the destruction of the enemies of the people of God. Here that thought remains in the background. The following lines of the psalm call upon the nations to rejoice as they anticipate the Lord's coming to judge the earth. God's saving act on behalf of Israel foreshadows the justice which he will effect among and for them.[11] The entire world, pictured as the distant islands, looks forward to God's saving act of judgment. We should not allow the first lines of this psalm to go unnoticed. The contention which implicitly informs the psalmist's statements involves not merely 'the house of Israel', but God himself: his 'holy arm and right hand' gain salvation *for him*. In revealing his righteousness, God was not only delivering his people, but establishing his own cause against those who contend against him.

It is currently quite common for scholars to interpret 'God's righteousness' as his 'covenant-faithfulness' toward Israel. In other words, God is 'righteous' in that he fulfils his promises to save his people.[12] Despite its initial appeal, this interpretation does not fit Psalm 98.[13] Although the Lord might be said to act out of covenant-faithfulness to his people, his action itself cannot properly be called covenantal. It rather represents the judgment of the King, who establishes justice in his creation (verse 6). As we have noted, his deliverance of Israel anticipates his 'coming' to judge savingly on

---

[10] On this topic see Stuhlmacher 1966: 117–184; Reventlow 1971: 37–102; Reumann 1982: 12–26. I shall differ from each of them in some ways, however. The biblical scholar Hermann Cremer used the Latin equivalent *iustitia salutifera* to describe this righteousness of God (Cremer 1900: 33). See Is. 9:7; 11:4; 32:16; 33:5; 41:10; 42:21; 45:8, 21, 23, 24; 46:13; 48:18; 51:5, 6, 8; 54:14, 17; 56:1; 58:8; 59:9, 16–17; 60:17; 61:10–11; 62:1; 63:1; Pss. 9:4; 22:31; 24:5; 31:1; 35:24; 36:6–7; 40:9–10; 51:14; 69:27–28; 71:15, 16; 71:19, 24; 72:1–3; 88:12; 89:15–17; 97:6; 98:2; 99:4; 103:6; 116:5; 118:19–21; 119:123, 140; 129:4; 143:1,11; 145:7.

[11] A similar image appears in Is. 51:4–8: 'My righteousness is near, my salvation has gone forth, and my arm shall judge the peoples. Upon me shall the coastlands wait, and for my arm they shall hope' (verse 5).

[12] So Westerholm 1997: 9–19, 41–49; Wright 1997: 118–133, and many others. I have discussed the biblical usage of 'righteousness' in 'Righteousness language in the Hebrew Scriptures and early Judaism: Linguistic considerations critical to the interpretation of Paul', in D. A. Carson (ed.), *Justification and Variegated Nomism* 1, *The Complexities of Second Temple Judaism* (Tübingen and Grand Rapids: Mohr [Siebeck], forthcoming).

[13] Schlatter 1935: 35–36 describes such an interpretation as a 'declaration of war' against Paul's letter to Rome.

behalf of the entire earth. The nations themselves expect to receive his saving justice (verses 7–9). For this reason the very elements of creation – the sea, the rivers and the hills – celebrate his coming.[14] The fidelity which God displays toward Israel is only one manifestation of the saving righteousness which he exercises as ruler of all.

The 'creational' context of 'God's righteousness' which appears in Psalm 98 is characteristic of biblical usage. The language of 'righteousness' appears with remarkable frequency in association with the vocabulary of 'ruling and judging', especially the root *špṭ*.[15] This activity of 'ruling and judging' extends well beyond God's relationship with Israel, as, for example, in the Genesis account of Abraham's intercession for Sodom and Gomorrah. Upon hearing of the coming destruction which God will bring upon these cities, Abraham raises the objection that there might be righteous persons who would be slain along with the wicked. For God to allow such an inequity is out of the question: 'Shall not the judge of all the earth render just judgment?' The narrative suggests that God might indeed find some 'righteous ones' among the pagans of these two cities (although he did not), and that they would deserve justice from him. God is expected to render judgment in favour of the righteous, whatever their national descent. The title given to God in the text, the 'judge of all the earth', is itself indicative of the context of biblical conception of righteousness. In the broader biblical witness, God repeatedly intervenes as the good and gracious ruler of all the earth to 'do justice and righteousness' for the weak and oppressed, who are unable to obtain justice for themselves.[16] Since evil prevails in the world which he made, God must again and again act to restore the right order of his good creation.[17] Early in Israel's history, he raised up 'judges' on behalf of his oppressed people, to work righteousness for them.[18] This task later fell to the king and to others in positions of power, who under the authority of God were to contend for the weak in society, whose rights were easily abused:

> Give, O God, your just judgments to the king

---

[14] See also, for example, Ps. 96; Is. 42:10–13; 49:13; 51:4–11.

[15] The *ṣdq* root and the *špṭ* root appear in close proximity in at least 142 contexts, a striking difference from the collocation of the *ṣdq* root with *bᵉrit*.

[16] See e.g. Pss. 9:1–20; 89:5–14; 97:1–12; 103:6; Jer. 9:23–24.

[17] See Schmid 1968 and 1974; Assmann 1990; Levin 1999. I shall offer a qualification of his views below.

[18] See Judg. 2:16–23; 5:11.

And your righteousness to the son of the king.
He will judge your people with righteousness,
And your oppressed ones with just judgment.

(Ps. 72:1–3)[19]

When this obligation was repeatedly violated, as the prophets charged Israel with doing, God determined to establish justice for himself, and to bring retribution on those who opposed him.[20] The messianic hope itself comes to expression within this framework: God promises his people a 'new' David who, unlike the previous rulers of Israel, will work justice and righteousness.[21]

In such biblical contexts the administration of justice is simultaneously judicial, legislative, and executive. The biblical authors are interested not in bare verdicts, but in the execution of justice. 'Righteousness' terminology, particularly the verbal forms, therefore often came to signify the (just) benefit which resulted from vindication in a contention or a legal proceeding. So, for example, God commands Zedekiah the king:

Perform just judgment and (do) righteousness,
Deliver the one who has been robbed from the power of the oppressor.

(Jer. 22:3)

'Justification' is viewed here as a definite action, the rectification of the weak in a particular dispute.[22] Furthermore, this usage of 'righteousness' terminology quite clearly includes the concept of a 'norm', an order within the world, which God graciously acts (again and again) to restore. 'Righteousness' therefore cannot be reduced to the idea of a 'proper relation', as often has been done in recent interpretation.[23]

The background of 'ruling and judging', together with the specificity of the biblical usage, substantially explains the idea of a 'saving

---

[19] See also e.g. 2 Sam. 8:15; 1 Kgs. 10:9; Jer. 22:3; Prov. 31:8–9.

[20] See e.g. Is. 1:10–26; 58:1–14; Amos 5:1–27.

[21] See e.g. Is. 9:1–6; Jer. 23:5–6.

[22] Hermann Cremer (1900) made this important observation regarding the biblical usage a century ago. When it is used in the sense of 'condemn', *hršy'* functions in much the same way as *hṣdyq*, often expressing the actual results of judgment. See 1 Sam. 14:47; Is. 50:9; Ps. 37:33; Job 10:2; Prov. 12:2.

[23] See Schmid 1968:166–186. The exclusion of any sense of a 'norm' from the significant 'righteousness' terms also goes back to Hermann Cremer.

righteousness' in the Hebrew Scriptures.[24] The concreteness of the biblical usage allows the biblical writers to appeal to God's saving righteousness:

> Give ear to my prayer;
>   in your faithfulness answer me, in your righteousness,
>   and do not enter into judgment with your servant,
>   for no living person shall be justified before you.
> For an enemy has persecuted my soul ...
>
> (Psalm 143:1–3a).

In this text, the psalmist petitions God to contend *for* him against his enemies, while at the same time asking that God might not enter into contention *with* him. Should God press his own claims, the petitioner himself would be undone. God's saving righteousness stands in juxtaposition to his retributive justice, without immediate explanation. This tension appears in a most striking way in Psalm 51, in which the psalmist appeals to God for mercy, even as he confesses that he has sinned against 'God alone'.[25] His confession does not represent an attempt to escape responsibility, but precisely the opposite, an admission of absolute and unmitigated guilt.[26] God is fully justified in this contention: there is no possibility of deliverance from divine judgment unless it comes from God himself.[27] In verse 14, the psalmist presents his petition accordingly:

> Deliver me from blood-guilt, God, God of my salvation.
> My tongue shall sing of your righteousness.

In a prayer of unsurpassed boldness, he asks God to act for him in God's contention with him. God's saving righteousness is to overcome God's righteous judgment. This opposition is softened somewhat in that the psalmist's guilt is personified and presented as a power from which he requires 'deliverance'.[28] Nevertheless, in the end the psalmist appeals to God against God.

---

[24] In some instances, e.g. Ps. 24:5, cultic ideas are present.

[25] As the superscript indicates, this psalm was traditionally associated with David's confession of his sin with Bathsheba after being confronted by the prophet Nathan.

[26] Cf. Gen. 39:9; 1 Sam. 2:25; 2 Sam. 12:13; Luke 15:21.

[27] Correspondingly, the psalmist's corruption extends to the very depths of his being, so that if he is to have a 'pure heart' it must come by a creative act of God (Ps. 51:10).

[28] Here we have an obvious anticipation of Paul's understanding of sin.

Several misunderstandings of the biblical references to the 'righteousness of God' should be avoided. The concept of 'God's righteousness' in the Hebrew Scriptures cannot be reduced to the meaning 'salvation' or the like, since it always functions within the context of a legal dispute or contention. When God works salvation for his people, he establishes justice for them (and for himself) over against their enemies and his. Saving righteousness and wrath parallel one another, since they are different aspects of the same event.[29] Correspondingly, along with the references to a 'saving righteousness' of God, there are a number of passages in which punitive or retributive conceptions are associated with 'the righteousness of God'. Often this usage represents a confession which appears as a formal element within a 'contention'.[30] After the crops of Egypt had been destroyed by hail in one of the ten plagues, the Pharaoh confesses, 'The Lord is righteous; I and my people are guilty' (Exod. 9:27). Similarly, in the great confession of Nehemiah, the people consider their lamentable condition and say to the Lord, 'You are righteous in everything which you have brought upon us, for you have acted in truth, and we have acted wickedly' (Neh. 9:33).[31] Here we have a striking confirmation that the biblical usage of 'righteousness' is essentially forensic in orientation. While the 'saving'. sense of 'God's righteousness' appears more frequently, the juridical orientation of the usage in the Hebrew Scriptures allows both positive and negative outworkings of that righteousness.[32]

In considerable measure the semantic distinction between 'saving

[29] E.g. Pss. 7:1–17; 89:5–18; Is. 11:3–5.

[30] See Bovati 1994: 103, who, however, overlooks that these confessions come after a punishment has been meted out. Following Bovati 1994 and de Roche 1983, I have described this setting as a 'contention' (*rîb*) rather than a 'lawsuit', since the dispute in all instances is a matter of two parties, and not a formal legal setting in which a third party decides the case. Nevertheless, because such 'contentions' constitute disputes over who is in the right, they are 'legal' in character. Furthermore, the 'contention' could involve the entrance of a more powerful third party who takes up the cause of the oppressed (e.g. Is. 1:17; 4:13–15). In this case something of the distinction which de Roche tries to maintain is lost (e.g. Is. 1:23). Against Bovati 1994: 392–393, the New Testament conception of justification and judgment does not fit a neat distinction between a present contention resolved in Christ (*rîb*) and a final judgment (*mišpāṭ*) where punishment is meted out.

[31] The remaining references to a retributive righteousness: Deut. 32:4–5; 2 Chr. 12:6; Pss. 7:10, 12; 11:5–7; 50:6; Is. 1:27; 5:16; 10:22; 28:17; Lam. 1:18; Dan. 9:7, 14, 16. Cf. Ps. 51:4; 2 Kgs. 10:9; Ezra 9:15; Neh. 9:8.

[32] The same understanding of justification appears in Luke's report of Jesus' words that 'the toll-collectors justified God, having been baptized with the baptism of John' (Luke 7:29).

righteousness' and 'retributive justice' follows lexical lines. The hi'phil stem of the verb and the noun *ṣᵉdāqâ* often denote an act of vindication or its result.[33] Usually the adjective *ṣaddîq* (which in all but one instance in the Hebrew Scriptures is applied to persons) is used to predicate righteousness of God, often with retributive or punitive overtones.[34] Perhaps this lexical distinction has contributed to the mistaken claim that 'the righteousness of God' always signifies a 'saving righteousness'. If one limits one's scope to the noun and verb, one takes into account only one aspect of the linguistic evidence.

The understanding of the biblical writers that injustice and wickedness are resident within the world goes a long way towards explaining why references to God's saving righteous appear roughly four times as frequently as those to his retributive justice. Only God's repeated intervention, whether mediate or direct, can effect righteousness. This is the will of God according to the Scriptures: to establish his righteousness within the creation and thereby to manifest that he is its Creator. Conversely, confessions of God as 'righteous' are not abstract statements in the biblical writings. They are acknowledgments by sinful human beings of their own acts of injustice. Consequently in the biblical literature they appear less frequently, and as responses to divine judgment.

The idea that God establishes and maintains 'righteousness' and proper order in the world requires some elaboration.[35] As we can see already in Psalm 98, God does not merely contend on behalf of those who have been oppressed. He also insists on his rightful claim to be God against the world which denies him.[36] Particularly in the book of Isaiah, God's saving action transcends the mere restoration of order within the world, as in 51:16:

> The heavens shall vanish like smoke,
>   the earth shall wear out like a garment,
>   and its inhabitants shall likewise die,
> but my salvation shall be for ever,
>   and my righteousness shall not pass away.

---

[33] The noun *ṣᵉdāqâ* in much of its usage very probably represents the transformation of the hi'phil stem into nominal form. In the same way, the noun *rišʿâ* (cf. *hršyʿ*) takes on the sense of 'guilt' or 'condemnation' in some contexts. See Deut. 9:4–5; Is. 9:17; Ezek. 5:6; Mal. 1:4; Prov. 13:6.

[34] The single exception of the use of *ṣaddîq* in reference to persons is the plural form found in Deut. 4:8.

[35] Here I want to expand the thesis of Schmid 1968.

[36] See the references to God's retributive righteousness in n. 31.

The punitive action which appears in this text obviously corresponds to God's saving activity, but clearly is not necessary to it: God need not destroy the world to save his people.[37] He acts not merely for them, but also for his own sake. His ruling and judging the world include his absolute right to be God, even to the point of the destruction of the old and the establishment of a new creation.[38] For this reason, when God has a contention with his people, it is only through wrath and condemnation that salvation and righteousness may come. Indeed, the prophetic oracles of salvation characteristically announce 'deliverance through destruction' (e.g. Is. 1:24–28; 5:1–30; 9:1–21; 51:1–23). As we shall see, Paul's understanding of justification follows these biblical lines of thought.

In this connection it is important to observe that we cannot adequately explain the biblical understanding of 'God's righteousness' simply by appeal to God's acting for his glory (against Piper 1983: 89–101). In biblical usage 'God's glory', like his righteousness, involves not only his vindication against his enemies, but also his bringing salvation.[39] In other words, the biblical understanding of divine glory also involves a tension between God's vindication over against the world and his bringing salvation to the world. As with God's righteousness, this tension is resolved not in a concept, but in a deed of God, which simultaneously establishes his right and in unfathomable mercy brings salvation.

The 'righteousness of God' revealed in the gospel

In light of these considerations, we may now return to Paul's allusion to the biblical usage of 'the righteousness of God' in Romans 1:17. In the first place, we must take note of a decisive difference between Psalm 98 and this text. The psalm speaks of an open manifestation of God's righteousness before the eyes of the nations. Paul, as we have seen, speaks of the revelation of the righteousness of God in the gospel to faith. This revelation is no less historical than the first, since the gospel announces the saving death and resurrection of Christ. Nevertheless, in contrast with the psalm, Paul has in view a 'hidden' revelation of God's righteousness, bound up with the demand for faith.

[37] Contra Schmid 1968: 177–179; Cremer 1900: 29.

[38] Cf. Is. 41:21–29; 45:18–25; 48:1–12; and see Pss. 11:1–7; 7:3–5; 97:1–6; 50:1–23, along with the references to God's retributive justice.

[39] E.g. Exod. 14:4; Num. 16:19; Is. 40:5; Is. 8. Paul himself speaks of 'God's glory' with salvific overtones: Rom. 3:23; 5:2; 6:4; 8:18; 9:4, 23.

It is also clear that Paul has in view a 'righteousness of God' which works the salvation of the human being, since this verse explains why the gospel is the 'power of God for salvation'. The revelation of God's righteousness fulfils the prophetic scripture in Habbakuk that 'the righteous one shall *live* by faith', that is to say, the revelation of 'righteousness of God' effects the life of the age to come.[40] As was common by his day, Paul transposes the prophetic promise of deliverance through – not from! – the Babylonian onslaught to the hope of resurrection from the dead, providing an important clue to the sense in which he speaks of 'the righteousness of God'. Paul speaks here not of an attribute of God, but of an act of God (Schlatter 1935: 36).[41]

The connection between God's saving intervention on behalf of Israel and the salvation of the world which we find in the psalm recurs in Paul's statement. The gospel is the power of God for salvation 'for the Jew first, and also for the Greek' (Rom. 1:16). The 'revelation of the righteousness of God' recalls not only God's promises for his people, but also his purposes for the nations. In speaking of 'God's righteousness' Paul has in view God's role as 'ruler and judge', who will savingly bring about 'justice and righteousness' for the world which he has made.

It is 'in the gospel' that the 'righteousness of God' is revealed. Paul's localizing declaration suggests that he refers to the resurrection of the crucified Christ, employing biblical language in order to convey its

---

[40] Since Paul speaks of the effecting of salvation, it is altogether likely that in the verb *zōn* he has in view the granting of eschatological life, and not the conduct of 'the righteous'. Cf. Rom. 2:7; 5:18, 21; 6:22–23; 11:15. Along with others, Hays 1997: 42–44, wants to read 'the righteous one' as a reference to Christ. But it is far more likely that Paul speaks generically here of the 'one who believes', explaining his opening statement in Rom. 1:16.

[41] I shall not elaborate the varied opinions regarding the meaning of the expression 'God's righteousness', on which one might conveniently consult Fitzmyer 1993: 255–263. Paul's language also reminds one of Luther, who found in the text a 'righteousness given to faith' rather than a mere divine quality. This passage was of considerable importance to Luther as he solidified his understanding of righteousness as a gift of God to faith in the gospel. In the preface to his Latin works published in 1545, he reflects on his struggle to comprehend the expression 'the righteousness of God' in this text. Through his education in the *via moderna* he had learned to interpret it as the 'active' righteousness of God by which God punishes sinners. Luther saw that Paul is speaking here of a 'passive righteousness', i.e., of a righteousness given to faith. He describes his response: 'I felt myself reborn, and carried through the portals into Paradise itself' (WA 54: 185). Scanning the predications of God in Scripture – 'strength of God', 'wisdom of God', 'truth of God' – he found that they are used not merely to describe God, but to describe what God gives to human beings.

saving significance. 'God's righteousness' is his 'vindicating act' of raising Christ from the dead *for us.* Here the biblical themes of God's deliverance of the oppressed, his vindication of his Servant, his faithfulness to Israel and his salvation of the world are implicitly present. That which is to take place at the day of judgment for those who believe is manifest here and now in the crucified and risen Christ (Rom. 2:6, 16; 3:5–6). For this reason, the 'righteousness of God' is simultaneously hidden and revealed. And it is *God's* righteousness which has been revealed: in Christ's resurrection God has been vindicated and has defeated his enemies. Salvation comes through destruction, justification through condemnation. Moreover, the gospel is 'the power of God unto salvation' because the 'righteousness of God' revealed in it entails nothing less than the resurrection from the dead. Habbakuk's promise of 'life' is fulfilled in the resurrection of Christ.

The broader context confirms this interpretation. In the opening verses of the letter, Paul names the resurrected Christ as the content of his gospel, which he likewise describes as the fulfilment of promise (Rom. 1:1–4). Even more significantly, he subsequently connects the justification of believers with the resurrection of the crucified Christ: '... who was delivered up on account of our transgressions, and raised on account of our justification' (4:25). Just as our sin brought Christ's condemnation and death, so his resurrection announces our justification. The close connection between verdict and vindication which one finds so prominently in the usage of the Hebrew Scriptures reappears here. The divine verdict 'for us' is present and manifest in the resurrected Christ. Later in Romans, Paul identifies Christ with the revealed 'righteousness of God' to which Israel refused to submit (Rom. 10:4). The theme appears elsewhere in Paul's letters and links his thought with the broader witness of the New Testament.

The justification of God and the ungodly

In the biblical imagery to which Paul alludes, God's vindication of his people is joined to his bringing retribution upon his enemies. That is true not only for his reference to the revelation of God's righteousness, but for the term 'gospel' itself, which may recall the same biblical background (e.g. Is. 40:1–31; 41:25–29; 61:1–4). Even Paul's declaration, 'I am not ashamed', may suggest the triumph of God and his servant over against their opponents (see Herold 1973: 28–69). Likewise, faintly, but definitely, in his emphasis upon the exclusivity of 'faith', Paul points to a 'contention' which exists between God and humanity, a 'contention' which is savingly resolved only by faith in the gospel (Rom. 1:17; Hab. 2:4).

This divine dispute with humanity provides the background to Paul's announcement of the justifying work of the gospel in Romans 1:16–17. Juxtaposed to the 'righteousness of God' in 1:17 stands the 'revelation of God's wrath' in 1:18. Although some have appealed to the parallelism between the two expressions as an indication that they represent opposing activities of God, Paul's subsequent argument shows that he regards them as interdependent.[42] In correspondence with its biblical background, for Paul God's saving righteousness does not abrogate his righteous judgment against the world, but brings it to completion. As we have noted, justification comes only through condemnation, life only through death. The way in which Paul connects the opening discussion in verse 18 to verse 17 signals this relationship: '... the righteous one shall live by faith, *for* the wrath of God is revealed from heaven ...' If he had been thinking of a strict antithesis, one would have expected here a concession, an 'even if'. God's saving righteousness is revealed in the gospel precisely because God himself comes to his own righteousness in the cross of Christ. This simultaneous justification of God and the sinner drives Paul's argument in 1:18 – 3:26.

The righteousness of God's wrath against idolatry (Rom. 1:18–32)

Often interpreters read Romans 1:18 – 3:20 as a logical demonstration running along these lines: 'All Gentiles have sinned and stand under God's wrath; all Jews have done the same; therefore all are under the wrath of God and all need the gospel.' Paul clearly arrives at the endpoint of this syllogism, but his argument does not follow this path. Much of what he has to say is lost if we attempt to read the passage in this manner.[43]

If we are to understand Paul's argument properly, we must closely observe his declaration: 'the wrath of God is revealed from heaven against all ungodliness and unrighteousness of human beings who suppress the truth in unrighteousness' (1:18).[44] His charge is directed

---

[42] Rightly, Schlatter 1935: 36; Herold 1973, despite considerable distance between their readings of the passage and that offered here.

[43] The argument which follows appears in substantially the same form in Seifrid 1998.

[44] The reference 'from heaven' carries overtones of coming judgment (cf. 1 Thess.

against the 'ungodliness and unrighteousness of human beings'.[45] At this juncture he makes no explicit accusation against all humanity, although in naming 'human beings' (and not merely Gentiles) as the perpetrators of injustice, he anticipates it. Here he asserts only that God's wrath has been revealed against all idolatry. Only later, in Romans 3, will he bring the accusation that all are idolators. It is significant, too, that at the very outset Paul characterizes 'ungodliness' as 'unrighteousness'. It is 'the unrighteousness of human beings' which calls forth the wrath of God (1:18). Paul's topic in 1:18–32 is the injustice of idolatry, and the justice of God's wrath against it.

He underscores this point by setting forth a series of charges, which he formulates in terms of paradoxes in order to convey their force: the 'unseen things of God' are clearly seen through what has been made, so that idolators are 'without excuse' (verse 20); although such persons profess to be wise, they have become fools (verse 22); idolatry is nothing other than 'the exchange of the glory of the incorruptible God for the image of the corruptible creature' (verse 23). In the first charge, the forensic orientation of Paul's argument is particularly clear: idolators are without excuse (verse 20). The divine surrender of idolators to their desires appears similarly in an emphatic, threefold 'law of retribution': (1) God has delivered over those who worship the image of the corruptible human to the dishonouring of their bodies (Rom. 1:24–25); (2) God has delivered over those who worship the creature rather than the Creator to corrupting the created order in their own persons (verses 26–27); (3) God has delivered over to a mind that is morally useless (*adokimos*) those who do not think it useful (*edokimasen*) to remember God (verses 28–29). Paul does not speak here of a progression of judgments, but a single act which expresses God's righteous wrath and anticipates God's execution of his 'just decree' of death on the 'day of wrath' (verse 32; 2:5).[46]

1:10; 2 Thess. 1:7), not salvation. Against Herold 1973: 302–329, Paul here speaks not of the cross, but of the world in the light of the cross. The divine contention which has been brought to a conclusion in Christ was and is present in the world. Rom. 1:20 – 3:20 speaks not simply of the time of God's patience, but of judgment already 'being stored up' (2:5).

[45] Paul does not name those of whom he speaks as Gentiles, and does not reintroduce the categories of 'Jew and Greek' until 2:9–10 (cf. 1:16–17). This delay must be intentional, since when Paul shifts away from the topic of idolatry at 2:1, he likewise refrains from describing his rhetorical addressee as a Jew, but speaks to 'anyone who judges another'. The parallelism is obvious: just as in Rom. 2 Paul asserts the justice of judgment upon the one who assumes the role of judge, in Rom. 1 he announces the righteousness of God's wrath upon all who worship idols.

[46] Paul obviously speaks of a past act of God, yet does not have a definite time in view.

We may freely admit that in 1:18–32 Paul primarily has in view Gentile society seen from a Jewish and biblical perspective. The orientation of his argument is clear not only from parallel descriptions of Gentile idolatry which appear in early Jewish literature (as, for example, in Wis. Sol. 13 – 14), but also from the attack upon 'wisdom so-called' which lies at the centre of his polemic: those who professed to be wise became fools (verse 22). Here Paul exposes the pretensions of Hellenistic society, just as he subsequently calls into question Jewish presumption of privilege in the possession of the law (17–29). Nevertheless, Paul does not bring a charge against Gentiles as such, only against all idolatry. He knows well enough that Jews also could be idolators (2:22).[47] Ethnic stereotypes are irrelevant to him.[48] Each one, whether Jew or Greek, will receive just recompense for his or her deeds at the coming day of judgment (2:8–11). God will judge the secrets of all hearts through Christ Jesus (2:16).

Paul's charge that idolatry is an act of unrighteousness rests upon the claim that the knowledge of God is imparted by creation. When he speaks of 'that which is known of God' (*to gnōston tou theou*), he does not have in view some residual, limited capacity within the fallen human being to know God (1:19). Paul's language makes it clear that he regards natural revelation as imparting a knowledge of God which is sufficient for the creature to worship him rightly. 'That which is known of God' is perceived in the difference between the creation and the Creator. His unseen being and eternal power distinguish him from that which he has made and sustains (1:20). It is incumbent upon the human creature to glorify and give thanks to this one eternal, beneficent and

---

He clearly does not equate Rom. 1 with his description of the fall of humanity in Rom. 5. There is something of a generic sense to his description: it is Adam's transgression reliving itself in all generations.

[47] *Hierosylein* ('to rob a temple'), whatever else it conveys, is obviously equivalent to idolatry for Paul in this context.

[48] His gospel is universal precisely because it meets the individual, the 'righteous one' who believes. The gospel in which the promises to Israel and the nations have been fulfilled also reduces them to nothing. We must not confuse 'individualism', in which each one constructs his or her own god, with the responsibility of each person before God. 'Individualism' generally is not absolute. It results in 'communities' of like persons, in which one hides oneself from God and neighbour. It cannot be overcome by the human attempt to form community, but only by God who reduces all to the community of Adam in order that he might place us in the community which he has created in Christ. Moreover, according to Paul, the communities of Israel and the nations are fundamental to the world whether we are aware of it or not. We shall return to the latter topic in chapter 6. On the former, see Bellah 1985: 219–249; Bonhoeffer 1954: 17–39.

unseen Creator. That is precisely what the idolator refuses to do. As Paul's further argument will make clear, natural revelation is complete and sufficient, but it does not issue in a true natural theology or knowledge of God. The fallen human being has been subjected to idolatry, which the gospel does not supplement but brings to an end.

The created order imparts not only a knowledge of God the Creator, but a knowledge of his will. Idolators 'know the righteous ordinance of God' that those who engage in vices are 'worthy of death' (1:32). The human being is not merely an observer of the enduring order of creation, but a participant in it: Gentiles sometimes 'by nature' perform the 'things of the law' (2:14).[49] As the creation of God, the human being remains a moral being and cannot become amoral, only immoral. Seen in this light, 1:32 reveals the considerable dimensions of natural revelation in Paul's understanding. The worship and thanksgiving which the creature owes the Creator according to 1:21 entail much more than lip-service. It includes that 'righteous decree of God' which encompasses the whole of our proper service to God with body and life. The judgment of God, his 'delivering up' of idolators, anticipates the mercies of God, which liberate us from idolatry and effect the worship of the one true God (12:1–2).

The impartiality of divine judgment (Rom. 2:1–16)

In Romans 2:1–11 Paul lays an accusation before everyone who acts as judge of another, using the same language that he applied to idolators: 'You are without excuse.' His argument here takes the same form as it did in Romans 1. He probably has a fault in view which was common to Jews of his day, since he reintroduces the distinction between Jew and Gentile at the conclusion of this passage (1:16; 2:9–11). Nevertheless, he is obviously not interested in attaching an ethnic label to his rhetorical addressee. He knows well enough that Gentiles, too, could be guilty of judging the other (14:10–13). As in Romans 1, Paul is not concerned with blaming particular persons or groups, but with displaying the righteousness of God's wrath.

Often the nature of the sin Paul has in view here is misunderstood. He certainly does not imagine that it is wrong to pass judgment upon sins. If that were so, his argument would collapse upon itself. He

---

[49] There is no reason to attribute this awareness of God's will to the presence of synagogues in the Hellenistic world, especially in the light of Paul's subsequent claim that 'the work of the law' is written upon the heart of Gentiles (Rom. 2:15).

himself anticipates that believers will in fact judge the world, and speaks of it later in this very chapter (2:27; see also, e.g., 1 Cor. 4:5; 6:2–3). It is rather the arrogation to oneself of the role of judge which Paul regards as a fundamental transgression, a theme which he draws from biblical tradition and which is present in other New Testament writings (see Matt. 7:1–5; Jas. 4:11–12; Jude 9; 2 Pet. 2:11). According to James, the one who judges another violates the law and usurps God's role as judge (Jas. 4:11–12). Paul presupposes something along these lines, since he assumes from the start that the one who passes judgment on another has an 'unrepentant heart' and is liable to God's wrath (Rom. 2:5). The self thus becomes the idol which replaces the one, true God. And the self-appointed judge is blind to personal sins which are no different from those which they see in others. Paul here exposes the rebellion against God which accompanies this judgment of others, and underscores the righteousness of God's wrath against it. Affirmations of God's righteousness, equity, and impartiality abound in this section of the letter (2:1–16).[50] The 'day of wrath' is nothing other than the 'revelation of the righteous judgment of God' (2:6). Paul is driving home the point that God's wrath is justified, and preparing for its resolution in the cross of Christ. To stand in judgment upon idolators and immoral persons does not remove one from participation in their transgressions. On the contrary, it only establishes the justice of God's judgment upon one's very self.

Interpreters usually regard Paul as making a statement about Gentiles in Romans 2:12–16, and then argue whether or not he has believing Gentiles in view. Of course, Paul does speak about Gentiles here, but his interest in them does not rest on their ethnicity as such, or on their status with respect to the gospel, but on their 'being without the law' (verse 14). He signals this concern not only in his description of them in these terms, but also in his introduction to this section in which he asserts that those who 'sinned without the law shall perish without the law' (verse 12). His immediately preceding declaration concerning 'the righteous judgment of God' concludes with a straightforward denial that God will make any distinction between Jew and Greek: there is no partiality with God (verses 9–11). Now Paul provides a warrant for that claim. A Jew might have pointed to Israel's possession of the law as a significant qualification of the divine impartiality which Paul has just

---

[50] Verse 2: 'the judgment of God is according to the truth'; verses 5–6: 'the day of wrath and of revelation of the righteous judgment (*dikaiokrisias*) of God, who shall render to each one according to their deeds'; verse 8: 'to those who obey unrighteousness [there will be] wrath and anger'; verse 11: 'there is no respecting of persons with God'.

asserted (verse 11). Paul therefore seeks to dispel the thought that lack of knowledge of the law might represent a disadvantage at the day of judgment. This becomes clear in his subsequent characterization of his imaginary Jewish dialogue partner, who supposes that because he discerns that which is morally excellent from the law, he may serve as 'a guide to the blind, a light to those in darkness, an instructor of the foolish, a teacher of infants' (verses 18–20). The fault of the Jew here lies not in the exclusion of Gentiles from salvation, or in the assumption of some 'national' certainty of blessing, but in the presumption that with knowledge of the law the Jew was privileged and had something to offer the Gentile. Paul exposes this fallacy from two different angles. In the text at hand, Paul makes clear that Gentile disobedience to God is not due to a lack of understanding of his will. While a Jew might have supposed that a Gentile had something to gain in becoming a 'hearer of the law' (verse 13), Paul insists that in this regard the Jew had nothing to offer. Subsequently, in verses 17–29, he will make it clear that knowledge of God's will has not secured Jewish obedience. There is no saving advantage to be found in awareness of the divine demands. Divine impartiality therefore is not in any way diminished by the *anomia* of Gentiles.[51]

Paul's argument in 2:14 turns upon the understanding of 'creational' revelation which we have described above: those who do not have *Torah* function as *Torah* for themselves. Paul does not argue that Gentiles are 'a law unto themselves', but that their occasional performance of the requirements of the law fulfils the role of the law of Moses. Although they lack the external address of the law, 'nature' supplies an internal witness, which equally conveys the divine demands, at least in the sense with which Paul is concerned. Those who sin without the law will perish at the final judgment (verse 12). This will take place justly and without diminishing divine impartiality, because the intended effect of the law ('the work of the law') has been written in their hearts (verse 15).

Paul does not speak of the *law* being written *upon* their heart, but of the *work* of the law written *in* their hearts. That is, he does not here allude to God's promise that he will write his law upon the hearts of his people (Jer. 31:31–34). We can hardly think that Paul speaks simply and particularly of believing Gentiles here, since he supposes that some of them will be condemned at the day of judgment: their thoughts will accuse them (verse 15). He uses the language of

---

[51] See the similar discussion of this passage in Bassler 1982: 139–149.

'inscription in the heart' because he sees in 'nature' a parallel to the law's role in addressing the human being with the demands of God, a function which he elsewhere describes as 'letter' (see esp. 2:27, 29). In short, Paul claims that occasional obedience to the demands of the law by Gentiles provides evidence (*endeiknymi*) that all that the law might accomplish in imparting the knowledge of God's will has been written in their hearts already by the hand of the Creator (2:15). As with his assertions concerning the knowledge of God in Romans 1, Paul's statement concerning this 'work of the law' is unqualified. The work of God the Creator within the fallen human being is equal to the manifestation of his will in the law of Moses.

This 'work of the law' is not to be identified with the witness of the conscience of which Paul speaks in verse 16. It is rather the object and content of that witness. As in secular Greek, the compound form *symmartyreō* ('bear co-witness') should be given its full weight (so also 8:15; 9:1). Alongside the Gentiles' occasional obedient deeds, the conscience also bears witness to the 'work of the law written in the heart' (cf. Eckstein 1983: 159–161). This reading is confirmed by the language of verse 15: Gentiles *display* the 'work of the law' written in their heart in their behaviour. Paul is not concerned to describe the function of the conscience within the present order.[52] When he explains this 'witness of the conscience', he speaks of the day of judgment at which the thoughts of the Gentiles will accuse or defend them (verses 15–16). At that time the consciences of Gentiles, along with their deeds, will serve as a co-witness to the work of God the Creator within each of their hearts. That work, as we have seen, is the impartation of the knowledge of his will. Of course, Paul does not imagine that the Gentile world generally embraces and accepts this knowledge. Quite the contrary: his statements in 1:28–32 and his need to argue the matter indicate just the opposite, that the Creator's imprint of his will upon the human creature is largely suppressed, just as the knowledge of God the Creator has been perverted by idolatry.

Paul's argument here is guided by the expectation that all human beings will be judged according to their works, and indeed, according to their obedience to the law. His statements stand in obvious tension with his subsequent declaration that God justifies sinful human beings by faith, apart from 'works of the law' (3:28). We shall return to this topic in our discussion of faith.

---

[52] On this topic see Eckstein 1983.

The possession of the law as no advantage (Rom. 2:17–29)

When Paul indicates that the 'work of the law' is inscribed in the hearts of Gentiles (Rom. 2:15), he does not have in view the requirements particular to Israel. In Romans 2:17–29 he takes up the ethnic dimension of the law and the privileges associated with it in the most remarkable way. As we shall see again in Romans 4, for Paul circumcision stands in a twofold relation to the law. On the one hand, he regards it as integral to the law, since possession of 'letter and circumcision' marks the disobedient as transgressors *of the law*. At the same time, circumcision is set apart in that it serves as an emblem of obedience: 'circumcision is profitable, if you obey the law' (2:25).

For Paul, circumcision is a promissory sign of the circumcision of the heart by the Spirit of God. On the basis of this circumcision, he refuses to concede the title 'Jew' to the one who 'trusts in the law and boasts in God'. In agreement with Deuteronomy and Jeremiah, he interprets 'being a Jew' as the result of the work of the Spirit of God in the heart.[53] Circumcision in the flesh, an outward sign for which one might receive praise, counts for nothing (2:28–29). Being a Jew and being circumcised are inward realities, visible only to God. God regards as circumcised the one who is uncircumcised according to the order of the present world (*ek physeōs*) yet keeps 'the righteous requirements of the law'. This one shall pass judgment on the circumcised transgressor of the law (verses 26–28). The sign of circumcision is fulfilled in the eschatological work of the Spirit, not in possession of 'the letter'.[54]

In this passage Paul clearly is concerned with something more than dismissing Jewish presumption of privilege in the law. At the centre of his argument stands the work of God by the Spirit. He presupposes that his addressees know that there is such a one as a 'hidden Jew', whose circumcision is of the heart. Indeed, this uncircumcised one 'keeps the righteous ordinances of the law' without the benefit of instruction in the law (verse 26). True obedience to the law comes from beyond the law, in the work of the Spirit of God who is given through the gospel.

[53] See Deut. 10:16; 30:6; Jer. 4:4; 9:25–26. 'Israel' likewise is made up of those 'born of promise' (Rom. 9:6–9).

[54] Paul's treatment of circumcision here is not at odds with his subsequent claim that Abraham's circumcision was a sign of his uncircumcised 'righteousness by faith' (Rom. 4:11). The two perspectives are united by the connection between justification and the gift of the Spirit. Paul is quite aware, of course, that circumcision is also demanded by the law of Moses (Lev. 12:3). Nevertheless, he interprets it as a sign of promise given to Abraham (and his descendants). In its fulfilment, however, it is a matter of indifference (Gal. 5:6; 6:15). It is no longer a commandment of God (1 Cor. 7:19).

For this reason, Paul speaks of some Gentiles whose thoughts will defend them at the day of judgment, when God examines the secrets of their hearts (2:15).[55] The gospel creates 'new obedience'.

The advantage of the Jew in the oracles of God (Rom. 3:1–18)

The advantage of 'the Jew' lies not in the possession of the law, but in the 'oracles' of God. Under this heading, Paul treats the human condition: only when the meaning of the law has been clarified does the fallen state of the entire world become apparent. As interpreters have long noted, Romans 3 anticipates Romans 9 – 11, where the emphasis is shifted and the faithfulness of God, rather than the failure of Israel, becomes the focus of attention. The central element of the present section is the charge which Paul now brings against all humanity, that Jew and Gentile alike are 'under sin'. God has a contention with humanity, that he is the true God and they all are idolators. His first and primary demand is that we believe this judgment upon us. The advantage of the Jew lies precisely here, in being entrusted with 'the oracles of God' which make known the human condition (3:1–2).

The term 'oracles' (*logia*) is highly unusual for Paul, appearing only here in his letters. Although Paul might have chosen to speak of God's 'promises' to Israel (as in 9:4), he does not do so in this context. While one cannot exclude the possibility of synonymy, his singular choice of *logia* suggests a sense other than that of 'promise'. In biblical usage, while the term *logion* may signify a promissory word of God, it generally carries the broader sense of 'utterance', and is also applied to commandments, divine threats, and pronouncements of judgment.[56] In this context Paul immediately speaks of the 'words' (*logoi*) of God, which announce God's contention that 'every human being is a liar' (3:4). The obvious repetition of the noun-stem implies that when Paul speaks of the *logia* ('oracles') he has these *logoi* ('words') in view. Likewise, in 3:10–18 Paul cites a string of scriptural 'utterances' which charge all humanity with godlessness. It is most natural to think that these are included among the 'oracles' to which Paul refers. At the same time, Paul speaks of Israel's failure to *believe* the oracles of God, which suggests that promises of salvation are included within the scope

---

[55] In view of his subsequent charge that 'all human beings are liars' (Rom. 3:4), he can only have in mind the justification of believing Gentiles at the judgment seat of God.

[56] See for example Num. 24:4, 16 (LXX); Is. 5:24 (LXX); Is. 28:13 (LXX); Is. 30:27 (LXX); Acts 7:38; 1 Pet. 4.11.

of the term (verse 3).[57] Further help in sorting out the meaning of the term comes from 11:4, where Paul returns to the unusual topic of oracular revelation. Citing Elijah's complaint, 'I alone am left!', Paul speaks of the 'oracle' which came to the prophet in response: 'I have kept for myself 7,000 who have not bent the knee to Baal'.[58] God knows better than Elijah and has accomplished his ends without the prophet. With his reference to oracular speech Paul underscores God's transcendent knowledge and power. It is likely, then, that Paul alludes to God's unfathomable ways in Romans 3:2 when he speaks of 'the oracles' with which Israel has been entrusted. As Paul makes clear in chapters 9 – 11, God's dealings with his people are beyond searching out. Salvation always comes in and through divine judgment: God calls those who are not his people to be his people (9:25–26); through bringing destruction and exile he saves a remnant by his grace (9:29); he hardens Israel and treats them as enemies in order to save them (11:25–26); he has shut up all in disobedience, so that he might have mercy upon all (11:32). From this perspective, the breadth of Paul's reference in Romans 3:2 is understandable. Salvation and judgment necessarily belong together in God's untraceable ways, and both come into view in the expression 'the oracles of God'.

Although 'some' have failed to believe these oracles, their unbelief in no way invalidates the faithfulness of God (3:3). Paul uses deliberate understatement here in order to emphasize his point.[59] That 'certain ones' have disbelieved merely confirms what the oracles of God proclaim, that God will yet be seen to be 'true' and that every human being will be shown to be a 'liar' (verse 4). Far from challenging God's truthfulness, the failure of 'some' Jews confirms what 'has been written'. In the accusation that 'every human being is a liar', Paul draws upon the words of Scripture (Ps. 116:11). His language also recalls his earlier description of the fundamental human sin, the

---

[57] In view of the manner in which Paul frames the divine dispute with humanity as a contention over the truthfulness of God and his words, it is best to understand the *apistia* of some Jews here as 'disbelief' (likewise, *apistein* in Rom. 3:2). Of course, disbelief is 'unfaithfulness', but it is so in a specific sense. This reading is confirmed by Paul's taking up the matter of Israel's unbelief in Rom. 9 – 11 (cf. 9:30–33). As most interpreters agree, Paul anticipates that discussion here. Furthermore, elsewhere in Romans Paul uses *apistia* in the sense of 'unbelief' (4:20; 11:20, 23), just as the New Testament and LXX generally use *apistia* and *apistein* in reference to 'unbelief' (Mark 6:6; 9:24; Heb. 3:12, 19; 2 Macc. 8:13; Wis. Sol. 1:2; 10:7; 12:17; 18:13; cf., however, 14:25).

[58] Paul here characterizes God as 'the one who gives an oracle' (*ho chrēmatismos*).

[59] In Rom. 9 – 11 he will lament the failure of practically the whole of Israel to believe in the gospel.

'exchange of the truth of God for a lie' (1:25). He now implicitly equates unbelief with idolatry. Even more remarkably and directly, Paul here declares that God somehow stands behind human transgression, including that of Israel. Building upon the wording of Psalm 116:11, he cites Psalm 51:4b: '(let every human being be a liar ...) in order that you might be justified in your words, and might triumph when you enter into judgment'. Just as the psalmist confesses that his sin effected the hidden and strange purpose of God, Paul expresses the expectation that all human beings will be made liars *in order that* God might be justified.[60] Even in idolatry and unbelief, God remains the sovereign Lord, announcing and bringing his word to pass, making manifest that the human being is a 'liar'.[61] For Paul, the unbelief of 'some' Jews represents nothing other than the divine 'delivering over' of humanity to sin, the revelation of God's wrath of which he spoke in Romans 1.

Correspondingly, when Paul speaks of God's being 'true' in this context (3:4, 7), he has in view his 'being God'. Paul's thought here corresponds to Romans 1, where he describes the rejection of God as the suppression of the 'truth', and idolatry as the rejection of the 'truth of God' (1:18, 25). The language of 3:4–7 likewise recalls the pattern of divine 'contention' or 'lawsuit' in Isaiah 40 – 48, where God's confirmation of his word manifests that he alone is God, and not the idols of the nations.[62] God's 'faithfulness' serves to establish that he is God (verse 3).[63] Paradoxically and profoundly, the human 'lie' establishes God's righteousness in his dispute with us. It causes the

---

[60] The LXX interprets the Hebrew text in the same way. This theme reappears in Rom. 9 – 11, where Paul contends that God is strangely at work in Israel's unbelief: God has consigned all to disobedience in order that he may have mercy upon all (11:32).

[61] Of course, Paul firmly rejects any suggestion that this divine operation reduces human culpability (Rom. 3:5–8). Although the manifestation of human evil merely confirms the divine pronouncement, God will still bring his wrath justly upon the world in judgment (3:5–6). Paul cuts off any attempt to push this question further in the same way that he abruptly curtails his discussion of the electing purpose of God (3:7–8; cf. 9:20–21). Just as the creature has no right to challenge the Creator, it is blasphemous to say that we should do evil so that good (i.e., God's justification) might come of it.

[62] See especially Is. 43:9–10, and 41:26 (LXX); 42:3 (LXX); 44:26 (LXX); 45:19 (LXX).

[63] Paul returns to this topic in Rom. 9 – 11. As Is. 40 – 66 in particular makes clear, God's faithfulness to Israel is the means by which it is manifest that he is the true God. Paul does not change topics as he moves from God's faithfulness to his deity. He rather sets forth the fundamental significance of God's 'announcing' and 'fulfilling' his word. Similarly in Rom. 15:8, where Paul speaks of Christ ministering to the 'circumcision' for the sake of the 'truth of God' he has in view something more than divine faithfulness, namely, the confirmation of the reality of the true God before the nations.

truth of *God* to abound.[64] Our very unbelief, which denies God, confirms that he is God, since he has already made known in his oracles that we are 'liars'.

The forensic setting which Paul presupposes differs considerably from a modern courtroom. Although the biblical 'contention' was forensic in as much as a matter of justice was at stake, it was not restricted to the setting of a formal trial. Moreover, while one might appeal to 'witnesses' or a powerful ally (particularly the king in the monarchical period), a 'contention' was essentially a two-party affair. Paul does not here imagine God in the role of an impartial judge, but as a party to the dispute, who seeks vindication over against idolatrous humanity: the justification of God entails our condemnation.[65] We miss something essential in Paul's conception of justification if we impose our image of a modern courtroom on the biblical texts.[66] For Paul, the justification of human beings takes place only through God's triumph and their defeat.[67]

Paul reinforces all that he has said concerning fallen humanity in a lengthy chain-citation of Scripture in 3:10–18. In introducing these texts, he refers to his preceding statements as a 'charge' against Jew and Gentile alike (verse 9), so that his forensic tone is unmistakable. In speaking of this 'charge' he in all likelihood refers especially to his assertion in verse 4 that 'all human beings are liars', which he now restates: Jews and Gentiles alike are 'under sin' (verse 9).[68] This dense

---

[64] Rom. 3:5, *synistēmi* (cf. 5:8); 3:7, *perisseuō*. Note that here Paul 'fronts' the genitive, using *theou dikaiosynē* instead of *dikaiosynē theou*.

[65] See, with some qualifications, Müller 1964: 57–72. This biblical background is not essentially at odds with the hearing before a Roman tribunal (*bēma*), with which Paul and his first readers were also familiar. Essential features of the Hebrew 'contention' continued in the Hellenistic and Roman periods. Often a single figure, either a (Hellenistic) king or a Roman official, was responsible for both the administration and execution of justice (see Thür & Pieler 1978, esp. 368–389). In civil disputes, the parties involved brought charges themselves (e.g. Acts 18:12–17). Furthermore, kings and officials freely took action and rendered judgments in their own interest or that of public order (e.g. Josephus, *Antiquities* 18:57; *War* 2:301). Consequently, it is no surprise that Paul speaks of the final judgment as 'our appearance before Christ's tribunal', and readily joins this appearance to the divine 'contention' with humanity described in the book of Isaiah (2 Cor. 5:10; Rom. 14:10–12; cf. Is. 45:23).

[66] Wright 1997: 96–99 falls into this error.

[67] Jesus likewise uses the image of a contention with an opponent to describe the human situation before God. He warns that it must be settled before it comes before the judge who will mete out punishment (Matt. 5:25–26; Luke 12:57–59). Although the figure of the judge enters the metaphor (thereby the picture of final judgment), that judge is assumed to take the side of the opponent, so that here again justice is a two-party affair.

[68] Here we have a confirmation of the reading of Rom. 1 – 3 as an argument for the

expression undoubtedly reflects the threefold divine surrender of idolators to transgression which Paul introduced in Romans 1.[69] He later describes the divine action upon the fallen human being in more direct manner as a being 'sold under sin' (7:14; cf. Is. 50:1). 'Being under sin' therefore signifies both guilt and condemnation, both human rebellion and God's sovereign judgment upon the human being in rebellion.

The passages which Paul cites in support of this claim are drawn primarily from the Psalms and Proverbs. Significantly, he begins with the declaration from Psalm 14:1–3 (Ps. 53:2–4) that 'no human being is righteous' and names the violation of the first commandment as the first transgression: 'There is no-one who understands, no-one who seeks God' (Rom. 3:11; Ps. 14:1–2). The introductory words of the psalm lie subtly in the background: 'The fool has said in his heart, "There is no God."' Subsequent scriptural citations in the chain depict human beings as transgressors of the 'second table of the law', those who fail to love their neighbour as themselves (Rom. 3:13–18).

The law of God and the righteousness of God (Rom. 3:19–20)

Paul here summarizes his discussion of Israel's privilege with a declaration concerning the law:

> We know that whatever the law says, it speaks to those in the law, in order that every mouth might be closed and all the world might be held guilty before God. Because by the works of the law no flesh shall be justified before him, for through the law comes the knowledge of sin.

At first sight, one might suppose that Paul here merely explains his prior chain-citation of Scripture. It is more likely, however, that he recalls his anticipatory discussion of the law in 2:17–29, forming something of an envelope (inclusio), which rounds off a discrete section of the letter (2:17 – 3:20). The term *nomos* ('law') reappears here for the first time since the end of Romans 2. Furthermore, Paul now speaks for the first time of the 'works of the law' which cannot justify, and of the 'knowledge of sin' which comes through the law.

---

justice of God's wrath followed by a charge that all humanity is guilty.

[69] The divine 'giving over' to transgression also implicitly lies behind the confession of Ps. 51:6, '[I sinned] in order that you might be justified', which Paul takes up (Rom. 3:4).

We have here a succinct description of the divine purpose for the law, in which Paul counters a misunderstanding of it attached to the expression 'works of the law'.[70] It represents a theological confession ('we know ...') which prepares for Paul's exposition of the justifying work of the cross in 3:21–26 and lays the groundwork for his further explication of the law in 3:27 – 8:39.

I have rendered *hypodikos* here as 'held guilty' (before God) rather than as 'accountable' (cf. NIV, NRSV), a reading which is to be preferred for several reasons. (1) The sense of 'guilt' or 'liability to judgment' is normally attached to this word.[71] (2) The preceding chain-citation obviously has to do not with accountability, but with guilt. Since it is fairly clear that Paul continues the thought of this citation when he speaks of 'whatever the law says', it is probable that he speaks here of condemnation, not mere 'accountability'. (3) Paul has just argued that the Gentiles are fully accountable to God without the law (Rom. 2:12–16). It hardly makes sense for him to reverse his position and make the law necessary to this accountability. (4) The word *hypodikos* is coupled with the clause, 'that every mouth might be closed', an expression which is regularly used in the Scriptures to describe the silencing of the wicked and guilty (Pss. 63:11; 107:42; Job 5:16).

In speaking of the law effecting the 'knowledge of sin', Paul does not have in view an immediate awareness of guilt imparted by the knowledge of the law's demands, but the experience of sin. Through our entrance into this experiential knowledge, God establishes his claim that we are 'liars'. Despite the objective character of this event, however, it is only in faith that we recognize it and the purpose of the law which brings it about (see Seifrid 1998: 115–129). We shall return to this topic in chapter 4. Here we wish only to adduce several considerations in favour of this reading of the expression.

First, the aim of Paul's argument begun at 1:18 has been to display the righteousness of God's wrath against humanity. If he had regarded the demands of the law as presently bringing a consciousness of guilt, he would not have found it necessary to argue the matter. As we have seen, he presupposes that Jews who know the law might well think of themselves as superior to others (2:17–29). Prior to his conversion, Paul himself must have thought in this way (Gal. 1:14; Phil. 3:4–6).

---

[70] Cranfield 1975: 198, among others, fails to see that Paul's assertion that such 'works' do not justify (Rom. 3:21) surely implies that a number of Jews regarded such works as justifying.

[71] See e.g. Philo, *Spec. Leg.* 2.249; Josephus, *Vita* 74.

Although the 'knowledge of sin' derives from encounter with the commandment of the law according to Rom. 7:7–25, nothing in that context or elsewhere in Paul's letters gives any support to the idea that his encounter with the law brought him an awareness of the sentence of death which was upon him.

Secondly, it is nevertheless clear from Paul's language in 3:19 that the 'knowledge of sin' compels the entire world to submit to God in the final judgment, where his contention with us is resolved. Despite its effectiveness in bringing the 'knowledge of sin', the aim of the law in bringing human recognition of guilt takes place only *in foro Dei*.

Thirdly, Paul's use of this expression subsequently in Romans 7:7 and 2 Corinthians 5:21 suggests that it reflects the biblical idiom in which knowledge fundamentally involves experience (as in 'Adam knew his wife Eve and she bore him a son', Gen. 4:1). To 'know sin' is to have experiential knowledge of sin.

Fourthly, Paul speaks of 'the knowledge of sin', not 'the knowledge of sins', and later describes the prohibition against coveting as effecting this 'knowledge of sin' (cf. Rom. 7:7). In this expression, then, he does not have in view the knowledge of particular sins, but the knowledge of the character of sin as a whole, even though it is transmitted through the encounter with the particular commandment. His perspective likewise makes it clear that he views the law as a unity, which is violated by the transgression of even one commandment. In saying that the law effects the 'knowledge of sin', Paul interprets the law and the human condition comprehensively.

Finally, Paul introduces his declaration in 3:19–20 with the formula, 'we know that …', which he uses regularly in Romans to indicate that the matter about which he speaks is basic to the gospel.[72] As we have noted, human submission to the divine charge takes place in the final judgment. As we shall see below, this judgment has been brought into the present in faith, and only in faith. Our recognition of the purpose of the law and of the knowledge of sin takes place only in Christ, in whom the veil which lies over the reading of the law is removed (2 Cor. 3:12–18).

A function of the law therefore emerges in 3:19–20 which is different from that of natural revelation. While the will of the Creator written in the heart will be manifest at the day of judgment, it is God's will that the law bring the final judgment into the open in the present. It is to transcend natural revelation, not by supplementing any particular

---

[72] See Rom. 2:2; 7:14; 8:22, 28; 1 Cor 8:1, 4; 2 Cor. 5:1, 16; 1 Tim. 1:8.

knowledge of divine demands, but in effecting our confession of G[
just claim against us here and now.[73] As we have seen above, Paul does
not suppose that this acknowledgment of God's right comes about in
every human being who encounters the law. In fact, he subsequently
speaks of the objective effect of the law quite apart from any human
recognition of its significance: 'the law works wrath' (4:15); 'the
commandment entered in order that the transgression might multiply'
(5:20). The law operates upon the fallen human being, replicating the
Adamic transgression against God in each one (5:14, 20). It was into
the world thus subjected to the power of sin and death that the Son of
God was sent as an offering for sin and in which he performed the
decisive act of obedience on the cross (8:3; 5:19). Nevertheless, for
Paul the law has a distinctly experiential goal, which it reaches only in
Christ. It is precisely this theme which Paul takes up in 7:7–25, and to
which we shall return.

The righteousness of God in Christ (Rom. 3:21–26)

The law is not God's final word to us. That last word is found in the
revelation of 'his righteousness': in 3:21–26 Paul returns to the theme
with which he began. At the outset of this section, he both draws a
distinction between the 'the righteousness of God' and the law of God,
and binds them together. The law of God stands apart from the
'righteousness of God' so that it may bear witness to it. Along with its
pronouncement of guilt and death it points to vindication and life. Even
now, in the hour of fulfilment, the law attests the 'righteousness of
God' which has been made manifest (verses 21, 26).

This section is marked by two pairs of references to God's righteousness, at its opening and at its closing:

> … the righteousness of God has been made manifest (verse 21)
> … the righteousness of God through faith in Jesus Christ (verse
> 22)
> … unto the demonstration of his righteousness (verse 25)
> … unto the demonstration of his righteousness (verse 26).

---

[73] We may well understand the law as bringing a reminder of the will of God, which
has been obscured in us. As we noted above, because the law is addressed to ancient
Israel and not to humanity in general, it has a particular aspect (note *aspect*: the law
cannot legitimately be divided into moral and ceremonial portions), which the New
Testament writers understand as promissory of the age to come (e.g. Paul on
circumcision, Hebrews on the Sabbath).

The passage as a whole represents an expansion of the thought which Paul introduced in his initial reference to the 'righteousness of God' (1:17). As a result, the individual occurrences of 'the righteousness of God' do not carry the same sense which the expression bears there, but collectively unfold it.

Although Paul again recalls Psalm 98 in Romans 3:21 by repeating his announcement that the 'righteousness of God has been manifested', he now has in view a gift given to the human being, rather than an act of God. This is clear from his statement that this righteousness is 'apart from the law': he has in view a righteousness which is given (or, respectively, acquired; see 2:17–24; 4:13–15; 9:30–33). Moreover, he immediately indicates that this 'righteousness of God' is distributed 'through the faith of Jesus Christ, for all who believe' and that those who believe are 'justified freely by his grace' (3:22–24).[74] His following description of the means of justification gives evidence that he has not set aside his earlier reference to God's saving action in Christ. Nevertheless, his thought has now moved from the justifying event to the justification of the believer, mirroring the latter part of 1:17, where he likewise speaks of 'the righteous one who lives by faith'. The work of God in Christ's cross and resurrection is 'for us' and therefore a gift to us.

Correspondingly, as in 1:17, Paul again announces that the cross performs its saving work in and through faith alone. The 'righteousness of God' is mediated 'through the faith of Jesus Christ' (3:22). God set forth Christ as a 'place of propitiation, through faith in his blood' (verse 25). He justifies 'the one who believes in Jesus' (verse 26). Accordingly, this 'righteousness of God' is for *all* who believe. The loss of the divine glory – Paul's characterization of idolatry – extends to all human beings (1:23; 3:23). Correspondingly, because faith alone justifies, the distinction between Jew and Gentile has been overcome (verse 24). Universal fallenness and redemption, not ethnic differences, define the human condition.

In the central section of the passage, 3:22b–25a, Paul specifically describes the justifying work of God.[75] We cannot help but notice the

---

[74] I shall discuss the current debate concerning the interpretation of 'the faith of Christ', *pistis Christou*, in chapter 5. Here I have left the genitive relation uninterpreted.

[75] Often interpreters suppose that here he borrows (and perhaps modifies) an early Christian confession. It is debated whether this material extends from 3:24 to 3:26a, or from 3:25 to 3:26a. We need not concern ourselves with this question. Undoubtedly Paul makes use of language which would have been familiar to the Roman Christians as a description of the work of the cross. Yet he has fully appropriated it, so that both the content and form of the passage represent his own thought.

emphasis which he here lays upon the gratuity of God's act in Christ. No human work, but rather 'God's unconditioned act brings justification: '... being justified freely by his grace, through the redemption which is in Christ Jesus, whom God set forward as a place of propitiation through faith in his blood ...' (verses 24–25a).

Precisely stated, God accomplished our justification through 'the redemption which is in Christ Jesus'. Paul has just declared that all are 'under sin' (verse 9), a condition which he later describes as 'bondage' to sin and to death (6:17–23; 7:14–25). Consequently, the 'redemption' of which he speaks implicitly includes the resurrection from the dead, of which he later speaks in the same terms (8:23; cf. Eph. 1:14; 4:30). As in his opening declaration, Paul understands justification as 'located' in the resurrection of Christ. Here the 'righteousness of God' is both made manifest and made ours.

It is, of course, in the resurrection of the *crucified* Christ that our re-demption is found. We noted in our discussion of Romans 1:17 that the biblical references to God's saving acts of righteousness imply that his enemies receive retribution in those same acts. Paul now gives that underlying assumption full expression.[76] Christ's atoning death constitutes a 'demonstration of God's *own* righteousness', which has been hidden until 'the present time' (3:25–26). This delay has taken place on account of God's 'patience', in which he passed over the sins which human beings have committed (verse 25). As similar expressions in Romans indicate, in speaking of God's 'patience' (*anochē*) Paul has in view the 'forbearance of God intended to lead human beings to repentance' (2:4). Paul here refers to God's earlier suspension of his wrath, not to some former forgiveness of sins. Whereas Paul's initial usage of the 'righteousness of God' refers to the act of God for us in Christ's resurrection, these latter occurrences of the expression have to do with God's own righteousness manifest in Christ's death. God 'demonstrates his righteousness' in the crucifixion of his Son (3:25). In variance from his earlier language of 'revelation', Paul now speaks of the 'demonstration' of God's righteousness. There will come a time when God the Creator will 'demonstrate his wrath and make his power known' (Rom. 9:22).[77] The cross is the prolepsis

---

[76] The two final occurrences of 'God's righteousness' in this passage stand in immediate parallelism to references to God's patience and justice (Rom. 3:25–26). They undoubtedly signify 'God's own righteousness', just as Paul speaks in 3:5 of God's righteousness in his 'contention' with humanity. Note that Paul here employs the simple pronoun, '*his* righteousness'.

[77] The terminology varies between 3:21 (*phaneroō*) and 3:25–26 (*endeixis*). The verbal

of that day of judgment, when God's contention with the world comes to its conclusion. In justifying the sinner God does not set aside his contention with humanity. He brings it to completion in his own Son.

God wills that this completion take place not merely outwardly in Christ's cross, but also in us. Paul concludes with the striking statement that the demonstration of God's righteousness, i.e. his right in his contention against humanity, took place in order that God might '*become* just and the justifier of the one who believes in Jesus' (3:26). The clause bears a telic sense: God demonstrated his righteousness so that he might 'come to be just'.[78] In this concluding statement we have a reflection of the 'confessions' which appear at the resolution of the biblical contentions which we examined above. God 'becomes' righteous in that his adversaries confess his right and their guilt.[79] In the same way, the justification of the one who believes in Christ and the justification of God are bound together. Christ's death represents an atonement (with implicit notions of fulfilment of promise), in which guilt is both acknowledged and removed: 'God set him forth as a place of propitiation through faith in his blood' (verse 25).[80] Faith is thus directed to the *crucified* and risen Jesus. In faith, one takes the side of God in his claim against oneself, giving God justice. At the same time, one takes hold of God's gift in Christ, whom he has 'put forward' as an atonement and in whom he has taken the side of the sinner.

---

form of the latter term appears in the reference to the 'demonstration of wrath' in 9:22. Probably there is a semantic distinction between the two words for revelation, with *endeixis* conveying especially the sense of 'public exhibition' (as opposed to more mental notions of revelation).

[78] *Eis to einai auton dikaion kai dikaiounta.*

[79] E.g. 'The Lord is righteous, but I and my people have sinned' (Exod. 9:27). See also Lam. 1:18; 2 Chr. 12:1–6; Neh. 9:33; Dan. 9:16, and especially Is. 41:26. This usage is roughly parallel to Achan's confession of guilt in Jos. 7:19–21, in which he is said to 'give glory to God' (cf. von Rad 1962: 1:357–358). Rabbinic usage shows that this form of acknowledgment of God's justice continued into and beyond Paul's time (e.g. *b. 'Abod. Zar.* 18a).

[80] This interpretation of Christ's death goes back through early Christian tradition to Jesus' own words at his last Passover meal with his disciples. See Stuhlmacher 1986: 16–29. It is not at all surprising, then, that Paul's language here shows connections with Hebrews, 1 Peter, and the Johannine writings. In accord with our observations above, and the thrust of Paul's entire argument from Rom. 1:18 – 3:20, *hilastērion* should be rendered as 'place of propitiation' (of divine wrath). Paul alludes to the 'mercy seat' (Exod. 25:17–22; Lev. 16:1–34). Cf. Stuhlmacher 1994: 58–59. For discussion and literature, see Moo 1996: 236–240. Note that *God* put Christ forward as *hilastērion.* Paul does not speak of Christ appeasing an unloving God on our behalf, but of a God who redeems humanity in his own Son.

Justification and hope (Rom. 3:27 – 8:39)

Righteousness by faith has its counterpart in the life of faith. This overarching theme guides Paul's thought in 3:27 – 8:39. Furthermore, as Paul's opening triplet of rhetorical questions and affirmations shows, the primacy of faith raises the issue of the proper function of the law: faith excludes boasting, includes the Gentiles and in an unexpected way establishes the law (3:27–31). Not merely the distinction between Jew and Gentile, but the law itself serves as the counterpoint to faith in this section of the letter. Ethnicity appears in Romans 4 as one aspect of a larger question, and comes into more direct focus only in chapters 9 – 11. Of course, Paul deals with the law explicitly in only certain portions of these chapters (4:13–25; 5:12–21; 7:1–25). But the limited discussion of the law is an expression of Paul's theology: he puts the law in its place, subsuming it under the promise of God given to Abraham.[81] As we shall discuss later at greater length, faith is based upon and arises from this promise of God, which has been fulfilled in Christ and will yet come to fulfilment for all creation. Faith lives between Christ's resurrection and ours.

Already in his initial reference to the justification of both Jews and Gentiles by faith, Paul alludes to the hope of the fulfilment of God's promise to Abraham (3:28–29).[82] His thought turns directly to the topic of hope in his discussion of this promise in 4:13–25, comes into prominence in his elaboration of justification in 5:1–11, and reappears in his closing description of Christian life in 8:12–39. Emphatic affirmations of Christian hope appear in the conclusions of Romans 5, 6 and 7, confirming the importance of the theme throughout this section of the letter. To be justified by faith is to live in hope.

Paul's rhetorical questions at the conclusion of Romans 3 concerning works, Gentiles, and the law are Jewish questions. He continues to speak to an imaginary Jewish partner through the first section of Romans 4, shifting at the end of it because of the points he has established (verses 1–12). Abraham was justified by faith, apart from works (verses 1–8). He received the blessing of righteousness while yet uncircumcised, so he is father to both circumcised and uncircumcised (verses 9–12).[83] We shall not pursue this matter except to note that

---

[81] Paul's thought here corresponds to his treatment of the law in Gal. 3:1 – 4:21.

[82] See the discussion of Rom. 9 – 11 in chapter 6 below. It is noteworthy that in this statement he changes his verbs to the future tense.

[83] The outline of Rom. 4 therefore follows the questions of 3:27–31: boasting (3:27–28; 4:1–8), inclusion of Gentiles (3:29–30; 4:9–12), and the place of the law (3:31; 4:13–

Paul treats 'works' and circumcision (with its obvious ethnic significance) as two distinct issues.[84] As his discussion itself reveals, 'works' held moral and religious implications, and cannot be reduced to ethnic concerns as some interpreters would like to do.

It is not merely for the sake of an *ad hominem* argument that Paul treats the figure of Abraham. Because he understands justification as the fulfilment of promise in Jesus Christ, he begins his argument by clarifying the significance of the one to whom the promise was given. Abraham is integral to his 'biblical theology' of justification.[85]

According to the Scripture, Abraham's faith was 'reckoned to him as righteousness' (verse 3; Gen. 15:6). For the moment, the promise in which Abraham believed recedes into the background as Paul deals with Abraham's justification. The divine reckoning is entirely different from human calculation, which gives another only that which is due. God counted Abraham's faith as righteousness. In believing, Abraham did not work, but let God work.

In this context God appears as 'the one who justifies the ungodly' (verse 5). The characterization implies an exclusive rule: God justifies *only* the ungodly. The reckoning of righteousness apart from works represents the forgiveness of sins, as Paul's appeal to David makes clear (verses 6–8; Ps. 31:1–2). Furthermore, Paul here anticipates his subsequent description of God as Creator, 'who makes alive the dead, and calls into being the things which are not' (verse 17). The two characterizations are materially linked: justification is necessarily a *creatio ex nihilo*, like the promise from which it proceeds. The divine reckoning alone makes us righteous, not by transforming us, but by re-creating our persons in God's sight. Paul's language suggests yet a further idea: in Abraham's justification God also was justified. In believing the promise, Abraham acknowledged God as the good Creator, and himself as the ungodly one on account of whom blessing and progeny were not already present. The excluded alternative, 'boasting in works', does not simply have to do with a failure to acknowledge God as the source of the good that one does (verse 2). Our deeper problem is that although we may perform 'works', we are transgressors. Boasting hides our ungodliness. Faith, passive though it

---

25).

[84] The same distinction appears again in Rom. 4:13–17.

[85] Against Hays 1985, Paul readily affirms that Abraham is the forefather of Jews 'according to the flesh', anticipating his discussion of Israel in Rom. 9 – 11 (4:1, 12). Although the Gentiles have now been included, the promise to him belongs to Israel. The gospel is 'to the Jew first, and also to the Greek'. See chapter 6 of this study.

is, is obedience, because it lets God be God and allows his judgment upon us to stand. Paul underscores this paradox by returning to Genesis 15:6 at the conclusion of Romans 4. *Because* 'in hope against hope' Abraham believed the promise of God, it was reckoned to him as righteousness.[86] Absolute gratuity and true obedience meet in the promise of God and the faith which possesses it.

Paul likewise is not merely concerned with the questions of his Jewish contemporaries in his discussion of Abraham's circumcision (verses 9–12). He himself regards the promise as belonging to the patriarchs and their believing descendants, as becomes clear in chapters 9 – 11. Gentiles share in it only by being incorporated into this 'Israel'.[87] It is therefore of importance to him that the righteousness belonging to the promise was given to the uncircumcised Abraham. The promise demands the 'righteousness of faith'. This righteousness includes the Gentiles. This faith is required of the circumcised, who must follow in the footsteps of faith of the uncircumcised Abraham (4:12).

Over against the law stands God's promise to Abraham that Abraham's 'seed' will inherit the world (4:13). In speaking of this inheritance, Paul alludes to the 'revelation of the sons of God' at the end of history, the 'redemption of the body' when the 'fellow heirs' of Christ are glorified with him, and all creation is liberated from its captivity to corruption (8:15–23; 5:17). It is no accident that Paul draws a connection between the birth of Isaac and the resurrection of the dead (4:17–19). The one born of the deadness of Abraham's body and Sarah's womb anticipates that resurrection. Isaac therefore foreshadows the resurrection of Jesus the Lord, the 'seed' to whom the world belongs (verses 23–25). In a sense, of course, the fulfilment of promise is not exhausted in Jesus: God will yet bring it to fulfilment in *all* the brothers and sisters of Christ, who share in his inheritance (8:29–30; cf. Gal. 3:16, 29). Christians therefore not only believe in the same God as Abraham; they grasp the same word of promise as he did, now as 'promise in fulfilment' in Jesus 'who was raised for our justification' (4:23–25; see Sass 1995: 503–514).

As Paul stresses at the outset of Romans 5, justification is *by faith*, like that of Abraham, which against outward appearance lays hold of the promise of the God who raised Christ 'for us'. By virtue of Christ, its object, this faith is nothing other than 'boasting' in the 'hope of the

---

[86] We shall return to this topic in chapter 5.
[87] See chapter 6 below.

glory of God' (5:1–2), a glory which entails the resurrection from the dead (cf. 6:4; 8:17, 21, 30). Those who believe have peace with God and 'stand' in grace (5:1–2). Faith lays hold of the love of God which has been established in Christ's death for us (verses 5–8). Those who believe have been justified by Christ's blood, reconciled to God through the death of his Son (verses 9–10).[88] Yet this justification of believers remains a paradox in the present. Those who are right before God are inevitably subject to tribulation in the world (verse 3). They 'suffer together with Christ' as they wait for deliverance from the coming wrath of God (verses 4–5). Like Abraham, they 'hope against hope', trusting in God and his promise despite their circumstances in the world (4:18). They possess the 'righteousness of God' in the form of hope and await the resurrection of the dead.

This 'Christological' understanding of justification is especially apparent in 5:12–21, where Paul summarizes his initial exposition of justification and hope and restates his preceding argument in a new form.[89] Up to this point in the letter he has presented justification as a matter of the standing of the individual before God. In this passage he sets it in the context of human history, which he defines in terms of divine judgment in Adam and grace in Christ.[90] Indeed, a single act of transgression and a single act of obedience determine the entire course of human history.[91] The entrance of sin and death into the world in

[88] Often interpreters read 'reconciliation' as a broadening of 'justification' to include the new life of obedience. Here, however, the social-political metaphor of 'reconciliation' is more limited in its significance than 'justification'. It describes the present reality of a right relation with God, but does not carry the overtones of eschatological redemption that 'justification' does. Nor does it convey the understanding that God himself has been justified in the justification of the believer.

[89] 'On account of this, just as through one man ...' (Rom. 5:12).

[90] Thielman 1993 misses Paul's point by attempting to read 'Israel' alongside Adam and Christ into Rom. 5:12–21: there is no third entity between Adam and Christ. Along with the nations, Israel is in Adam. The promises to Abraham are fulfilled in Christ. The distinction between the Gentiles and Israel, fundamental though it is to this present world, is a mere tool in God's hand. We shall take up this topic in chapter 6.

[91] We cannot discuss here the extensive debates which at least since the time of Augustine and Pelagius have surrounded Rom. 5:12. For a survey of views see Fitzmyer 1993: 413–417. Pace Blocher 1999: 76–81, Theodor Zahn has offered the most plausible reading of the controverted *eph 'hō*, namely, 'under which circumstance', which is confirmed by Paul's usage elsewhere (2 Cor. 5:4; Phil. 3:12; 4:10). 'All sinned' under the condition of their subjection to sin and death which the one man, Adam, introduced (Rom. 5:12b). Sins were committed prior to the law (because sin was present as a 'power' in the world), but they were not 'reckoned' by God: they had no condemning effect of their own (5:13). This interpretation corresponds fully with the obvious point of Paul's larger argument, that 'through one trespass condemnation came to all human beings' (5:18).

Adam has its counterpart in the arrival of righteousness and life in Christ. He is the incarnate Son of God, who as the 'last Adam' reverses the 'pattern' of the first.[92] What we 'are' and 'become' as individuals is the mere outcome of their deeds. Just as Adam's transgression resulted in condemnation and death, Christ's 'free gift' brought justification and life (verse 16). In this affirmation, Paul presupposes the resurrection of Christ and its distribution: those who receive the 'gift of righteousness' will rule in life *through the one*, Jesus Christ (verse 17).[93] His single act of righteousness has brought 'the justification which issues in life' (*dikaiōsis zōēs*) for all humanity (verse 18).[94] The '*gift* of righteousness' (verse 17) is nothing other than Christ's '*act* of righteousness' (verse 18) in its saving significance for all who believe. Our 'justification' has been accomplished outside of us, in Christ incarnate, crucified and risen.

It is no surprise, then, that Paul again speaks of the resurrection from the dead as the immediate effect of justification (verses 17–18, 21). This is also the case in verse 19, where he promises that 'the many' will be instated (*katastathēsontai*) as 'righteous ones' as the result of the obedience of 'the one'. The topics which control Paul's argument in this section, namely the beginning and end of human history, strongly suggest that we should render this verb as a 'real' future, a reading which is confirmed by its immediate parallels (verses 17, 21; pace Moo 1996: 345–346). Furthermore, the opposition between 'justification' and 'condemnation' in context indicates that the verb bears a forensic significance (i.e. 'instatement'), which is well within its range of usage (rightly, Moo 1996: 344–346). Of course, Paul is not thinking merely of a verdict here, but of the enactment of that verdict in our resurrection. Commentators regularly go astray in supposing that Paul speaks of the obedience of believers here, a mere (present) 'righteousness of conduct'. That is to miss entirely the point of his

---

[92] Against Dunn 1980: 98–128, 209–212, as Rom. 8:3; 9:5, Gal. 4:4 and other passages show, Paul fully embraces a doctrine of incarnation, which informs his teaching on justification. Dunn himself has nearly conceded as much: Dunn 1998: 204–206.

[93] As this statement shows, Paul does not envisage here the salvation of all humanity. He deals here only with the manner in which justification comes to those who do believe, i.e. 'those who receive the gift of righteousness'. Elsewhere in the letter he speaks quite directly of the demand for faith (e.g. 1:17) and the division of humanity into saved and lost (e.g. 2:6–16).

[94] Paul's prior contrast between 'condemnation' and 'justification' (Rom. 5:16) indicates that he continues (as in 3:24–25; 5:8–9) to regard Christ's 'deed of righteousness' not merely as an act of obedience (which it was, of course), but as a bearing of our condemnation.

argument: the obedience of the *one* has secured *life eternal* for the many (verse 21).

Paul is well aware that his 'locating' justification in Christ's cross and resurrection might suggest that the present conduct of the believer may remain unaffected by the grace of God. He has spoken to this matter already in a fundamental, although indirect, way in his description of Abraham's faith and Christian hope. In Romans 6 he deals with the matter explicitly, taking up the topic first from the perspective of the death and resurrection of Christ, and then from that of the fallen human being (verses 1–14, 15–23).

He derives his understanding of obedience from grace itself, which he again defines entirely in terms of Christ and his work. Baptism into Christ entails baptism into his death and *thereby* participation in his resurrection. Paul reiterates this relation in several forms, concluding with the confessional statement, '*if* we have died with Christ, we believe that we also shall live with him' (verse 8; cf. verses 4, 5). The resurrection of believers in the future – their 'life with Christ' – is predicated upon their death with Christ in the past. That death set us free from sin and its power. Consequently, 'bodily obedience is necessary as an anticipation of bodily resurrection' (Käsemann 1980: 177).[95] The obedience of believers is a 'walking in the newness which is [eschatological] life' (verse 4). The resurrection of Christ is distributed to us here and now in the form of service to God.

As Paul makes clear, this resurrection cannot be understood apart from Christ's cross. Fallen humanity, 'the old human being', was crucified with the incarnate Son of God, whose death did away with the 'body under the power of sin' (*sōma tēs hamartias*; verse 6). This release took place, according to Paul, because 'the one who has died has been justified (*dedikaiōtai*) from sin' (verse 7). This statement has remained obscure to most interpreters, who generally have not seen that for Paul justification carries associations of power. Modern translations, for example, have made the unwarranted decision to render Paul as saying that 'the one who has died has been *freed* from sin', a reading which captures only a part of his intent.[96] 'Righteousness' language cannot be reduced to the mere notion of liberation, particularly not in this context, where Paul uses the forensic expression 'crucifixion' (and not merely 'death') with Christ (cf. Gal. 3:13). The

---

[95] Paul returns to similar formulations when he describes the work of the Spirit (Rom. 8:9–11, 12–13).

[96] So, for example, both the NRSV and the NIV.

'justification from sin of the one who has died' must be interpreted specifically in terms of life in the body, since Paul obviously does not suppose that everyone who dies attains forgiveness. His point is that the authority of sin over the body is exhausted at death: sin has no claim upon a corpse, so to speak.[97] Our 'crucifixion with Christ' has satisfied the 'right' which sin had over our body, and hence its power (cf. 1 Cor. 15:56). Henceforth, those who believe must present their bodily 'members' as weapons of righteousness for God (6:13).

Paul does not presuppose a sort of magical effect in baptism, since in that case he would hardly need to instruct his readers.[98] His treatment of this matter is rather entirely didactic and confessional: his readers must know and understand what Christ has done, and what baptism and belonging to him entails. They are to 'reckon' themselves 'dead to sin but alive to God in Christ Jesus' (verse 11). His derivation of the 'imperative' from the 'indicative' rules out any mystical conception: Christ's saving benefit must be grasped by faith.[99] We have to do here with a 'theology of the word of God'.

In conjunction with his taking up the perspective of the fallen human being, in the latter portion of Romans 6 Paul shifts away from the imagery of battle. On account of 'the weakness of the flesh' he now employs the imagery of slavery (verse 19).[100] Moral terms (sin, obedience, righteousness, impurity) appear here in the form of personified powers. Our conduct reveals to whom we belong and what our destiny will be: 'for the wages of sin is death, but the free gift of God is eternal life in Christ Jesus our Lord' (verse 23). The moment of liberation, or more precisely, 'change of lords', comes about in receiving the 'pattern of teaching' which constitutes the gospel. This doctrine itself is the power of God which creates true obedience within the heart. Paul provocatively reverses the expected locution here and speaks of the Roman Christians being 'delivered over' to the gospel, and not it to them (verses 17–18). The gospel with the 'righteousness of God' which it announces is now their lord.

---

[97] In Rom. 7:2–3 he similarly appeals to the case of the death of a husband which ends the law of marriage for the wife. The law likewise has no jurisdiction over us beyond our death.

[98] Modern interpretation has generally focused too narrowly upon the theme of participation in Christ's saving power in Rom. 6:1–14, granting religio-historical questions too much weight.

[99] Likewise, as Schlatter 1905: 353 observes, the mystery religions could not speak as Paul does of a 'universal' event in Christ.

[100] The old, fallen being remains with the believer! Already here Paul presupposes the *simul justus et peccator*.

It is important to see that when speaking of Christian obedience, Paul speaks of 'righteousness' as a reality which stands outside the believer, which the believer is to serve and obey, rather than some quality imparted to the believer. 'Righteousness', like 'sin' and 'death', signifies a state of affairs which holds sway in the world, a 'right order' – the saving righteousness of God foretold by the prophets (verses 12, 16, 18, 19, 20). Moreover, although those who believe have been enslaved to 'righteousness', they require admonition and instruction on account of the abiding lordship of sin. 'Righteousness' exercises its lordship in the present (verse 18), yet its reign is still to come: slavery to obedience *issues* in 'righteousness', just as slavery to sin issues in death (verse 16). Again here, Paul speaks of 'righteousness' as the new creation, which is a reality in the risen Christ, although it is yet to come in the world. We are to reckon ourselves 'dead to sin and alive to God *in Christ Jesus*' (verse 11). 'The gift of God is eternal life *in Christ Jesus our Lord*' (verse 23). Again, the 'new obedience' is the resurrection of Christ projected into the present, the earthly dimension of justification by faith alone.

Romans 6 therefore represents the point of transition between Paul's thought in chapter 5 and in chapter 8.[101] God's triumph over the world runs directly through the heart and life of the believer, where the old lordship of sin must be conquered anew in every situation and circumstance. The human being stands under the judgment of God, and therefore can be granted eschatological life and freedom from sin only when the sentence of death has come to completion. This judgment has come to pass for us 'in Christ Jesus'. We have life in him, not in ourselves. His resurrection represents the end of the lordship of sin, the entrance of the new creation. In 'presenting ourselves to God as those alive from the dead' (6:13), we do nothing but apprehend what has already taken place in Christ's death and resurrection for us, in the hope of its final realization. Obedience for Paul is essentially and necessarily a matter of faith, which does nothing other than lay hold of Christ. Conversely, faith which lays hold of Christ and his work is necessarily a matter of obedience. 'Justification' and 'ethics' meet in Christ crucified and risen for us. We shall have more to say about this matter, and about Paul's understanding of final judgment in our discussion of the law and of faith in subsequent chapters.

---

[101] In Rom. 4:1 – Rom. 5:21, Paul focuses upon the promise of God and its fulfilment in Christ. In Rom. 6:1 – 8:39 he focuses upon the fulfilment of the promise in those who believe.

Paul describes the life of hope more fully at the conclusion of Romans 8, where he returns to the themes of tribulation and justification. Here the framework of his thought shifts dramatically from his earlier discussion: now he speaks of believers having been placed – on behalf of God – in the contention between God and the world. Those who believe must 'suffer with Christ' in the 'present time' (verses 17–18), and must be conformed to the image of God's Son, not merely in glory but also in suffering (verse 29). For this reason Paul takes up the Septuagintal reading of Psalm 44:11, which speaks of the people of God given over to death on God's account (Rom. 8:36). He likewise here draws upon the imagery of Isaiah 40 – 66, where the servant of God is set in the midst of the conflict between God and the idols. It is this one whom God predestines, calls, justifies, and glorifies, just as he does all believers, and in so doing he establishes his claim that he is God (verses 28–30; see esp. Is. 49:7–9; 54:1–17). The questions which Paul subsequently raises in this passage are not merely rhetorical. They rather outline the 'contention' into which believers have been thrust by God:

> 'If God is for us, who is against us?'
> 'Who shall bring a charge against God's elect?'
> 'Who shall separate us from the love of Christ?'
>
> (verses 31–35)

For this reason, too, Christ now appears in the role of vindicator ('Who is the one who condemns? Christ Jesus is the One who died ...'; verse 34). Whereas earlier Paul spoke of justification before God, he now speaks of justification by God before the world. That is, he describes God's verdict on behalf of his elect (verse 30). The 'glorification' which Paul attaches to this 'justification' ('those whom he justified, these he also glorified'; verse 30) does not represent a subsequent act, but the vindication which accompanies the divine verdict. It consists in the resurrection from the dead, in which the children of God are glorified with Christ (verses 17, 18, 23). The triplet of questions concerning boasting, Gentiles and the law which began this section of the letter is replaced by a corresponding triplet concerning boasting in God, the suffering elect, and the love of Christ.[102]

---

[102] 'Therefore the friends of the cross say that the cross is good and works are evil, for through the cross works are destroyed and the old Adam, who is especially edified by works, is crucified.' Luther, *Heidelberg Disputation*, Thesis 21, cited from Lull (ed.) 1989: 44.

Again Paul understands the justifying work of the cross in terms of God's contention with the world as to whether or not he is God. To be justified before God is to be placed in conflict with the world, and vice versa. Here again the justification of the human being – now the one in Christ – represents the justification of God. Despite the difference in setting, the framework of thought remains constant: 'justification' has to do with God's contention with the world and his claim upon it. Likewise, in verses 28–39 verdict and vindication are again joined in 'justification'. Those whom God justified, he also glorified (verse 30). The one who delivered up his Son will freely give us all things (verse 32). 'Justification' necessarily brings with it the resurrection from the dead, and nothing less. The display of God's saving righteousness in the resurrection of Christ anticipates the end of history, when he will triumph over the world in bringing his 'sons' to glory.

Chapter Three

Beyond Romans: justification by faith in the letters of Paul

Although Paul's theology of justification is developed at greatest length in Romans, it is not absent from his other letters.[1] His language varies according to the occasion of his writing, but the underlying structure of his thought remains constant. In Christ's death God has passed judgment upon sin, and has brought his contention with fallen humanity to its end. In Christ's resurrection God has granted righteousness and life to those who believe. These children of God live in hope of the new creation which has entered the world in Christ. As we shall see, the 'Christ-centred' understanding of justification which we saw in Romans appears again and again in Paul's letters.

The Thessalonian correspondence

In the opening of 1 Thessalonians, Paul describes the report which had gone out among his churches concerning the conversion of the Thessalonian believers: 'They themselves report what sort of reception we found with you, how you turned to God from idols to serve the living and true God and to wait for his Son from heaven, whom he raised from the dead, Jesus, who delivers us from the coming wrath' (1 Thess. 1:9–10).

The risen Son of God delivers 'us' from the wrath of God. His resurrection effects life for those who are his. The basic elements of Paul's teaching on justification are present in this affirmation.[2] Paul subsequently assures the Thessalonians that 'if we believe that Jesus died and rose, so also God will bring those who have fallen asleep with

---

[1] We cannot examine every passage in which righteousness language appears. For a survey of the usage of Paul's letters see Reumann 1982: 41–123, which differs from our analysis at various points.

[2] See also 2 Thess. 1:4–10.

the Lord at his coming' (4:14). He died for us, that we might live with him (5:10). Believers already share in the age to come: 'you all are sons of light and sons of day; we are not of the night nor of the darkness' (5:5). Through faith in the crucified and risen Christ, the Thessalonians were delivered from God's wrath and granted salvation.

Here again we cannot avoid touching upon the topics of faith and the law, which we shall discuss further in subsequent chapters. In believing in Christ the Thessalonians believed in God and 'turned to God from idols to serve the living and true God'. Their faith was obedience. And their obedience was faith. Paul's exhortations to them are based upon the salvation given in Christ. Because we are 'sons of the day', we are to live as 'sons of day' with moral alertness and sobriety (4:4–5). Paul does not address the Thessalonians in terms of what they were in themselves: some of them could behave quite badly (e.g. 2 Thess. 3:6–7). He calls them to be what God in Christ made them to be. He makes no appeal whatsoever to the law, although he might well have done so in the matter of sexual morality. His instruction is based upon the call of God in the gospel, which effects the holiness of his people. Those who reject this apostolic instruction reject salvation itself (1 Thess. 4:1–6).

Faith in God meant a life of hope for the Thessalonian believers, a 'waiting for his Son from heaven' (1 Thess. 1:10). They waited for that 'Day' of which they had become children (5:4–5). The confusion which entered the congregation was due not to an excess of hope, but to a loss of it. Not all eschatology is hope! The Thessalonians were tempted to make the coming of the Lord a matter of human reckoning. Hope, however, is unseen and incalculable, a waiting in faith for the resurrected life which has been promised in Christ (1:3; 5:8). It was from this hope that some were tempted to stray, using the expectation of Christ's coming for their advantage, withdrawing from the responsibilities of everyday life.

In distinction from the synagogue in Thessalonica, Paul proclaimed salvation in Christ apart from the law to these Gentiles. It is therefore likely that he had instructed them concerning God's saving work in Christ in terms of justification, although the language does not appear in these letters. The traditional material in the Corinthian correspondence shows that Paul transmitted this teaching to congregations which were composed primarily of Gentiles. In the Thessalonian letters, however, Paul had no need to address the issue as he did in his letter to Galatia. There had been a decisive break with the synagogue already during Paul's mission in Thessalonica, so that the Gentile believers there did not face the temptation to adopt the law as the mark of piety.[3] The faith of the Thessalonians, which has obviously come under trial, lies at the centre of Paul's concern.[4] In this context, it was much more important for him to affirm the effectiveness of God's saving work in Christ than it was to set forth its basis. He takes a similar approach elsewhere when he addresses Christian suffering, as for example in Philippians (excepting Phil. 3). Even in Romans 5 and 8, new categories for understanding salvation enter alongside just-ification: peace and reconciliation with God, sonship and redemption, the intercession of the Spirit and the Son, predestination and calling. When God's contention with fallen humanity is not his sole concern, Paul quite willingly communicates the gospel in terms other than justification and righteousness. As these letters show, he is quite able to present the essential elements of God's justifying work without having to resort to a fixed terminology.

Galatians

The main lines of Paul's response to the crisis in Galatia do not seem to have been substantially shaped by his opponents, even though they obviously were called forth by them. His extensive rehearsal of his contact with Jerusalem was almost certainly occasioned by charges from the 'agitators' that he had been dependent on Jerusalem. Yet even this portion of the letter is no mere defence. Paul's account of his con-duct, particularly his confrontation of Cephas, serves as a model of how one should respond to a corruption of the gospel (2:11–12). The body of the letter and its theological argument do not appear to be de-termined by the claims of the adversaries (3:1 – 4:31). Already in 2:19 Paul declares that it was 'through the law' that he died to the law, an-ticipating his use of scriptural proofs, in which he finds the law subordinated to the promise and transcended by its fulfilment in Christ (3:15–29). We can scarcely suppose that Paul was forced to treat the figure of Abraham because his adversaries appealed to him as the model of circumcision: Abraham's circumcision never enters the debate (cf. Rom. 4:9–12)! Paul's attention is fixed on the promise given to Abraham. In it he finds the basis for rejecting circumcision and observation of the law. From this foundation he develops his argument,

---

[3] His statement that 'the Jews drove us out' (1 Thess. 1:15–16), probably recalls his experience in Thessalonica (Acts 17:5–10).
[4] See 1 Thess. 3:1–10; 2 Thess. 1:3, 10–11, 13–15.

not by offering a point-by-point refutation of opponents, but by a 'biblical theology of the promise' which provides an overarching basis for understanding Scripture.

Paul begins by presenting Abraham as the paradigm of salvation, much as he does in Romans. The scripture concerning Abraham sets the terms of divine blessing, 'Abraham believed God and it was reckoned to him as righteousness' (Gal. 3:6; Gen. 15:6). As Paul's subsequent argument reveals, he understands this divine word to bear both exclusive and universal implications. On the one hand, *all* who believe are sons of Abraham; on the other, *only* those who believe are sons of Abraham (Gal. 3:7). The promise which 'preached the gospel in advance' to Abraham is universal in scope: 'in you shall all the nations be blessed' (verse 8). Yet Abraham also provides the pattern to which all who receive the blessing must be conformed: they are blessed *with* the believing Abraham (verse 9; cf. Rom. 4:12). In his second appeal to Scripture in this passage, Paul very probably echoes the conclusion of the Genesis narrative of the promise given to Abraham (Gen. 12:3; 22:18).[5] Implicitly, therefore, he has in view both the beginning of Abraham's faith and its final testing in the offering of Isaac, even if the latter is very much in the background. The blessing of faith is simultaneously unconditioned gratuity and the reward of obedience, just as it is in Romans.[6]

Paul follows his appeal to Abraham with a contrasting rejection of the law and the 'works of the law', which he likewise bases on Scripture. Those who are 'of the works of the law' are under a curse, since the law demands absolute obedience (Gal. 3:10; Deut. 27:26). The law is not of faith, and therefore according to Scripture cannot justify (Gal. 3:11–12; Hab. 2:4). By his substitutionary death, Christ redeemed us from the curse of the law, so that the blessing promised to Abraham might come to the Gentiles (Gal. 3:13–14; Deut. 21:23). Rather than serving as a vehicle for the reception of the promise (as Paul's opponents might have claimed), the law represents an obstacle which had to be surmounted in order for the promise to come to fulfilment.

The second movement of Paul's argument resolves the opposition between the promise and the law by making the latter subservient to the former. The distinction between the two remains firmly in place,

---

[5] Paul's choice of the term *ethnē* in place of *phylai* reflects the latter verse. So, rightly, Sass 1995: 281.

[6] As we shall see, in this matter there is theological continuity between Paul and James.

but now God's saving purposes are viewed in their historical dimensions. This takes place in two different ways. First, Paul underscores the priority of the promise to the law and its inviolability. Just as no-one changes a human covenant once it has been completed, no-one can alter the divine granting of the inheritance through the promise (3:15, 17–18). The course of the biblical narrative from Abraham to Sinai reinforces the distinction Paul already has drawn between faith and the law, except that now he speaks in terms of the promise in which faith has its basis. Secondly, the promise now appears as a plurality of 'promises' to Abraham's seed, whom Paul identifies as Christ (verse 16). Correspondingly, the promised 'inheritance' now comes into view, pointing to the life of the age to come as the substance of Abraham's blessing (verse 18, cf. 26–29). Paul's earlier statements imply that the promise to Abraham had to wait for its fulfilment (verse 8). He now makes that span of time clear: the promise awaited the arrival of the eschaton in Christ. It is within this 'history of the promise' that the law finds its proper function. It was added in order to effect a curse, to prevent the realization of promise before the promised seed arrived (verse 19). By 'enclosing all things under sin' the law points to Jesus Christ, the one in whom the promise has come to fulfilment (Gal. 3:22). In this way Abraham's faith has come to the Gentiles who believe in Christ, and with it Abraham's blessing.

Underlying Paul's theology of promise and fulfilment is the stark contrast between 'the present evil age' and the 'new creation' (1:4; 6:15). The promise has come to fulfilment apart from and in opposition to fallen humanity (4:21–31). That fulfilment represents the entrance of the eschaton into this world in Jesus Christ (3:27–29). The instatement as sons has arrived in him (4:4–7).[7] The law brought servitude under the present fallen world and its 'elements' (4:3, 8–11). In Christ, eschatological freedom is now here (4:26; 5:1). The Spirit who has been sent into the hearts of believers is the prolepsis of the resurrection, the presence of the age to come here and now (3:14; 4:5–7; 5:25). At the same time, Paul speaks with marked eschatological reserve. The 'not yet' stands undiminished alongside the 'already'. It is the unseen Jerusalem above which is 'our mother', not the present, visible city (4:25–26). Those who believe have yet a course to run, a harvest which must yet be reaped at the final judgment (5:7; 6:7–10). Paul's body bears the marks of Jesus, but not yet the glory of the risen Lord (6:17). His theology of justification clearly follows this pattern of

---

[7] Cf. Rom. 8:23, where Paul speaks of the instatement as sons as yet to come.

thought, as we shall see in some brief reflections on selected texts.

Paul's report of his confrontation of Cephas at Antioch provides a theological summary of the letter as a whole. Just as Cephas' behaviour adumbrated the troubles which were to emerge in Galatia, Paul's response to it presents the gospel in abbreviated form.[8] It is significant that after speaking of 'justification by faith', Paul speaks of believers 'seeking to be justified in Christ' (2:16–17). He obviously does not speak in this way from a lack of certitude, but because he here views justification as a future event. As he will later say, 'we through the Spirit, by faith are waiting for the hope of righteousness' (5:5). In a critical sense, the justification of believers is yet to come. The 'being justified through faith' is nothing other than a 'seeking to be justified in Christ'. This understanding is implicit in Paul's continuing explanation of justification: 'I have been crucified with Christ. I live, but no longer I. Rather, Christ lives in me. And what I now live in the flesh, I live by the faith which is of the Son of God, who loved me and gave himself up on behalf of me' (2:19b–20).

The believer has been crucified with Christ. And – Paul's reserve is significant – the risen Christ dwells in the believer, in place of the sinner who once was there. Paul does not say, 'I have been resurrected with Christ'.[9] We presently 'live by faith' which has its source in the Son of God.[10] Unlike the 'works of the law', which bring an outward righteousness, the righteousness of the believer is hidden in hope (cf. 1:14; 5:5). Our justification *in spe* awaits our justification *in re*, the resurrection from the dead.

This essential connection between justification and resurrection appears repeatedly in Galatians. It is especially clear in 3:19–29, where Paul draws a distinction between law and promise: 'If a law had been given which was able to effect resurrection (*zōopoiēsai*), righteousness actually would have been by the law' (verse 22). The law performs the necessary, first step on the way to justification, 'imprisoning all things under sin' (verse 22). Before the promise can be 'given', i.e. fulfilled, the law must condemn and put to death (verse 22; 2:19; cf. Rom. 1:24–

---

[8] In my view it is likely that Paul reports his speech to the end of Gal. 2. Even if he shifts to analysis of that event (at Gal. 2:15), his statement is a summary of his response.

[9] Likewise, in Rom. 6:4 it is probable that he speaks of a future resurrection of believers (see verse 8). Where he speaks of our resurrection with Christ, he does so with the qualification that this resurrection is *extra nos*, 'in Christ' or 'with Christ in God' (Col. 2:12; 3:1; Eph. 2:6). This reserve guards against the problem of an 'over-realized' eschatology which emerges in the later letters: some claim that the resurrection has taken place already (2 Tim. 2:18).

[10] We shall treat the 'faith of Christ' in chapter 5, below.

32). It is therefore by no means contrary to the promises of God (verse 21)! Yet the law cannot bring the resurrection of the dead. That comes about only through the promise (verses 22, 24).

In the latter part of this verse Paul speaks of 'righteousness' as the result of resurrection, as a reality belonging to the age to come. His language again recalls the theme of God's saving righteousness in the Psalms and the book of Isaiah, and parallels his description of the new obedience in Romans 6. The world will be right with its Creator and will be set right within itself. This blessing and life, which God promised to Abraham, has come to fulfilment 'in Christ Jesus', the seed of Abraham (3:16, 29). Those who believe find their justification in him (verse 24). In baptism they have 'clothed' themselves with Christ: 'There is no longer Jew nor Greek. There is no longer slave nor free. There is no longer male nor female. For you are all one in Christ Jesus' (verse 28). 'In Christ' the life of the resurrection is present.[11] It belongs to those who believe in him, who have been justified by faith (verse 24). In hope they possess the righteousness of the age to come.

Justification is found in the crucified and risen Christ, who is present in justifying faith. For this reason Paul follows his statement concerning the indwelling Christ by declaring, 'What I live ... I live by faith in the Son of God' (2:20). He subsequently says that he suffers birthpangs until 'Christ' is formed within the Galatians (4:19). Not two pregnancies, but one, is in view. Paul is giving birth to Christ within the Galatians. Correspondingly, being justified in the law means being *severed* from Christ (5:4). Christ is really present in those who believe: 'those who belong to Christ', Paul later says, 'have crucified the flesh with its passions and desires' (5:24). The marks of suffering upon Paul's body are not his own, but the marks of Jesus (6:15). The Christ-centred understanding of justification which we saw in Romans reappears here.

The Corinthian correspondence

The language of justification appears primarily in brief formulas in the Corinthian correspondence. Even in 2 Corinthians 3, where Paul speaks of the 'ministry of righteousness', he does not engage in extended discussion concerning justification, but recalls prior instruction, using traditional language.[12] This absence of argument on

---

[11] Need we say that Paul knows that Jesus was a free, Jewish male?

[12] Here we have evidence that Paul instructed his Gentile congregations concerning the

justification clearly has to do with the problems in the Corinthian church. Under the influence of Hellenistic culture, the Corinthians had reinterpreted the gospel as the means of present blessing and success.[13] A variety of failures resulted: they evaluated ministers of the gospel by human standards, failed to exercise discipline within the congregation, took one another to court, engaged in immorality under the banner of freedom, and more. The false standards of the congregation led to a widening rift between them and Paul. They were increasingly attracted to Hellenistic Jewish missionaries who, as signs of their authority, boasted of their rhetorical prowess and wonder-working powers. Second Corinthians is largely a defence of the apostolic ministry of the cross in the face of these opponents.

In other contexts, including the Thessalonian correspondence, Paul could assume that his readers lived in the expectation of the coming of Christ and final judgment. In the letter to Rome (e.g. 3:6) it is a commonplace to which he could appeal. At Corinth this biblical understanding of the world itself was under attack. It would have served no purpose for Paul to argue the means of justification, when final judgment, resurrection, and the age to come themselves were in doubt. For this reason Paul speaks so often in terms of 'holiness' in these letters. He is reasserting the biblical understanding of salvation, which is not in the first place a matter of my empowerment or pleasure, but of God's reclamation of 'this piece of earth' for himself.[14] Similarly, he uses traditional statements on justification in the Corinthian correspondence as frontal assaults upon disobedience to the gospel. They appear in the form of declarations, sharp reminders of the truth which the Corinthians had abandoned. Despite their brevity, therefore, they are basic to Paul's thought. In them Paul calls the Corinthians to return to Jesus Christ, the irreplaceable foundation which he had laid among them (1 Cor. 3:11).

In another way, too, Paul's teaching on justification in these letters reveals that it was of fundamental significance to him. He here applies it not to relations between Jews and Gentiles, but to the pride which had emerged within the Corinthian congregation. It is not the problem

---

justifying work of the cross, probably from the very beginning of his work.

[13] The Corinthian error should not be characterized as 'over-realized' eschatology, as is often done. They did not take Paul's eschatological teaching to an extreme, but discarded it. The text which is usually used as a starting-point for this thesis represents Paul's ironic characterization of their thinking (1 Cor. 4:8).

[14] This expression appears frequently in Käsemann's essays. On the topic of 'holiness' as God's possession of the earth, see Peterson 1995.

of nationalism or ethnicity, but the divine contention with fallen humanity which calls forth his statements on justification here – and elsewhere. This background is especially apparent in the first formulaic statement concerning justification which appears in 1 Corinthians: 'But by him you are in Christ Jesus, who became for us wisdom from God, and righteousness, and holiness, and redemption, in order that, just as it is written, "Let the one who boasts, boast in the Lord"' (1:30–31; Jer. 9:23). The crucified Christ is the wisdom of God which, according to Scripture, has 'destroyed the wisdom of the wise' (1:19; Is. 29:14). Isaiah's announcement of divine judgment upon Israel extends to the nations. The passage from Jeremiah which Paul cites likewise reflects God's decision to send Israel into exile for its sins. For this reason, Jeremiah warns that the wise should not boast in his wisdom, nor the strong in his strength, nor the wealthy in his wealth (Jer. 9:22). None of these will deliver when destruction comes. This judgment has now been rendered on the world – proleptically – in the crucified Christ. In him God has brought human wisdom, strength, and privilege to nothing, so that 'no flesh might boast before God' (1:26–29).

This Christ is the 'wisdom and power of God' (verse 24). The resurrection of the crucified Christ is implicit in the saving significance which Paul ascribes to him. The triplet of descriptive nouns which Paul uses in our text represents varying perspectives on a single divine act. He speaks in the category of 'being' here, or more precisely, 'coming to be': Christ *became* for us righteousness, holiness and redemption' (verse 30). Consequently, it is clear that the formula reflects Christ's incarnation, cross and, especially, his resurrection – his 'coming to be' righteousness from God for us. In other words, Paul here declares that Christ, crucified and risen, is the 'wisdom from God'.[15] As we suggested above, his terms represent an assault on the understanding of salvation which had infected the Corinthian congregation, a call to return to biblical truth. 'Sanctification' (or 'holiness') and 'redemption' respectively speak of the establishment of God's ownership of the human being and of deliverance from slavery and disaster. And as Paul's implicit reference to the risen Christ suggests, 'righteousness' here again signifies God's saving righteousness, which rectifies the world and its relation to him. This 'saving righteousness' comes about only through God's triumph in his contention with the world. The risen Christ is the crucified Christ in

---

[15] Note that Christ does not make us wise; rather, Christ *is* our wisdom! For this reason boasting is in 'the Lord', not in ourselves (1 Cor. 1:30–31).

whom the world has been condemned.[16]

A similar triplet of terms appears later in the letter. After listing various unrighteous persons who will not 'inherit the kingdom of God', Paul declares: 'And some of you were such persons. But you were washed, but you were sanctified, but you were justified by the name of the Lord Jesus Christ and by the Spirit of our God' (6:11). As in the earlier passage, Paul's language here reminds the Corinthians of the biblical understanding of salvation from which they had strayed. The terms vary only slightly from the first triplet. The reference to 'washing' no doubt recalls baptism. The placement of 'justification' in final position yields an inclusio, by which Paul recalls his initial statement concerning the exclusion of the unrighteous (*adikoi*) from the kingdom of God (6:9). 'Justification' again signifies the life and righteousness of the new creation, as its association with the kingdom of God suggests. It creates new persons, who no longer are what they once were. For this reason, too, Paul speaks of justification 'by the Spirit of God', the agent of the resurrection and the new creation. In this formula he admonishes the Corinthians to believe in the work of God in Christ, without which they will not see the kingdom.

The same understanding of justification appears in a traditional formula in 2 Corinthians: 'On behalf of us [God] made him who knew no sin to be sin, that we might become the righteousness of God in him' (5:20). This confession is a summary of Paul's apostolic message, through which God's reconciling work in Christ is distributed to the world. It therefore recalls his characterization of the work of Christ which precedes his description of his ambassadorial role: 'If anyone is in Christ, there is a new creation. The old things have passed away. Behold, new things have come to be!'

The 'new creation' reflects the promise of the book of Isaiah, in which God effects his saving righteousness for his people (Is. 43:14–21, 6–11; 51:4–8; 65:17–25). In this passage again Paul identifies the saving righteousness of God with God's work in Christ. Moreover, it is Christ's resurrection in particular which he has in view. Just as God's making Christ 'sin' is an indirect means of speaking of his death, so God's making us 'the righteousness of God' implies the resurrection from the dead. The conclusion of the statement contains a significant imbalance, which reinforces this point: God made Christ sin on our

---

[16] The verse from Jeremiah which Paul cites ('Let the one who boasts boast in the Lord') also anticipates the establishment of righteousness through the exile (1 Cor. 1:31; Jer. 9:23).

behalf, so that we might become the righteousness of God *in him.*[17] It is *in Christ* that there is a new creation. From this perspective Paul's following appeal to Isaiah makes sense: '[God] says, "In an acceptable time I heard you, and in the day of salvation I helped you". Behold, now is the acceptable time! Behold, now is the day of salvation! (6:2; Is. 49:8). God's promise to his Servant has been fulfilled in the resurrection of Jesus. The 'day of salvation' therefore has arrived, to which the Corinthians must respond. Indeed, Paul subsequently describes the Corinthians as *being* 'righteousness'. Here we find not a mere quality, but a state of affairs. They cannot share in unrighteousness, not because of what they are in themselves, but because of what God has made them to be in Christ (6:14).

The extrinsic character of the gift of righteousness is likewise apparent in 2 Corinthians 9:9. Citing Psalm 112:9, Paul urges the Corinthians to complete their contribution for the saints in Jerusalem: 'He scattered, he gave to the poor; his righteousness endures for ever.' Paul places the Corinthians in the role of the righteous person in the psalm, using the passage to support his claim that through the grace of God the Corinthians may have 'all sufficiency, in all ways, at all times' so that they might abound in 'every good work' (verse 8). Such 'sufficiency' corresponds to the 'righteousness [which] abides for ever', and implicitly points to the life of the resurrection. This 'righteousness' therefore represents not the result of giving, but its basis. In the following verse, Paul speaks of 'righteousness' itself producing 'fruits' (note the plural). The term therefore presupposes a foundational, creative work of God. God the Creator, who 'supplies seed to the sower and bread to the one who eats', shall 'supply and multiply your seed, and the fruits of your righteousness' (verse 10). So Paul promises. God's sovereign rule over creation becomes a sign of his effecting eschatological salvation. Paul here alludes to Isaiah 55:10, which describes the all-powerful, redeeming word of God in terms of the Creator's providential care for the world.[18] Redemption from sin is an act of creation, as are all God's works. In it human beings come to recognize God as Creator and therewith embrace their creaturely roles as vehicles of his good purposes. In this way they become participants in the work of God. Paul therefore prays that God might increase the

[17] It is this final prepositional phrase in particular which shows that Paul views Christ's death not only as representative, but also as substitutionary.

[18] Is. 55:11, 'So shall my word be, which goes forth from my mouth. It shall not return to me empty, but it shall accomplish my pleasure and cause to prosper that for which I sent it.'

Corinthians' 'seed' and the 'fruits' of their righteousness, joining the petition for present blessing with its eternal end (verse 10). He has already encouraged them to give generously, since 'the one who sows sparingly' shall reap in the same way at the arrival of the eschaton (verse 6). In a twofold sense this harvest is merely the crop which God himself has produced. In his care for the present world, God the Creator provides the means to give. In the gospel he has effected a new creation, with an everlasting righteousness from which generosity flows from his people. For this reason, the collection does not merely meet the needs of the saints, but results in thanksgiving to *God* (verse 12). It is proof of the Corinthian confession of the good news of Christ and their 'participation' (*koinōnia*) with all believers (verse 13). Because of the grace of God 'upon' the Corinthians the believers in Jerusalem will long for them (verse 14). In conclusion, Paul breaks into an exclamation of praise to God for 'his indescribable gift', Christ himself (verse 15). He is the righteousness which 'abides for ever'.[19]

As we have seen, the traditional formulas concerning the gift of righteousness in the Corinthian correspondence speak without exception of justification in terms of 'being'. Believers *are* 'in Christ Jesus', and he *is* to them righteousness, sanctification and redemption (1 Cor. 1:30). The Corinthians *were* immoral, greedy and idolatrous persons, but have been washed, sanctified and justified (1 Cor. 6:11). Christ was made *to be* sin, in order that those who believe might *be* the righteousness of God (2 Cor. 5:21). These ontological statements correspond to the extrinsic character of righteousness and justification which we have seen already. The new creation and its righteousness have come to reality in the resurrected Christ.

Philippians

The topic of justification appears in a discrete section of Philippians which is sometimes treated as an independent composition (3:1 – 4:1). This is highly unlikely, however, since the themes which dominate the earlier part of the letter are integral to this section as well (see esp. Garland 1985). The letter is Paul's thanksgiving for the gift which he received from the Philippians, and deals with difficulties associated with Paul's imprisonment. Paul's purpose throughout is to set forth

---

[19] Notice that Paul describes the gospel here as the 'gospel [i.e. good news] of Christ'. We might even say, using Johannine language, that he is the Word and bread which came down from heaven, the locus in which creation and redemption meet.

believing life as conformation to Christ in both humiliation and
exaltation. It is this pattern, not his circumstances or possible execution, with which Paul wants the Philippians to concern themselves.
Philippians 3 therefore is closely linked with the rest of the letter,
particularly the 'hymn to Christ' in 2:5–11. Paul measures loss and
gain in terms of Christ alone (1:21; 3:7–8). He wishes to share in the
power of Christ's resurrection, and to know the fellowship of his
sufferings (2:8–11; 3:10–11). He awaits Christ as the Saviour from
heaven who will bring his present humiliation into conformity with his
glory (2:7–8, 9–11; 3:20–21).

In this chapter, then, Paul is not combating opponents within the
congregation. Those who would urge Judaizing represent more of a
general danger than a specific and immediate problem. Paul's teaching
here is a reminder of instruction he had provided earlier (verse 1). We
cannot discern from his statements whether he has in mind Jewish
Christians who advocate the circumcision of Gentiles, or Gentile
Christians who have adopted circumcision and now themselves seek to
further the practice, or both.[20] We need not suppose that Paul deals
with two different threats in the chapter, legalism and libertinism
(verses 2–6, 17–19). As Galatians (5:13 – 6:10) shows, legalism itself
is fleshly behaviour in which various vices are likely to manifest
themselves. Those who advocate Judaizing represent a false and
destructive piety, against which the congregation must be protected.

Within this context, Paul speaks of justification by faith. On account
of the knowledge of Christ, he has set aside his former 'righteousness
from the law' (verses 6–8). He regards it not merely as inferior, but as
'loss' and 'dung' (verses 7–8). It represented a false confidence in
fallen humanity and a distortion of true worship (verse 6). The
elements of his former righteousness (on which I have commented
already) were outward and visible. He has set them aside, not for an
inner virtue, but for Christ. Here a tension emerges. Paul has Christ and
knows him: for this reason he regards all else as rubbish (verse 8). But
he does not yet have Christ and does not yet know him: for this reason
he longs to gain Christ (verses 8, 10–12). This knowledge of Christ is
found in the 'power of his resurrection' in which Paul longs to share
and to which he presses forward (verses 10–12).[21] The tension

---

[20] It is in any case unlikely in the extreme that Paul is thinking simply of Jewish people
here.

[21] *Hoc est Christum cognoscere beneficia eius cognoscere* (Melanchthon). Paul's
earlier reference to 'the knowledge of Christ Jesus my Lord' likewise points to the
resurrection from the dead (Phil. 2:9–11; 3:20–21). The path to the resurrection

therefore arises from the hope of the resurrection, which has come to reality in Christ the Lord, but is yet to come in those who belong to him.[22]

Faith spans the gap between the present and the day of judgment. It is the true worship, which sets the believer in constant movement forwards, and which counts as righteousness before God (verses 3, 9). Paul has it as his aim 'that I might be found in him not having my own righteousness which is from the law, but the righteousness which is through "the faith of Christ", the righteousness from God on the basis of faith' (verse 9). Here he has in view the day when God will examine him, and hopes to meet that judgment with the 'righteousness of faith'.[23] The righteousness Paul desires comes from God, 'on the basis of faith' (*epi tē pistei*). Faith, not the righteousness from the law, constitutes true piety before God. Yet this righteousness accorded to faith is an 'alien righteousness', which does not belong to Paul as his righteousness from the law once did. Faith and its righteousness are present only 'in Christ'. The 'faith of Christ' is faith which has its source in him, in his death and resurrection (verse 9).[24] Paul's thought here is very close to his discussion of Abraham's faith in Romans 4. The 'righteousness from God on the basis of faith' is at once absolute gift and recompense of obedience.

Justification in the later letters of Paul

Paul's teaching on salvation takes on new forms in Colossians, Ephesians and the Pastoral Epistles.[25] Nevertheless, in the Pastoral Epistles we encounter formulations which reflect the theme of justification as it appears in his earlier letters: 'And great, according to (our) confession, is the mystery of piety: the one who was manifest in the flesh, was justified by the Spirit, was seen by angels, proclaimed

---

necessarily passes through 'the fellowship of his sufferings (3:10).

[22] There are overtones of God's saving righteousness here. God's raising Jesus from the dead was an act of vindication, a note which is sounded in the well-known hymnic passage of Phil. 2:6–11 ('*Therefore* God exalted him highly'). In sharing in Christ, Paul shares in that verdict and act of power.

[23] As elsewhere in Paul's letters, 'finding' involves examination and judgment (1 Cor. 4:2; 15:15; 2 Cor 5:3; Gal. 2:17).

[24] See the discussion of *pistis Christou* in chapter 5 below.

[25] The differences between these letters and Paul's earlier epistles have been sufficient to raise doubts for many scholars regarding the authenticity of these letters. Nevertheless, we think there are good reasons for supposing that Paul was the author of all these letters. We shall leave the brief letter to Philemon out of consideration here.

among the nations, taken up in glory' (1 Tim. 3:16). Here Christ's resurrection is described as his 'justification'. God's judgment is joined to his vindicating action, as in other letters of Paul and their biblical antecedents. Most significantly, God's work in Christ (which is traced from incarnation to exaltation) is the basis of piety or godliness. The confession closely corresponds to the understanding of justification we have seen already.

The same is true in a second text which speaks of justification in relation to the believer: 'When the kindness of God our Saviour and his love for humanity appeared, he saved us, not by works which we did in righteousness, but according to his own mercy, through the washing of rebirth and renewal by the Holy Spirit, whom he richly poured out upon us through Jesus Christ our Saviour, that being justified by the grace of that One we might, according to hope, be heirs of eternal life' (Titus 3:4–7).

Not 'works which we have done in righteousness' but the 'grace of Christ', through whom the Spirit has been 'poured out', justifies us.[26] Justification here is equated with 'rebirth and renewal' by the Spirit, and is a prolepsis of the 'eternal life' which belongs to believers in hope. It is the establishment of the righteousness of the new creation.[27] The passages which speak of the pursuit of righteousness (which, of course, has an ethical dimension) fit into this framework very well.[28] Likewise, the relationship of the believer to the law appears in the same manner as in the earlier letters of Paul: 'We know that the law is good, if one uses it lawfully, knowing that law is laid down not for a righteous person, but for the lawless and disorderly, for ungodly persons and sinners ... and whatever else lies opposed to sound doctrine according to the gospel ...' (1 Tim. 1:8–11).

A familiar passage from Ephesians comes very close to the language of Romans and Galatians: 'For by grace you have been saved through faith, and this [entire event] is not of yourselves; it is the gift of God, not by works, that no-one might boast. For we are his creative work, created in Christ Jesus for good works, which God prepared beforehand, that we might walk in them' (2:8–10).

Instead of the more frequent contrast between 'works' and 'faith' we

---

[26] The grace of Christ is his surrender of himself on the cross for our sins. Cf. Rom. 5:15; Gal. 1:4; 2:20; 1 Cor. 11:23–26. In his earlier letters Paul is concerned to deny the saving value of 'works'. Here it is disobedience which stands in contrast to the mercies of God. The sole means of justification is the 'grace of Christ'.

[27] See also 2 Tim. 4:8, which speaks of the hope of righteousness.

[28] 1 Tim. 6:11; 2 Tim. 2:22; 3:16; Titus 1:8; 2:12.

find here a contrast between 'grace' and 'works'.[29] Faith is the means by which grace operates. But neither of these formulations is new.[30] Paul's shift from 'justification' to 'salvation' is more significant.[31] The change in terms involves not a broadening, but a narrowing of scope. As we have seen, 'justification' for Paul comprehends the new creation and the resurrection from the dead. In speaking of 'salvation' Paul surrenders the forensic context of justification, that is, the divine contention with the world and his triumph over it in the resurrection of Christ. That is not to say that these ideas have been discarded in Ephesians. They appear in other forms, even in the immediate context. The Ephesians had been 'children of wrath' with the rest of fallen humanity (verse 3). In Christ, God has done away with the law which separated Jew and Gentile from one another and from God (verses 14–18).[32] He has triumphed over the powers of the present world (verse 2). In his saving work in Christ, God has abolished all boasting (verse 9).

This dispersion of the conceptual elements of justification into the theology of the letter is characteristic of Colossians and Ephesians. Paul generally speaks of the forgiveness of sins rather than justification. But this forgiveness encompasses the whole life of the believer, not merely past deeds: by it God gives life to the dead and freedom from the powers of evil.[33] As such, the theme of forgiveness approaches that of justification in the earlier letters. Paul interprets justification in terms of forgiveness in Romans 4:6–8, so this change in

[29] This pairing appears regularly in the later letters (Eph. 1:6–7; 3:2; Col. 1:6; 1 Tim. 1:14; 2 Tim. 1:9; Titus 2:11).

[30] On 'grace' and 'works' see Rom. 4:4; 11:6. Paul often speaks of faith as the means by which Christ's work is mediated (e.g. Rom. 3:25; 1 Cor. 2:5; 15:14; Gal. 3:14). The 'works' to which Paul refers here are substantially the same as those in his earlier letters (likewise 2 Tim. 1:9; Titus 3:5). As we saw in Romans, Paul moved between the two forms, 'works of the law' and 'works' with only a slight shift in meaning. Naturally, the expression now carries new significance, since the new obedience takes its orientation from the gospel (Eph. 2:10). Nevertheless, it is simply not true to say (as some interpreters do) that here 'works' refer to 'works in general'. The will of God expressed in the law neither requires nor allows generalization (Eph. 6:1–3; 1 Tim. 1:8; cf. 2 Tim. 3:15–16).

[31] It is not the case, pace Marshall 1996, that 'salvation' is Paul's usual term for God's work for humanity. The usage of 'salvation' noticeably increases in the later letters, while that of justification nearly disappears.

[32] Literally, 'the law of commandments in injunctions' (Eph. 2:15; cf. Col. 2:14). Probably the idea here is that the commandments come in the form of injunctions carrying sanctions (*dogmasin*; cf. Dan. 6:13, LXX).

[33] Eph. 1:7; 2:1; 4:32; Col. 1:13–15; 3:13; 2:13–15. The description of salvation as 'life from the dead' differs from the earlier letters, where believers are said to be put to death and raised to life with Christ. But it has precedents in the earlier letters (e.g. Rom. 7:9). There is no loss of eschatology here (cf. Eph. 1:14; Col. 3:4–6).

vocabulary is not unprecedented, nor does it involve a major semantic shift. 'Forgiveness' lacks, of course, the theme of God's justification in his contention with the world. But as we have just seen, this element of the gospel appears in God's triumph over the powers of evil and the exclusion of the human boast (Eph. 1:19–23; 2:2, 9; 6:10–17; Col. 2:15).

Paul, then, does not set aside his earlier teaching on justification in his later letters, but unfolds and elaborates it in new circumstances. Particularly in the traditional statements of the Pastoral Epistles, it becomes clear that this understanding of God's work in Christ is the foundation upon which Paul builds. If the writing of Philippians is to be ascribed to the same period of Paul's ministry as Ephesians and Colossians, it shows that Paul was prepared to present his teaching on justification by faith whenever the threat of Judaizing arose.[34] Furthermore, as Ephesians (2:11–22) and 1 Timothy (1:8) make clear, the church requires continuing reminders that Gentiles have been made partakers of the promises to Israel, and that the law serves the gospel and finds its end there. The situation of the later letters is not essentially different from that of the Thessalonian and Corinthian correspondence. Paul presents his gospel as a 'word on target', in terms that fit his audience and their needs.[35] He is not bound to the language of righteousness and justification to express the ideas which those terms convey. His freedom of expression is a mark of his understanding of the gospel.

---

[34] Similar themes appear in Colossians, where Paul wards off an asceticism which carried Jewish overtones (2:11–15, 16–23). In Titus certain heretical teachers, especially 'those of the circumcision', are a threat to the churches (1:10).

[35] I borrow this expression from my teacher, J. Christiaan Beker, in thankful memory of him.

Chapter Four

The righteousness of God and the law of God

As we have seen, Paul speaks of a twofold relation of the law to justification: 'Apart from the law the righteousness of God has been manifest, being witnessed by the law and the prophets' (Rom. 3:21). The law is excluded from the gift of righteousness given through Christ, yet it shares in the prophetic witness to that righteousness (cf. Rom. 3:31; 7:1–6; Gal. 2:19). Paul never calls into question the divine origin of the law, its holiness, its goodness, or its authority, but nevertheless unequivocally declares that believers are no longer subject to it.[1] In anticipation of our following discussion, we may say that Paul's surprising statements concerning the law make sense given his view of the fallen state and moral inability of the human being (Laato 1995). In the light of the work of Christ, the purpose for the law becomes clear (see Westerholm 1988). There is no need to speak of contradictions in Paul's thought (Räisänen 1986), or of development in his understanding of the law in the course of his mission.[2]

Paul's legal terms

We shall proceed by exploring the significance of several terms which Paul uses in reference to the law, which are potentially confusing and have been matters of debate.

---

[1] They are not 'under the law' (Rom. 6:14; 1 Cor. 9:20; Gal. 3:25; 4:5, 21). They have died to the law (Rom. 7:6; Gal. 2:19).

[2] E.g. Drane 1975; Hübner 1984. It is largely because he does not recognize the dimension of sin in biblical understanding that Fuller 1980 cannot understand how the law, which demands obedience, serves the larger purpose of God's grace.

'Law' and related terms

It is useful in examining Paul's use of the term *nomos* ('law') to distinguish between 'meaning' and 'reference'.[3] Words not only 'refer' to things but 'signify' concepts. The word 'constitution', for example, may refer to a national constitution, or signify the more general idea of a body of fundamental rules, or serve both purposes at once. If we bear this phenomenon of language in mind, we may more easily understand Paul's usage of the Greek term *nomos*. Most of the occurrences of *nomos* in Paul's letters refer to the law of Moses. They therefore convey not only ideas related to 'law' in general, but also those associated with the law of Moses in particular. We may summarize them in a general way as follows:[4] *The law which was given through Moses[5] to Israel[6] announces the demands of God for life in the present, fallen world[7] in written words[8], which offer life and blessing on the condition of obedience,[9] but death and a curse for disobedience.[10] Those who know the law shall be judged by it.[11]*

Clearly, not all of these ideas come into play in every passage, but Paul generally assumes one or more of them each time he uses *nomos* (as may be seen in the citations in the preceding footnotes).[12]

In a few instances Paul uses *nomos* to signify the concept of 'divine ordinance' or 'regulation' in word-play upon its usual reference.[13] One group of these texts has to do with the gospel as expression of the will

---

[3] See Silva 1994: 101–108, who differs slightly from my presentation. Winger 1992 makes an important contribution here, although he attaches far too much importance to the observation that for Paul 'law' usually refers to 'the Jewish law'.

[4] See Moo 1983: 82–83; Westerholm 1988: 106–109.

[5] Rom. 10:5; 1 Cor. 9:9; Gal. 3:17, 19.

[6] Rom. 2:14, 17; 3:19; 9:4.

[7] Rom. 7:1–3; Gal. 2:19; 4:3.

[8] Rom. 10:5; Gal. 3:10.

[9] Rom. 7:9–10; 10:5; Gal. 3:11.

[10] Rom. 1:32; 7:9–13; Gal. 3:10.

[11] Rom. 2:12, 27; Gal. 5:3.

[12] In describing Paul's usage in this way, we are rejecting the view that Paul uses the term *nomos* to refer to 'legalism' (as, for example Cranfield 1979: 2:845–862; Fuller 1980: 65–120). It is likewise unlikely that the Greek term *nomos* distorted the sense of *twrh* (Dodd 1935: 30–31). *twrh* does sometimes mean 'instruction', but its significance is already conditioned when it refers to the Sinaitic code in the Hebrew Bible. For a discussion of these issues see Moo 1983: 83–84; Westerholm 1988: 136–140.

[13] We are thereby rejecting the proposal that Paul sometimes refers to the law itself in some particular form or another in such expressions as the 'law of sin and death' or the 'law of the Spirit of life' (Rom. 8:2).

of God. The gospel represents a 'law of faith' which transcends the 'law of works', that is, the law of Moses (Rom. 3:27; see 10:5; Gal. 3:12). Likewise, although Paul is not 'under the law' and may live 'without law' (*anomos*), he indicates that he is not without a divine norm (*mē ōn anomos theou*): Christ himself is his 'law' (*ennomos Christou*; 1 Cor. 9:20–21). Those led by the Spirit are not 'under the law', according to Paul (Gal. 5:18). Yet the Galatians, to whom Paul wrote these words, were under obligation to fulfil 'the law of Christ', that is to say, 'the law which is Christ himself' (Gal. 6:2).[14] In other passages, Paul describes the divine judgment which delivers the human being over to sin as a 'law'. The 'law of sin' overpowers and enslaves the law of Moses which is mirrored in the mind of the fallen human being ('the law of my mind'; Rom. 7:23, 25). This 'law of sin and death' is overcome by the gospel, that is, the even more powerful 'law of the Spirit of life in Christ Jesus' (Rom. 8:2).

In other instances Paul uses *nomos* to refer to Scripture or the books of Moses, rather than to the demands of the law themselves. That is to say that Paul occasionally speaks of the Scripture as 'law' when it performs the functions of the law, that is, when it expresses God's demands, or testifies to divine judgment.[15] This extension of the range of *nomos* signals that Paul does not think of the law as an isolated or aberrant entity within the body of divine revelation, but integral and central to the biblical message. It is significant that he refers to the Mosaic law only in the singular, unlike his contemporaries Philo and Josephus, or the author of Hebrews.[16] Paul views the law as a unity, not merely as a collection of individual demands.[17]

---

[14] See Gal. 2:20; 4:19; 5:6, 24; 6:17. Rightly, Eckstein 1996: 250—251. Although some interpreters wish to find in these passages a sort of 'Christianized law' to which Paul regards believers as being obligated, his clear statement that believers are not subject to the law argues against this view (Gal. 5:18). It is unlikely that Paul would introduce this weighty qualification of his bold declaration concerning freedom from the law in such an obscure and indirect manner.

[15] On the former, see 1 Cor. 14:34: wives 'are not permitted to speak, as the law also says'. It is possible that Paul has the Pentateuch specifically in mind, but my point remains the same. On the latter, see 1 Cor. 14:21; Gal. 4:21–31.

[16] Stuhlmacher 1992: 261; Moo 1983: 75. Cf. e.g. Heb. 8:10.

[17] Of course Paul knows that the law consists in individual demands (e.g. Rom. 7:7–13). He refers to these as 'righteous requirements' (*dikaiōmata*) or as 'commandments' (*entolai*) With its emphasis upon 'righteousness' (or 'justice'), the former term carries with it ideas of judgment and recompense (e.g. Rom. 1:32; 2:26; 5:16, 18; 8:4). 'Commandment' conveys primarily the idea of 'demand' or 'requirement', but when it refers to the law of Moses, it may naturally be associated with notions of recompense as well (e.g. Rom. 7:8–13; Eph. 2:15; 6:2).

As we shall see, for Paul the law of Moses has a limited role. It presents the demands of God upon humanity under its fallen condition, and in so doing bears witness to God's larger work in Christ.[18] This distinction between the law and God's final purpose is clear already in Paul's provocative application of the term 'law' to the gospel: the law of faith transcends the law of works (Rom. 3:27). For this reason Paul exhorts his congregations with 'commands of the Lord' not contained in the law of Moses (1 Cor. 9:8–14; 14:37; cf. 1 Tim. 6:14), and likewise excludes the requirement of circumcision from 'the commandments of God' (Rom. 2:26; 1 Cor. 17:19). That is not to say that Paul regards the law as something less than the word of God. It is simply not God's final word to us.

'Letter' in Paul's usage

The limited function of the law within the fallen order is especially apparent in Paul's further reference to the law as 'the letter' (*gramma*), or, as the RSV renders it, 'written code' (see Hays 1989: 130–131). *Gramma* always stands in opposition to the work of the Spirit (Rom. 2:27; 7:6; 2 Cor. 3:6–7 twice). This antithesis is not one of literal meaning versus a figural sense. And it obviously does not involve an absolute rejection of written address, since Paul then would not have written letters with instruction, exhortation and demands.[19] Furthermore, Paul's usage lends no support to the claim that the 'letter' signifies a misuse of the law.[20] Rather, as the rendering 'written code' suggests, 'letter' is best understood as a reference to the will of God in the form of written demands.[21] 'Letter' and 'Spirit' represent two different ways in which God addresses the human being. The written code encounters the human being from without, requiring obedience as a condition of life ('do this and you will live'; Lev. 18:5; Rom. 10:5; Gal. 3:12). In contrast, the Spirit writes the will of God upon the heart through the proclamation of what God has done for us in Christ.[22]

---

[18] Paul regards the law as having been given to Israel for the world (Rom. 3:19–20).

[19] On the former, see Luther's lively response to Jerome Emser, 'Concerning the Letter and the Spirit', *LW* 39: 175–203. On the latter, see Käsemann 1971: 139–140.

[20] Rightly, Westerholm 1988: 209–216; against, e.g. Käsemann 1971: 146–147; Furnish 1984: 200–201.

[21] Westerholm 1988: 211 speaks of *gramma* as 'the commandments in written form'. 'Commandments' by definition are written, for Paul. With *gramma* he speaks of the will of God in the form of commandments.

[22] See the discussion of Rom. 10:5–8 below. It is only with respect to the granting of righteousness that Paul draws the distinction between the *written* law and the promises

Unlike 'the written code', the Spirit performs a 'circumcision of the heart' (Rom. 2:28–29; cf. Deut. 30:6; 10:16; Jer. 4:4). Those who believe in Christ render service to God in 'the newness of the Spirit'. They share in the new creation which has been inaugurated in Christ. Their obedience does not derive from 'the oldness of the letter' by which God addresses the fallen human being (Rom. 7:6). Of course, Paul does not imagine that the new creation has come in its fullness. That will not take place until we are raised from the dead. The life of the believer therefore is one of battle between the Spirit and the flesh, between the new creation in Christ and the fallen human being which we remain in ourselves (e.g. Gal. 5:17–26). This very battle confirms the reality of the new obedience. Its outcome is certain already.

The 'works of the law'

We now return to the expression 'the works of the law' which we left unexplored in the first chapter. We there rejected the view that Paul opposes these works because they served simply as 'ethnic boundary markers', and suggested that they bore a broader significance for him.

Paul does not oppose the works of the law in and of themselves. In at least one instance he speaks of them in neutral terms, when he describes 'the person of the works of the law' (Gal. 2:16). He does, however, regard these 'works' as deficient, and opposes the false opinion which supposes that such works contribute to a right standing before God, whether personally or nationally.

We recall that Paul's rejection of the 'works of the law' is rooted in his understanding of God's work in Christ:

> ... because by the works of the law no flesh shall be justified before him, for through the law comes the 'knowledge of sin'. But now apart from the law the righteousness of God has been manifest, being borne witness to by the law and the Prophets, the righteousness of God through faith in Jesus Christ ...
>
> (Rom. 3:20–22).

We find no suggestion in this context that such 'works' are wrong in themselves, as would necessarily be the case if they illegitimately marked off an ethnic boundary to God's grace. Nor does the expression

---

and gospel which *speak*. Elsewhere the law itself speaks (e.g. 3:19), and the promises have been written (e.g. 1:17).

have to do *merely* with 'Jewish national boundary-markers' (circumcision, Sabbath-keeping and the like), since Paul subsequently appeals to the justification of Abraham and David to show that God justifies the *ungodly* and *transgressors* (and not merely Gentiles or pagans) apart from 'works' (Rom. 4:1–8). In fact, Paul treats Abraham's circumcision in Romans 4 somewhat independently of the topic of 'works', interpreting it as a sign of the righteousness of faith (4:9–12).[23] His usage indicates that the expression 'works of the law' refers to 'deeds done in obedience to the law of Moses',[24] and differs from the simpler term 'works' only in its designation of the source of the divine demand.[25] We may think of 'works of the law' in general terms as including adherence to the prohibitions against murder, adultery, theft, idolatry and the like, along with circumcision, Sabbath-keeping and food laws (cf. Rom. 2:17–24).

Nevertheless, Paul obviously regards the 'works of the law' as bearing an ethnic and national significance. Only a Jew may boast in 'the works of the law' or be identified as one who is 'of the works of the law'.[26] It was by 'works' that Israel vainly sought to establish its

---

[23] Against Dunn 1990: 183–241; Dunn 1992. We should probably think of 'circumcision' as hyponymous to 'works of the law', given the connection which Paul assumes between circumcision and 'works of the law' in Gal. 3:1–14.

[24] See Moo 1983: 90–99; Westerholm 1988: 109–122. The expression appears in two clusters in Paul's letters: Rom. 3:20, 27, 28; Gal. 2:16; 3:2, 5, 10. Although Gaston 1984 has argued that the expression 'works of the law' refers to the 'works which the law does' (i.e. he takes *nomon* to be a subjective genitive), his reading is unlikely and few have followed him.

[25] Moo 1983: 95. See Rom. 4:2, 6; 9:32; 11:6; Eph. 2:9; 2 Tim. 1:9; Titus 3:5. Some interpreters suggest that Paul uses the term 'works' to speak of '(good) works in general', in contrast with those works which the law demands. This shift in reference is unlikely, however, since the law remains for Paul an expression of the holy will of God against which all 'good' is measured (Rom. 2:14–16; 13:8–10). Moreover, Paul's argument in Rom. 4 (where he switches from speaking of 'works of the law' to 'works') has to do with the validity of the law (4:13–16), not a generalized 'good'. David, who was justified apart from 'works', transgressed the law (4:6–8). Likewise, Paul later speaks of the believing remnant of Israel being preserved by grace, not by 'works' (11:6).

[26] Gal. 2:16; Rom. 3:27–30. Schreiner 1993: 51–57 attempts to avoid the conclusion that 'works of the law' bore an ethnic significance, by arguing that the expression 'works of the law' refers to all the works which the law of Moses commands. Precisely here, however, his argument fails, since Paul's designation of the source of the demand inescapably brings national identity into view. Who followed the law of Moses but Israel? And if 'works of the law' entail *all* the demands of the law, then circumcision, Sabbath observance and the like are included. Furthermore, the 'works of the law' were the basis of Jewish boasting and a matter of Jewish identity (Rom. 3:27–28). The expression therefore does not refer indiscriminately to any and all demands of the law, but to outward deeds which might be performed and seen by others.

righteousness before God (Rom. 9:30 – 10:3). Clearly, then, Paul rejects these works as markers of 'religio-national' identity, i.e. as signs of the people who are righteous, and not merely as signs of national privilege.

But why, we may ask, are such 'works of the law' insufficient to justify the human being if they represent conformity to divine demands? This question is particularly pressing, since Paul himself affirms that God will 'render to each one according to that one's works' at the final judgment (Rom. 2:6). This divine recompense entails conformity with the demands of the law: the uncircumcised one who keeps the requirements of the law will judge the circumcised transgressor (2:27). We must wonder how Paul can affirm that the doers of the law will be justified (2:16) and deny that believers are justified by works (4:2) within the space of two chapters in Romans.

The resolution to this difficulty comes from Paul's understanding of the last judgment and of the law itself. Final recompense will involve not a 'weighing' or 'counting' of works, but a manifestation of persons by their works: 'It is necessary that we all become manifest before the judgment seat of Christ, that each one should be recompensed for the things done through the body, whether good or evil' (2 Cor. 5:10; see also Rom. 4:10-12).

The day of judgment will reveal the secrets of human hearts (Rom. 2:16; see also 2:27–29; 1 Cor. 4:5). Correspondingly, Paul speaks of the judgment of a person's 'work' (note the singular) as a comprehensive matter. The 'work' of one's life will appear as a whole, either as perseverance in seeking 'glory, honour, and immortality', or as obedience to unrighteousness (Rom. 2:7–8).[27] From this vantage point, we can understand why Paul regards 'the works of the law' as inadequate for justification. As individual, outward acts, the 'works of the law' do not comprehend the whole of the person, or the whole of the law, which, it is to be recalled, Paul regards as a unified demand.[28] The 'works of the law' do not overcome the coveting which is present within the heart (Rom. 7:7–13). This distinction between mere 'works of the law' and true obedience comes to expression in Galatians 3:10, where Paul declares that a curse rests on all those who are 'of the works of the law'. He supports this charge by appealing to

---

[27] Paul knows of poor and inadequate Christian obedience. He is also able to distinguish between the salvation of a person and the rejection of his or her labour (1 Cor. 3:13–15). In this case, however, he speaks of the danger of damnation: if someone destroys the temple of God, God will destroy that person (1 Cor. 3:16–17).

[28] On this topic see Schreiner 1991.

Deuteronomy 27:26: 'Cursed is everyone who does not abide in all those things written in the book of the law to do them.' Paul cites the text freely, interpreting the verse by adding the word 'all' (the things written) from the immediate context in Deuteronomy (Deut. 28:15, 58). The 'works of the law' are inadequate to save, because no-one fulfils all the demands of the law. Often this citation is read as a mere 'quantitative' statement, as if one merely needed to increase the percentage of one's acts of obedience in order to avoid the curse of the law. There is, however, a decisive difference between partial obedience and doing that which the law demands. Paul's perspective becomes clear in his further alteration of Deuteronomy 27:26. In variation from the Hebrew text, he speaks of 'abiding in those things written [in the book of the law]'.[29] Usage of the expression 'to abide' elsewhere suggests that it carries covenantal overtones, so that in this strict interpretation of the demand of the law, Paul appears to have fidelity and love toward God in view.[30] For Paul, to violate one commandment is to violate the whole law.[31] In viewing the requirement of the law in this way Paul is in full agreement with the Hebrew Scriptures, particularly Deuteronomy. To listen to God's voice, to fear God, and to love him is to keep *all* of his commandments.[32] Anything less is disobedience.[33] It is precisely this unqualified love toward God and neighbour of which the fallen human being is incapable.

Here is a decisive dividing-line between Paul and his Jewish contemporaries, who embraced the ideal of full obedience to the law.[34] For them, this aim could be sufficiently realized in the practice of piety: various provisions for atonement compensated for partial failure. Taken as a whole, this way of life could be described as 'perfection'.

[29] Paul may follow the LXX here. The Masoretic text speaks of 'establishing the words of this Torah by doing them'.

[30] See Sirach 28:6–7 and Jer. 38:32 (LXX). Although one may find rabbinic utterances to the same effect, only Paul insists that love for God and neighbour is to be reflected in complete obedience. See Sanders 1977: 107–125; 1978: 109–119.

[31] Paul was not alone in early Christianity in taking this strict stance. See especially Jas. 2:10–11; Heb. 2:2.

[32] See e.g. Deut. 4:1–2; 5:29; 6:1–5, 13, 24; 8:6, 20; 10:12; 13:4, 18; 17:19; 26:16–17; 30:4–10; 31:12–13; Jos. 22:5; Judg. 6:7–10; 2 Kgs. 18:11–12; Jer. 11:1–8; Dan. 9:4, 9–14.

[33] We should remind ourselves, too, that Jesus summarized the law in this way, in the double commandment of love toward God and neighbour (Mark 12:28–31).

[34] See Laato 1995. Garlington 1991 surveys the theme of obedience in selected writings of early Judaism, finding it close to that of Paul, apart from its nationalistic orientation. He fails to come to grips with the profound difference between Paul's understanding of the human being and the 'anthropological optimism' of early Judaism.

The Qumran community used this language, as Paul apparently did prior to his conversion. Obedience from the heart thereby becomes an ideal, a goal to which – with divine assistance – one might attain. For Paul, in contrast, this obedience of the whole person is God's immediate, justified demand. It is not that the human being desires to obey God and is only too weak to enact it. We are rather in rebellion against our Creator, and do not wish to seek him or to serve our neighbour. The sacrifice of Christ does not supplement partial failure, but ends radical disobedience. The 'works of the law' cannot satisfy the demand of the law, because they cannot change the idolatrous human being from whom they proceed. As we have noted, Paul himself, prior to his conversion, attained outward perfection. In retrospect, however, he views this former 'righteousness' as inadequate.[35] The Galatians, who measure their righteousness on the basis of 'works of the law', engage in self-deception and 'foolishness' (see e.g. Gal. 3:1–5). To seek righteousness in the 'works of the law' is to hide from the fallenness of one's own heart: 'by the works of the law, no flesh shall be justified before him, for through the law comes the knowledge of sin' (Rom. 3:20).[36]

This false opinion comes to the fore in Romans 3:27–28, where Paul associates the 'works of the law' with 'boasting': 'Where then is boasting? It is excluded. Through what kind of law? A law of works? No, but through the law of faith. For we reckon that a person is justified by faith, apart from works of the law.' Paul undoubtedly draws the term 'boasting' from the Scriptures. More than once he alludes to the divine pronouncement in the book of Jeremiah, which must have served as a source of his understanding: the one who boasts must boast in the Lord, not in human wisdom, might, or wealth.[37] Indeed, in the Psalms 'boasting' serves as a synonym for 'trusting' and 'worship'. Effectively, that in which one boasts is one's 'god': 'Some

---

[35] One is reminded not only of Paul (Phil. 3:6), but of various accounts from the Gospels. Jesus' charge against the Pharisees who were concerned with ritual cleansing comes especially to mind (Mark 7:1–23; Matt. 15:1–20). It is possible to observe the law quite precisely in an outward manner, and yet fail to practise 'justice, mercy, and faithfulness' (Matt. 23:23). Likewise, Jesus' encounter with the rich young ruler comes to mind (Mark 10:17–22; Matt. 19:16–22; Luke 18:18–23). Upon hearing the second table of the law, he could in honesty say to Jesus, 'All these things I have kept from my youth.' Yet Jesus' word to him revealed his true state. Despite his great obedience, he did not love God from the heart: he went away sad because he placed his earthly wealth above discipleship to Jesus.

[36] We shall discuss the 'knowledge of sin' further below.

[37] 1 Cor. 1:30; 2 Cor. 10:17; Jer. 9:23–24. The psalmists make the saving deeds of God their boast (e.g. Pss. 5:11–12; 34:1–3; 44:4–8).

boast in chariots; some boast in horses; but we shall boast in the name of Yahweh our God' (Ps. 20:7; see also Pss. 44:6; 49:5–6; 97:7).

As in the broader biblical usage, for Paul 'boasting' involves both a relation between oneself and others and a relation between the self and God. Unfortunately, the dominant approaches to this topic have been one-sided. Bultmann (1990: 3:646–654) stressed self-trust as the primary element of 'boasting'. He was thereby able to comprehend the biblical paradox that legitimate boasting is always a boasting in God, but failed to see that for Paul proper boasting has its correlate in the work of God in the world, so that 'boasting' cannot be reduced to a matter of self-understanding. The 'nationalistic' reading singles out Paul's objection to the illegitimate 'boasting' of Jews over against Gentiles, and thus recognizes the social dimension inherent in boasting (e.g. Dunn 1988: 1:185). Yet this interpretation fails to take into account that for Paul 'boasting' also involves a claim for the self before God: 'If Abraham was justified by works he has a boast. But he has no such boast before God' (Rom. 4:2).

The two-sided character of 'boasting' is readily apparent in Paul's usage. The Corinthian boasting in various leaders, by which they asserted their personal superiority, involved a failure to acknowledge that everything they possessed came as a gift from God (1 Cor. 4:7). Likewise, God's negation of all boasting, in the cross, entails the destruction of worldly wisdom, strength, and honour (1 Cor. 1:26–31). Paul's determination to boast only in the Lord meant that he refused to enter into comparison with false apostles (2 Cor. 10:12–18). All human boasting is a violation of the love of God and neighbour which the law demands. Legitimate 'boasting' is paradoxical, pointing away from oneself and one's community to God and his work. The boasting of faith, which appears so prominently in Romans 5:1–11, is a boasting in hope, which, looking beyond outward circumstances, exults in the work of God (verse 3). Against this background, Paul's boast in 'heart' (2 Cor. 5:12; 10:8–17) becomes understandable: the saving work of God presently takes place here, and not in mere appearances, which are subject to human manipulation.

As with the contrast between the 'letter' and the Spirit, we find here the distinction between the work of the human being and the work of God. The boast in the law is empty because it is misplaced: the law can bring only an external righteousness, not a transformation from within (Rom. 2:17–29). The human being requires the new creation which the gospel effects. God alone sees the heart where such work takes place. Praise comes to this person from God himself at the final judgment, not from human beings here and now (Rom. 2:28–29). In rejecting the 'works of the law' in justification, Paul attacks the assumption that outward conformity to the law may secure God's favour and bring salvation (Rom. 3:27–28).[38]

The law as witness to the righteousness of God in Christ

When Paul rejects the saving value of the 'works of the law' in Galatians and Romans, he does so with full recognition that he is dealing not merely with a misreading of the law, but with the law itself.[39] The law is a 'law of works', which demands deeds of obedience in order to obtain the offer of life (Rom. 3:27; cf. 10:5; Gal. 3:12). The misuse of the law lies in the refusal to confess the reality of sin and guilt which it exposes, a refusal which entails seeking to be justified before God by the 'works' which lie within our power (Rom. 3:20). In its manifestation of sin, the law bears witness to Christ. That is its divine purpose, which we shall now explore in selected texts from Paul's letters.

Selected passages from Galatians

As we briefly discussed earlier, although Paul's letter to Galatia obviously was prompted by controversy, his argument appears less shaped by the immediate problem there than by his own 'biblical theology'. At least initially, he formulates his attack upon the Galatians' acceptance of circumcision in terms of the 'works of the law'. Nevertheless, as we have just observed, Paul recognizes that the law itself requires works. When he speaks of the 'works of the law' in Galatians, he immediately turns to discussion of the law proper, first in his brief description of his rebuke of Peter at Antioch (2:15–21), and then in his extended argument in 3:1 – 4:7. His adversaries have rightly grasped the obvious demand of the law upon which blessing or curse follows. They have failed, however, to see the extent of the law's claim

---

[38] Rom. 3:27–28. We need not think that Paul supposes that Jews or Jewish Christians regarded their 'righteousness' as *entirely* self-attained. He argues rather that a righteousness based on the performance of works is *incompatible* with the grace of God. This suggests that in Paul's view many Jews regarded their obedience as a necessary *supplement* to their election by God. Cf. Rom. 11:6.

[39] See especially the discussion of Rom. 3:27 – 4:25 above.

upon their persons and the place of the law in service to the promise.[40]

Galatians 2:15–21

Since we have already discussed the 'works of the law' and the connection Paul draws between life and righteousness, we shall here focus upon a single, significant statement about the law in 2:15–21.

In elaborating his confrontation of Peter at Antioch, Paul asserts: 'If seeking to be justified in Christ we ourselves are found to be sinners, is Christ then a servant of sin? By no means! For if I again build those things I have done away with, I establish myself as a transgressor. For through the law I died to the law, that I might live to God' (verses 17–19).

In context, Paul has just distinguished between 'we who are Jews by nature' and 'sinners from among the Gentiles'.[41] Now he makes them equal. Even 'a person of the works of the law' is justified through the 'faith of Christ' alone.[42] 'We' Jews who 'seek to be justified in Christ' have been revealed by God as sinners.[43] We need not suppose a technical use of the term 'sinner' in this context.[44] Paul does not have in view mere ethnic status, but the judgment of the law. As we have seen already, Paul here speaks of the justification of believers as lying in the future: they seek to be justified in Christ. In the meantime they are also sinners according to the law. Paul's question, then, as to whether Christ serves as a minister of sin is entirely understandable.

His answer is based upon faith in Christ: 'I' have done away with 'those things', i.e. my existence as a sinner and my relationship to the law.[45] If I should reconstruct them (as Peter had done) I make myself, not Christ, a transgressor. Paul regards the law itself as sanctioning the

---

[40] For a thorough treatment of this topic in Galatians see Eckstein 1996.

[41] This statement need not be regarded as the invalid opinion of Jewish Christians who would urge Judaizing. Paul himself regards Israel 'by nature' (but not 'of nature') chosen by God. See the discussion in chapter 6 below.

[42] In Gal. 2:16 *ex ergōn nomou* most likely should be read with *anthrōpos* (not with the verb). Paul speaks of 'a person of the works of the law' (cf. Gal. 3:5, 10, *hosoi ex ergōn nomou*) in analogy to 'a man in Christ' (2 Cor. 12:2), and the various references to 'those of the circumcision', and 'those of the law' (e.g. Rom. 4:16). Despite the contrary insistence from a number of interpreters, a scan of usage of *ean mē* (and *ei mē*) shows that these particles here introduce an exceptive clause. This resolution of the difficulty is more straightforward than the supposition of an ellipsis (Walker 1997). We shall discuss the 'faith of Christ' in the next chapter.

[43] The passive 'we have been found' almost certainly presupposes God as the agent.

[44] Against Dunn 1993: 132–333, 141. Rightly Eckstein 1996: 36.

[45] The active sense itself, which is surprising at first sight, derives from the act of faith, which lays hold of Christ's work (Gal. 2:16, 19).

severance of his relation to it: 'through the law, I died to the law' (verse 19). In a very compressed manner, Paul expresses the thought which we encounter in Romans 7:1–6, that the law finds its limit in its sentence of death. Once that punishment has been meted out, its jurisdiction ceases. Consequently, to re-establish a relationship to the law after having believed in Christ is to violate the law itself. The one who returns to the law is a transgressor of it.[46]

The end of our relationship to the law arises from our participation in the cross and resurrection of Christ: 'I died to the law, in order that I might live to God' (verse 19). As in Romans 7:1–6, we here meet an 'either-or'. Life before God and service to him are possible only where there is freedom from the law. Although Paul does not develop the thought here, he is preparing already for his instruction of the Galatians concerning the 'new obedience' brought by the Spirit of God. Paul, and all who believe, live 'by the faith of the Son of God' and know the reality of Christ living in them (verse 20). Before the law we are sinners. In him sin has been overcome.

Galatians 3:1 – 4:7

As we have seen, in Galatians 3:1 – 4:7 Paul describes the law as the means to the fulfilment of God's promise to Abraham. Its purpose is therefore circumscribed. Those who believe are justified with Abraham and receive his blessing (3:9).[47] This blessing is mediated through Christ, Abraham's seed, in whom God's promises have been fulfilled and through whom they are distributed (verse 16).[48] Those who have been 'clothed' with Christ and belong to him are Abraham's seed (verses 26–28, cf. 19). They are heirs of sonship and of the age to come (verse 29).[49] The law cannot displace or add conditions to God's

---

[46] Similarly, Eckstein 1996: 66.

[47] Although Abraham's justifying faith serves as Paul's starting-point, he is more interested here in the promise of God to Abraham than in the character of Abraham's faith which appears so prominently in Rom. 4.

[48] It is likely that Paul identifies himself and other Jews with 'Gentiles' in Gal. 3:14, since he has just spoken of the curse of the law as resting upon all who disobey it. Consequently, Jews, too, are effectively 'sinners from among the Gentiles' (Gal. 2:15).

[49] Throughout the passage, Paul is focused on the promise of God fulfilled in Christ. For this reason he ascribes the 'coming' of faith to God's work in Christ, even though he has already spoken of the paradigmatic faith of Abraham at the outset of his argument (Gal. 3:6–9, 22). We shall return to this theme and current questions concerning the meaning of the expression 'the faith of Christ' (verse 22) in the next chapter. Here it is sufficient to note, against Hays 1983: 193–196, that Paul's argument in 3:1 – 4:7 is quite coherent once one recognizes that Christ is the sole object of the promise of God in which Abraham believed, according to Paul.

promise to Abraham, since it represents an unalterable 'decree' or 'ordinance'.[50]

This priority of the promise raises a serious problem, of course. If the promise is unchangeable, the law seems to serve no purpose: 'Why then the law?' (verse 19). Paul has a simple answer to the question. The law serves the promise, and not vice versa (cf. Rom. 4:13–15). The law performs this ministry, moreover, in a backwards and contrary way, effecting the very opposite of what the promise offers. It was given in order to effect transgressions and has brought about the curse which it threatened (verses 10, 19).[51] In a strange work of God, the law has brought condemnation so that redemption itself might come: 'The Scripture has imprisoned all things under sin, *in order that* the promise might be given to those who believe' (verse 22). The curse of the law is the precondition to the fulfilment of God's promise in Christ. It imprisoned humanity for the 'faith that was to be revealed' (verse 23). Now that Christ has come, it has become a guardian who temporarily confined us, so that we might be justified by faith (verse 24).[52] The law, which offered life on the condition of obedience, could not impart life (verse 21). As Paul indicates in the opening of this letter, the entire 'age' in which we live is evil (1:4). Redemption comes only from beyond, from Christ, who was sent forth from God and became human, coming to be born of a woman, under the law (4:4–5; cf. 1:1–4).

Paul's line of thought is very similar to that which we saw in Romans 3:19–20. He gives no indication that the demands of the law in themselves create a sense of guilt within the human being.[53] Indeed, he

[50] I have chosen to render *diathēkē* here in a general sense, and not as 'testament'. I cannot here enter into the debate concerning the background of Paul's statement that such a *diathēkē* is unalterable. Paul appears to have something of the order of an 'oath' or 'vow' in view.

[51] Given Paul's following statement about the law's imprisoning humanity under sin, this reading of *tōn parabaseōn charin* in Gal. 3:19 is the most natural. Although interpreters often construe Paul's statement that the law was ordained through angels as a criticism of the law, the phrase is rather honorific. Angels are associated with the presence of the divine glory at the giving of the law (e.g. Deut. 33:2; Ps. 68:17; Acts 7:53; cf. Gal. 1:8; see Stuhlmacher 1992: 264–265). The objective effect of the law is especially apparent in this context: it imprisons *all things* under sin.

[52] The significance of the *paidagōgos* has been the subject of continuing debate. It seems clear enough from the context that Paul draws upon only three aspects of the guardian's function: (1) that those under a guardian are deprived of freedom; (2) that those under a guardian have the status of minors; (3) and that therefore the guardian's role is temporary. Paul thereby is construing imprisonment under sin in a positive way, as a stage in God's redemptive purposes. He does not regard the law as serving an educative function here, nor does he imagine that the law restrains sin.

[53] So also Eckstein 1996: 205–245, 254–255.

could hardly suppose that it would do so, given the Galatians' desire to take the obligations of the law upon themselves. The law rather provides the visible context for the incarnation, death and resurrection of Christ: 'When the fullness of time came, God sent forth his Son, born of a woman, born under the law, that he might redeem those under the law, that we might receive the instatement as sons' (4:4–5).

Galatians 4:21–31

Paul also finds the witness of the 'law' to the gospel in the story of Hagar and Sarah in Genesis 21.[54] The exclusion of Ishmael from Isaac's inheritance corresponds to the work of the law in 'shutting up everything under sin' (Gal. 3:22). Not the son born according to the flesh and under slavery, but the son born according to promise and in freedom, is the heir of salvation. Paul perceives the pattern of law and promise in God's dealings with the sons born to Hagar and Sarah. The former corresponds to human inability and failure despite the greatest of efforts, the latter to the triumph of the divine word despite all outward appearances. The distinction between them lies again in the difference between the work of the fallen human being and the work of God. Hagar, the slave, signifies the 'covenant from Sinai', whose children are begotten 'according to the flesh'. It corresponds to the 'present [mount of] Jerusalem', which, according to Paul, is 'enslaved along with its children'. In contrast, those who believe are children of the free woman, the heavenly Jerusalem. As we have seen, the law is neither God's first nor last word to us. That first and last word is the promise to Abraham which has been fulfilled in Jesus Christ.

2 Corinthians 3:1–18

The contrast between the 'written code' and 'the Spirit' which we examined above reappears in extensive form in 2 Corinthians 3. We will not concern ourselves here with the background of this passage, except to say that it seems best to read the text as a response to the Corinthian insistence upon letters of commendation. Paul defends his apostolic ministry in biblical terms, taking the misplaced Corinthian focus on external standards to their ultimate implications by

---

[54] In speaking of 'the law' in Gal. 4:21 Paul *refers* to the Scripture (or perhaps more narrowly, the books of Moses), a usage which, as we observed above, appears only where the Scripture functions as 'law'. The 'Scripture' here represents law in narrative form.

contrasting the ministry of the gospel with the ministry of the law.[55] The Corinthians are Paul's letter of commendation. They are a letter 'of Christ' himself, written through the agency of the apostle, not with ink, but with the 'the Spirit of the living God', not upon stone tablets, but upon tablets of 'fleshly hearts' (verse 3).[56]

With this last phrase Paul probably alludes to Jeremiah 17:1, which speaks of 'the sin of Judah ... written with a pen of iron and inscribed with a tip of diamond on the stone tablet of their hearts'. Despite the law which had been given them, Judah was entirely given over to evil, unable to love and obey the Lord. Nevertheless, God promises to overcome this incorrigibility by inscribing his law upon their heart (Jer. 31:31–34). Paul recalls both the negative and ironic passage from Jeremiah and its promissory supplement with his reference to the 'tablets of hearts'. The Spirit of God performs his work not upon 'human hearts' (as both the NIV and NRSV translate *kardia sarkinai*) but upon 'fleshly hearts', that is, hearts hardened in rebellion against God, stony counterparts to the tablets of the law.[57] The Spirit of God transcends the 'plates of stone' given at Sinai by writing the will of God upon hearts formerly inscribed with sin. Subtly, but firmly, Paul speaks to the Corinthians about their fallen state, and sets the question before them as to whether or not their minds have been penetrated by the light of the gospel.

This promised inscription of the will of God upon the human heart is effected through the apostolic ministry, which Paul speaks of here as 'the new covenant' (Jer. 31:31–34).[58] Actually, the use of the term 'covenant' is somewhat misleading, since it may call to mind notions of a contract or mutual obligations into which two parties enter. In

[55] Therefore no theories of opponents who were advocates of Judaizing, or who claimed to be divine men, are necessary. Nor need we suppose that there has been an interpolation into the letter.

[56] It is distinctly possible that the 'letter of Christ' involves an epexegetic genitive. Christ is being written on the hearts of the Corinthians through the ministry of the apostle.

[57] Hays 1989: 128–129 and Hafemann 1995: 145–148 (along with others) interpret the phrase as an echo of Ezek. 36:26, 'I will give you a new heart and put a new spirit within you, and remove the heart of stone from your flesh, and give you a heart of flesh.' But the passage in Ezekiel does not use the metaphor of 'tablets' to describe the heart, or speak of inscription upon the heart. The interpretation of *sarkikos* as a reference to the fallen state of humanity better fits Paul's theological usage of the *sark-* stem and of this adjective in particular (cf. Rom. 7:14; 1 Cor. 3:1), and best corresponds to Paul's description of the human condition in this context.

[58] The Corinthians naturally would have been familiar with this expression through the tradition of the Lord's Supper which Paul handed on to them (1 Cor. 11:17–34).

biblical usage, the terms $b^e r\hat{\imath}t$ and *diathēkē* generally signify an 'ordinance' or 'decree' which is undertaken by or imposed upon one party. So, for example, God takes an obligation upon himself in his promise to Abraham in Genesis 15 and in contrast places an obligation upon his people in the giving of the law at Sinai (Kutsch 1978). In the passage from Jeremiah, God promises a new $b^e r\hat{\imath}t$, 'not like the one I made with your fathers when I took them by the hand to bring them up out of the land of Egypt' (Jer. 31:32). This reference to the exodus $b^e r\hat{\imath}t$ signifies the law given at Sinai, obedience to which was the condition for blessing, and of which Jeremiah speaks in an earlier prophecy: 'But this command I gave them, "Obey my voice, and I will be your God, and you shall be my people"' (Jer. 7:23, NRSV).[59]

In Jeremiah 31:31–34 God announces that he will make a new $b^e r\hat{\imath}t$, different from the earlier 'covenant' broken by the fathers. Now he lays an obligation upon himself, not upon them. The content of the $b^e r\hat{\imath}t$ therefore changes.[60] The law no longer represents the substance of the $b^e r\hat{\imath}t$, but has become an object of it: God will write the law upon the hearts of his people.[61] He promises to replace the former commandment with an act which will accomplish that which the commandment could never achieve.[62] God himself alone will effect obedience within his people. He will then truly be their *God*.[63] The people themselves will no longer need instruction or admonition: to put the matter in Paul's terms, no 'written code'! Each one from the least to the greatest will know the Lord.[64] This new $b^e r\hat{\imath}t$ which God takes upon himself is predicated upon his utter mercy. He will forgive the iniquity of his people and remember their sin no longer.

Here we may remind ourselves again that Paul does not suppose that the fallen world has passed away, or that Christian struggle is over. Believers live in the early dawning of the eschaton, not at its high noon. Indeed, Paul *writes* to the Corinthians on account of their

---

[59] See Deut. 29:25; 1 Kgs. 8:9, 21; 2 Chr. 5:10.

[60] Hafemann 1995: 119–128, among many others, obscures this distinction.

[61] The content of God's will expressed in commandments or written in the heart does not enter into discussion, and may be assumed to be constant. Given the prophetic elevation of the moral over the cultic and formal elements of religion, the Jeremianic conception of the law approximates to that of Paul (Jer. 4:4; 7:22–23; 14:12).

[62] Kutsch 1978: 43–44 unfortunately misses the paradoxical shift of obligation to God.

[63] Note the implicit connection between disobedience and idolatry, and the manner in which Jeremiah conceives of salvation as having Yahweh as one's God. In chapter 2 we saw that the same line of thought governs Paul's argument in Rom. 1 – 3.

[64] As Paul tells the Thessalonians, they will be *theodidaktoi* ('ones taught of God'; 1 Thess. 4:9).

'fleshly hearts', and subsequently appeals to them to accept the gospel as if they never had done so (2 Cor. 6:1–13). His sufferings as an apostle are a testimony to the battle between the new creation and the old which is taking place in the world (2:14–17; 4:7–18). Nevertheless, through the apostolic proclamation, the Spirit of God is imparting the new life of the age to come (3:6; 5:17).

Having defined apostolic ministry in terms of this 'new ordinance' or 'covenant', Paul contrasts it with the former covenant.[65] The 'letter', that is, the written code, 'kills' (3:6). Moses' ministry is one of death and condemnation (verses 7, 9). Many interpretations of this passage fail at precisely this point, supposing that the sentence of death which the law effected represents merely something to be escaped.[66] For Paul, however, Moses' administration is divinely ordained and represents an essential precursor to the gospel. The Spirit gives life to nothing other than that which has been put to death (2 Cor. 3:6). The ministry of righteousness arrives only where the judgment of condemnation has been rendered (verses 7–11). The administration of death is a divine *ministry* (verse 9). Paul speaks here of the rightful power of the law to condemn and kill, not merely its weakness.[67]

---

[65] Hafemann 1995: 156–173 attempts to distinguish between 'covenants' (which he maintains are essentially the same) and 'ministries' (which he views as differing according to the presence or absence of the Spirit). In part this reading rests on a misunderstanding of the 'new covenant' or 'ordinance' which we have discussed above, and in part on a misconstrual of 'ministry' (*diakonia*), which for Paul is nothing other than the administration of the divine ordinance (2 Cor. 3:6). The *covenant* from Sinai brings servitude (Gal. 4:24).

[66] According to Hafemann 1995: 265–313, Paul must defend both the glory of the law and its ministry of death. For this reason he understands Moses' veil as a means of shielding the Israelites from the glory of God which would bring their death. But for Paul, the very purpose of the law is to bring condemnation and death. The veil does not inhibit this ministry. It only obscures the vision of the law's goal. Furthermore, according to the narrative of Exod. 34:29–35 the Israelites are made to look upon Moses' shining face as he delivers divine ordinances to them, despite their fears. On each occasion he unveils his face before going before the Lord, and covers it only *after* conveying the instructions he has received. Similarly, at Sinai the people fear that they will die upon hearing God's voice, only after they hear it utter the ten commandments (Exod. 20:18–21; Deut. 5:22–27). God commends the fear which accompanies this seeing and hearing, since on account of it the Israelites will keep his commandments (Deut. 5:28–33). Only it will not last! Israel cannot continue to hear God's voice or see his glory. It cannot, so to speak, live in God's presence. It can receive the good law from God himself, but it cannot keep it. It requires a mediator, the role which Moses fills for a time.

[67] Hafemann 1995: 156–184 treats the entire section as a discussion of the ineffectual nature of the law apart from the Spirit – as if Paul anywhere speaks of an effectual law through the Spirit!

The ministry of death, inferior though it was to that of the 'new covenant', bore a glory of its own. Indeed, it is precisely the glory associated with the law that becomes the focus of Paul's interest: 'If the ministry of death came with glory, how much more shall the ministry of the Spirit be attended by glory?' (verses 7–8). The glory associated with the apostolic ministry so exceeds the glory of Moses' face as he descended from Sinai, that in comparison the former glory is no glory at all (verse 10; Exod. 34:29–35). This eclipse of the glory associated with the promulgation of the written code corresponds to the temporary function of the law. Paul repeatedly makes the point in this passage that the Mosaic covenant and the ministry which proceeds from it have been 'done away with' or 'annulled' (verses 7, 11, 13, 14).[68] Yet the earlier glory of the law was actual glory, and establishes its continuity with the gospel. Although the work of the law is God's 'alien' work, not his 'proper' work, it remains *God's* work. Consequently, the law points beyond itself to a greater end: 'Moses used to place a veil upon his face in order that the sons of Israel might not behold the goal of that which is annulled' (verse 13).

The glory of Moses' face prefigures the surpassing glory of the 'new covenant', and represents the unseen 'goal' (*telos*) of Moses' ministry ('that which is annulled'). The administration of death was accompanied by a portent of the better things to come. At that time Moses enjoyed access to the divine presence, yet he enjoyed it alone. He thereby bears witness that the law is not God's final word: the first glimmerings of God's 'proper work' appear already in the face of the minister of God's 'alien work'. Now through the work of the Spirit all

---

[68] Recent interpreters have recognized that the verb which Paul employs, *katargeō*, signifies 'to annul, to do away with'. Often 2 Cor. 3:13 has been interpreted as speaking of the sons of Israel being prevented from gazing 'at the goal of *that which was fading*' (*eis to telos tou katargoumenon*). Not only does this misrepresent the meaning of the verb, but its reference is misconstrued. 'That which is done away with' (*tou katargoumenou*; note the neuter) is Moses' ministry of death and the covenant upon which it is based, not the glory of Moses' face (to which *telos*, 'goal' refers). 'That which abides' is the ministry of life and the new covenant from which it arises. Against Hafemann 1995: 310, both participles in 2 Cor. 3:11 (*to katargoumenon* and *to menon*) signify present time, and the 'annulment' does not refer to the function of the veil, which is not mentioned until 2 Cor. 3:13, but the old covenant and Moses' ministry. Likewise, against Hafemann 1995: 380, in 2 Cor. 3:14 the implied subject of *katargetai* is 'the old covenant' (2 Cor. 3:13), not the 'veil', which is associated symbolically only with the action of the participle *mē anakalyptomenon* ('not being revealed [or uncovered]'). There is no reason why the subject of *katargetai* must be the same as that of *menei*. Paul has already spoken of the ministry of Moses and the old covenant as being annulled (2 Cor. 3:11), and reiterates the point here.

who believe behold the glory of the Lord (verses 17–18). In the ministry of the new covenant the intermediary has been removed, or, more properly stated, replaced by Christ.[69]

'The sons of Israel' could not endure the former glory, and were afraid to come near Moses (Exod. 34:29–35). He accordingly covered his face with a veil in order that, in Paul's words, 'they might not gaze upon its glory' (2 Cor. 3:7). Paul interprets Moses' placement of the veil as an act of judgment, signifying the hardening of the minds of the sons of Israel. They remain so, in Paul's words, 'until this day' (verse 14). The law brought condemnation upon them in the fullest sense. God had not yet opened their 'fleshly hearts' to perceive the end of his dealings with them through Moses. Paul does not thereby call into question the capability of Israel to understand the requirements of the law. Nor does he suggest that the condemnation which came upon Israel was due to some sort of misunderstanding or misuse of the law. Quite the opposite: the very purpose of the law was to bring death. Rather, the 'veil upon the hearts' of the Israelites represents their inability to see the purpose of the law. Only by the Spirit, who is given forth in the apostolic proclamation, is one able to see that the law which puts to death has the gospel which gives life as its goal.[70] Those who believe gaze at the glory of God not as it is dimly reflected in the face of Moses, but as it shines forth from Christ, the image of God (verse 18; 4:4–6).

Romans 7:1 – 8:11

Paul has dealt with the purpose of the law already in a relatively thorough manner earlier in Romans (3:27 – 5:21). The law is subordinate to God's promise to Abraham, effecting God's wrath in preparation for God's grace in Christ (2:12-13; 4:13–17; 5:20). Yet he

[69] Cf. 2 Cor. 3:18, *katoptrizomenoi*, 'beholding in a mirror'.

[70] In siding with those who recognize the hermeneutical implications of Paul's statements in 2 Cor. 3, we must at the same time offer some corrections of their views. Hays 1989: 122–153 offers a discussion of this text which in many ways is excellent, but fails to indicate that the Spirit directs believers outside themselves to Christ (as is quite clear in 2 Cor. 4). He therefore places the church, rather than Christ, at the centre of interest, and speaks in terms of a 'hermeneutics of freedom' rather than properly of one of constraint to Christ. Käsemann 1971: 138–166 regards Christology as central to hermeneutics, but introduces confusion by describing that Christology in terms of the (earthly) 'presence of the risen Lord'. He is therefore no less 'ecclesiocentric' than Hays, even if he is critical of the visible church. Paul's understanding of Scripture is centred upon Christ's death and resurrection.

has ascribed a divine purpose to the law which he has not yet explained in this letter: 'through the law comes the knowledge of sin' (3:20). Up to Romans 7, he has been primarily concerned to place the law within the course of God's dealings with humanity. Now he completes his treatment of the law by returning to the theme with which he began, the effect which the law is to have within the human being.[71] His immediate point of departure lies in his discussion of freedom from sin in Romans 6. He there interjects a declaration which is as startling as it is direct: 'Sin shall not be lord over you, for you are not under law but under grace' (verse 14).[72] Freedom from sin has its basis in freedom from the law. This is the theme which Paul takes up in Romans 7. At its opening he suddenly shifts from speaking of the 'wages of *sin*' to the topic of the law: 'Or do you not know … that the *law* has lordship over a person [only] as long as that person lives?' (6:23 – 7:1).

The law and sin are joined in the fallen human being: 'When we were in the flesh, the passions of sins which come about through the law were active in our members so as to bear fruit for death' (7:5).[73]

Our release has been secured in Christ, in whose death we have died to the law (Rom. 7:1–4).[74] The law has its sphere of jurisdiction only within the present, fallen world. Once we have passed through death, it has no claim upon us. Consequently, those who have died with Christ to the law 'serve in the newness of the Spirit, and not in the oldness of the letter' (verse 6). Service to God takes place only where there is freedom from the law.

Although 7:1–25 constitutes a distinct unit within Paul's argument, it

---

[71] The obvious verbal and thematic correspondence between Rom. 3:19–20 and 7:7–25 confirms the connection between them. Paul speaks directly of 'coming to know sin' through the law (Rom. 7:7, cf. verse 13), and extensively explores the reality of guilt (7:14–25; cf. 3:19).

[72] Cf. Rom. 4:15, 'the law brings wrath, but where there is no law, neither is there transgression'.

[73] It may be that Paul speaks of 'the passions of *sins* effected by the law' (plural), because he has in view the manifold individual commandments contained within the law.

[74] The line of Paul's thought here is the same as that of Rom. 6. It is sometimes wrongly thought that Paul employs in a clumsy way the metaphor of the married woman whose husband dies. Paul appeals to this law straightforwardly. We need only recognize that he presupposes that the union of husband and wife in one flesh corresponds to the relation between the believer and Christ (cf. Gen. 2:24; Eph. 5:29–33). Note that he speaks of the 'under-a-husband woman' (*hē hypandros gynē*) who is bound to the 'living husband' (*ho zōn anēr*) (Rom. 7:2). Christ serves the same role as the husband who dies: through his body we have been put to death to the law, so that we might be joined to another (Rom. 7:3–4). Only here does Paul expand the metaphor of the marriage law, by identifying the one who died with the one who was raised. We are joined to the risen Christ.

is quite clear from this last statement concerning service 'in the newness of the Spirit' that Paul's discussion of the law is not complete without his treatment of the work of the Spirit in 8:1–11. His description of the 'wretched person' who knows condemnation by the law obviously corresponds to 7:5, just as his statements about those who 'walk according to the Spirit' in 8:1–11 correspond to 7:6. Consequently, the two units belong together and must be interpreted together.

In the narrative section of the chapter, Paul is concerned with the bondage of the human being to sin. The text falls into two distinct sections: a retrospective concerning the encounter with the law followed by an assessment of the human being under sin (7:7–13, 14–25). The change in tense usage between the two parts has to do with Paul's shifting of his focus from the encounter with the law, to the fallen person who knows the law. He does not speak of a specifically Christian struggle in verses 14–25. The decisive 'present' of God's work in Christ appears only at the beginning of Romans 8. He is not merely contemplating his preconversion life either. The confessional introduction to this section and its seemingly anticlimactic conclusion make it clear that he is speaking about a reality which continues in him, even though it has been overcome in Christ.[75]

At the outset of his narrative, Paul quickly brushes aside as unthinkable the idea that the law of God has somehow served an evil purpose. It rather effects God's good intent: 'Is the law sin? By no means! Rather, I would not have known sin, except through the law' (verse 7). The law imparts the 'knowledge of sin', as Paul has announced already in Romans 3:20. The commandment against coveting awakened 'all coveting' within him (verse 8).[76] As a result, says Paul, 'I died' (verses 9–10). Sin deceived him, and through the commandment killed him (verse 11).[77] In each one who is confronted with the law, Adam's transgression is recapitulated, not as a fall from a pristine state (or Paul would not speak of indwelling sin), but as a re-enactment of the primal sin.[78] This recapitulation takes place, moreover, as the violation of our responsibility toward our neighbour.

---

[75] See Rom. 7:14, 25. For further arguments see Seifrid 1992b: 313–333.

[76] It is worth noting that Paul again in this context speaks of the law as consisting in concrete commandments, which offer life and threaten death (Gal. 3:12; Rom. 10:5).

[77] Paul here recalls the deceit of the serpent, 'You surely shall not die!' (Gen. 3:4, 13).

[78] The law entered in, in order that *the* transgression (*ho paraptōma*) might increase (Rom. 5:20). The articular form probably refers to the transgression of Adam (Rom. 5:14; cf. verses 15, 17).

All other transgressions against others (the dishonouring of parents, murder, adultery, theft and false witness, and so on) have their root in coveting, which is the antithesis of the love commandment. In this commandment the whole weight of the law comes to bear on us. No-one can hide from this commandment in outward deeds or apparent piety. The law with its offer of life and blessing has become a tool of sin and death (verse 13).

Nevertheless, the divine purpose of the law has not been thwarted. Sin itself remains a tool in God's hand. In deceiving the human being and bringing about death, the reality of sin is manifest. It openly effects death through the good commandment which offers life. In Paul's words, sin thereby becomes 'sinful beyond measure' (verse 13). Here we may speak with Luther of sin as the *annihilatio Dei* which the law exposes. The human being acknowledges that the law is good, but does otherwise. The cause of our disobedience lies in our desire to do away with God, who gives the commandment (see Iwand 1991: 23–25).

The first-person pronouns notwithstanding, Paul's tone is dispassionate well into his narrative, more like a physician's diagnosis than personal reflection. Although Paul speaks of the coveting which the commandment awakened within him, he treats this encounter and its results in a detached manner: 'This commandment unto life was found for me to be unto death' (verse 10); 'Sin deceived me and through the commandment killed me, so that the law is holy' (verse 11). The reality of sin established itself in his encounter with the law independently of any appreciation of it on his part.[79]

The second section of Paul's narrative begins with a confessional statement: 'We know that the law is spiritual, but I am fleshly, sold under sin' (verse 14).[80] His following reflection and analysis are nothing more than the personalizing of the truth with which he begins. The 'we' becomes an 'I'. Paul recognizes that which he has confessed as true in him, and implicitly true in his readers and all human beings – although they must come to own it themselves. Here the fallen human being comes to a knowledge of the self in the light of the law: 'I do not do what I will, but I do what I hate' (verse 15).[81] This rent in the fabric

---

[79] As we have noted, his stance fits what we know of his preconversion life. It is quite clear that he could never have boasted of his accomplishments as a Pharisee or his 'progress in Judaism' had he recognized that the law effected his death (Phil. 3:6; Gal. 1:14).

[80] We may note that Paul's closing exclamation of praise also has a confessional form, in which he returns to the use of the plural: 'Thanks be to God through Jesus Christ *our* Lord' (Rom. 7:25).

[81] Paul probably still has in view here the transgression of the prohibition against

of the human being between the approval of the law and the practice of evil forms the basis of the entire analysis.[82] That I 'will' to do contrary to what I actually do shows that I confess the goodness of the law (verses 14–16). That I act contrary to what I 'will' shows that sin has possessed me (verses 17–20). I know that the law is good. I know that there is no good in me. Before the law, then, I stand guilty and condemned: 'Wretched person that I am! Who shall set me free from the body of this death?' (verse 24). The one who approves the law with his mind is subject to a 'law of sin' which makes him, the one who wishes to do good, a prisoner to the evil which indwells him (verses 21–25).

In this anguished exclamation, the law has fulfilled its divine purpose. The divine contention which was brought to an end in the cross has been brought to an end in the human heart (cf. 3:5–8, 21–26). Here we see that 'sin' has overpowered us in such a way that we are united with 'sin'. What sin does, 'I' do. Sin works coveting, and, in disobedience to the commandment, *I* covet (verses 8, 11). 'For *me*' the commandment which offers life brings about death (verse 10). I am guilty before God. Nevertheless, the 'self' remains paradoxically passive. 'Sin' takes the active role, effecting coveting, deceiving me, killing me. In the latter part of Romans 7, Paul states quite directly, and more than once, that 'I am not the one effecting it [transgression], but sin which indwells me' (verses 17, 20). It is 'I' who perform the evil, and yet not 'I' but sin which indwells me. All transgression is Adam's transgression recapitulated in humanity under condemnation, just as all obedience is Christ's obedience in the humanity justified in him.[83] The confession recalls Paul's earlier announcement that God has 'surrendered' the idolators to transgression (1:24, 26, 28). The 'I, but yet not I' in Christ has its counterpart in Adam (cf. Gal. 2:20). The person in whom sin dwells is both guilty and enslaved, and for this reason 'wretched'.

This confession of sin does not exist in isolation, but in conjunction with the knowledge of Christ. Paul's shout of joy immediately follows his lament: 'Thanks be to God, through Jesus Christ our Lord!' (verse

---

coveting which he has just described.

[82] Paul's language becomes remarkably abstract in this passage in that he speaks of 'good' and 'evil', not merely of the law and sin. He thereby approximates, although never quite joins, ancient philosophical debate concerning the basis of moral inability.

[83] Here we may remember the echoes of Gen. 3 in Paul's description of the encounter with the law (Rom. 7:7:13), and his earlier reference to Adam's transgression being multiplied with the entrance of the law (Rom. 5:20).

25a).[84] The deliverance God has accomplished in Christ becomes manifest only where the full reality of sin and guilt are also manifest, and vice versa. Freedom from the law is present only where the law arrives at its divine purpose of effecting our acknowledgment of guilt. Paul's final statement on the matter in Romans 7, which has seemed to many interpreters to be strangely anticlimactic, in reality summarizes his main point: 'So then, I myself with my mind serve the law of God, but with my flesh the law of sin' (verse 25b). This final confession is no retreat. Just the opposite: in manifesting the reality of sin and the nature of redemption, it exposes the battle in which believers are engaged. Anything less is self-deception.

With this background, Paul continues to speak of the theme of deliverance in Romans 8. In sending his Son as an offering for sin, God 'condemned sin in the flesh', accomplishing that which the law could not do for us (verse 3).[85] In this manner Christ's death is to bring to 'fulfilment in us' the 'righteous ordinance (*dikaiōma*) of the law' (verse 4). For a number of reasons, it is best to understand this 'righteous ordinance' as the 'life' which the law offered on the condition of obedience. Paul begins and ends his thought in this section with a declaration that believers will be raised from the dead, so that it is quite natural to think that he is speaking of it indirectly in verse 4 (see 8:1–2, 10–11). We have also seen that Paul characterizes the law in Romans 7 as 'good' and beneficial (verse 12), and that he describes the commandment concerning coveting as 'the commandment unto life' (verse 9). It therefore makes sense that he now speaks of the resurrection from the dead as the 'fulfilment of the righteous ordinance of the law'. We have here a counterpart to 1:32, where Paul uses this term to refer to the sentence of death. The same law, after all, both threatened death and promised life (7:10). In 8:4, then, Paul is simply completing the thought with which he began in verse 3: what the law could not do, God did in Christ. He vindicated us and gave us the life which the law offers by first effecting the sentence of death which it pronounces upon us.

---

[84] On the eschatological character of Paul's thanksgiving see Banks 1978.

[85] Paul's juridical language ('condemnation') again combines the pronouncement of judgment and the execution of the sentence. The law establishes our guilt, but only in Christ is the sentence executed.

Romans 9:30 – 10:13

While in 1:18 – 3:20 Paul treats the guilt of all humanity, in 9:30 – 10:13 he treats Israel's failure in particular.[86] In a strange turn of events, while many Gentiles have come to faith in Israel's Messiah, Israel has largely remained unresponsive to the gospel. Those who were not the least concerned with the pursuit of righteousness have attained it (9:30). Israel, which pursued 'a law of righteousness', failed to arrive at the law (verse 31). Its guilt therefore consists not simply in its rejection of the gospel, but in its failure to heed the law itself. Rather than (pursuing) and attaining to the law (i.e. righteousness) 'by faith', it pursued the law (and its righteousness) 'as if attainment of it were by works' (verse 32).[87]

This 'pursuit of the law by faith' does not constitute some special form of accomplishment of the demands of the law.[88] We can hardly set aside the message which Paul has presented thus far in Romans when we arrive at this passage. He surely has not forgotten his declaration that 'apart from the law ... the righteousness of God has been manifest' (3:21), or his assertion that 'the law works wrath' (4:15). This same understanding of the law is implicit in Paul's citation of Leviticus 18:5 in 10:5 ('the one who does these things shall live by them').[89] Furthermore, 'faith' for Paul cannot be regarded as the

---

[86] This discussion of the law appears within Paul's larger response to the human challenge to God's right as God (Rom. 9:14 – 10:21), which we shall take up in chapter 6.

[87] It is somewhat difficult to render this verse, since Paul leaves the verb(s) here unexpressed. The verbal idea is undoubtedly to be drawn from the preceding clause, where Paul says that Israel 'pursuing did not attain' (*diōkōn . . . ouk ephthasen*). Yet the phrases of Rom. 9:32 demand a shift in emphasis from one to the next, i.e. from 'attaining' to 'pursuing'. The primary topic of the passage is the attainment of righteousness (cf. 10:3–10). When Paul shifts from speaking of 'righteousness' in 9:30 to 'the law' in verse 31, he has in view the law as a source of righteousness. Therefore the typical Pauline distinction between 'righteousness by faith' and a 'righteousness from works' appears in verse 32.

[88] For various reasons, the reading of the law as an offer of grace which is to be fulfilled 'in faith' has become widespread in evangelical biblical scholarship (e.g. Fuller 1980). In robbing the law of its proper function, this theology diminishes the gospel, which can be properly understood only on the basis of the condemnation and death ministered by the law. Furthermore, it implicitly adds a second demand to the law: one now must not only fulfil the law, but fulfil it in faith. When the law becomes gospel, the gospel becomes law. See Iwand 1991: 51–56.

[89] As we have seen, Paul uses this very passage from Leviticus in Gal. 3:12 clearly to distinguish the law from faith: 'the law is not of faith'. Against Cranfield 1979: 2: 521–522, Paul is not referring to Christ's perfect obedience of the law in his citation of Lev. 18:5. When Paul speaks of Christ's obedience in his letters, he always has Christ's

special means by which one may obey the law properly, since it is not a mere disposition of the human being. Faith is defined by its content: Israel stumbled against the stone which God placed in Zion and did not submit to Christ, the righteousness of God (9:33; 10:3; cf. 2 Cor. 1:20).[90] To 'pursue the law from faith', as Israel might have done, would have been to look for and expect 'Christ', who, Paul says, 'is the goal (*telos*) of the law' (10:4).[91]

What 'Moses writes' is transcended by that which 'the righteousness of faith says' (10:5-8; see Seifrid 1985). 'Speaking' stands in opposition to 'writing' here, just as the Spirit does to 'the letter' in 2 Corinthians 3. The written commandment addresses the fallen human being with the offer of life on the basis of obedience: 'The one who does these things shall live by them' (Rom. 10:5; Lev. 18:5). The 'righteousness of faith' speaks of what God has done in sending his Son (10:6-8). This is no repudiation of the righteousness of the law which Paul has characterized as 'holy' (7:12). It is rather an announcement that it has been superseded by the higher, greater righteousness of faith. Whereas the former righteousness, were it possible, would belong to the human being, the latter is God's alone, revealed in Christ (10:2-4). Righteousness comes through faith in Christ, and not performance of the demands of the law (10:9-13). This saving righteousness accords with the promise of Isaiah: 'No-one who believes in him shall be put to shame' (Is. 28:16; Rom. 10:5; cf. 9:33). This allusion to the very speech of Moses in Deuteronomy 30:11-14 does not contradict Paul's preceding reference to what 'Moses writes'.

---

obedient death on the cross in view. That is to say, he never treats what has traditionally been called Christ's 'active' obedience (to the law) as an entity distinct from his 'passive obedience' (in dying on the cross). In the text at hand, Paul speaks of Christ's incarnation and resurrection from the dead as the content of the gospel (Rom. 10:6-8), thus implicitly making the cross central to salvation. Furthermore, it is clear in the context that the righteousness of the law (10:5) stands in antithesis to the righteousness of faith (10:6-8).

[90] We have seen this aspect of faith already in Gal. 3:1 - 4:7, and shall discuss it further in the following chapter.

[91] Again Paul chooses this term to describe the relation between law and gospel. Badenas 1985 shows that it is best to render *telos* as 'goal', but in the process obscures the exegetical issue at stake. It is not sufficient to say that *telos* means only 'object/purpose, fulfilment' (never 'abrogation, termination, cessation)': in purpose or fulfilment the means or vehicle is secondary, and may well be temporal (e.g. Rom. 6:21). He misinterprets the passage largely because he construes *nomos* as a reference to 'Scripture', i.e. written, divine revelation in a general or prophetic sense. Paul, however, refers to 'Scripture' as 'law' only when he views it as functioning as 'law', i.e. in pronouncing a regulation, or bringing condemnation. Paul's citation of Lev. 18:5 (Rom. 10:5) makes it clear that he refers to the law of Moses in 10:4.

Rather, it again places the law within its biblical context. The law which brings death is subservient to Christ in whom there is life (10:5; 4:15). The law, after all, is *God's* law and serves his purposes. Paul sees in the gift of the law to Israel (the gratuity of which is emphatic in Deuteronomy) an anticipation of God's greater gift in Christ. The *nomothesia* through Moses anticipates the *huiothesia* in Christ (9:4).[92] As in 2 Corinthians 3, the ministry of death bears witness to the ministry of life.

In the context of Deuteronomy 30:11–14, Moses' declaration of the 'nearness of the word' serves to prevent Israel from evading its responsibility toward the Lord. In delivering them from Egypt, God had bound them to himself and placed upon them the obligation of love and obedience. If they do not follow him, they will perish. For this reason, the commandments which they receive represent God's good gift. By them they will ensure their well-being and preserve their life in the land. Disobedience will bring destruction, exile, and servitude (Deut. 4:7–8; 5:29; 6:18, 24; 27:1 – 28:68). Moses' appeal to the 'nearness of the word' therefore simultaneously reminds Israel of God's gracious revelation of his will and binds Israel to its obligation. Yet this good law is given to a stubborn and rebellious people (Deut. 9:4). 'To this day', Moses warns, 'the LORD has not given you a heart to understand, nor eyes to see, nor ears to hear' (Deut. 29:4). The promised 'circumcision of the heart' which brings obedience lies in Israel's future, on the far side of judgment, curse, and exile (Deut. 30:1–6).

Paul joins one of these passages from Deuteronomy which speaks of Israel's waywardness to his use of Deuteronomy 30:11–14. The introductory admonition in Romans 10:6, 'Do not say in your heart', echoes a pair of warnings related to Israel's possession of the land. In one of these, Moses charges the nation not to forget the Lord in the midst of future blessings by saying, 'My might and the strength of my hand have got me this wealth' (Deut. 8:17). Similarly, when Israel dispossesses the peoples dwelling in Canaan, she is not to say, 'Because of my righteousness the LORD has brought me in to possess this land.' Only the wickedness of the nations dwelling there caused Yahweh to drive them out. And only because of the promise to the patriarchs will he bring Israel, 'a stubborn people', into the land (Deut. 9:4–7). By appending this warning to Deuteronomy 30:11–14, Paul turns it into an admonition. While Moses had simply instructed

---

[92] The giving of the law through Moses anticipates the instatement as sons in Christ.

Israel that it need not ask idle questions about discovering God's demands, the personified 'righteousness of faith' warns against pride. In this way Paul renders the text applicable to his larger purpose of responding to the challenge to God's right as Creator. Israel must not foolishly put itself in the place of God:

> Do not say in your heart, 'Who will ascend into heaven?' That is to bring Christ down. Or, 'Who will descend into the abyss?' That is to bring Christ up from the dead. But what does [the righteousness of faith] say? 'The word is near you, in your mouth and in your heart.' That is the word of faith which we preach (Rom. 10:6–8).

Righteousness comes as a gift from God who sent forth his Son, delivered him up to die, and raised him from the dead. No-one can scale the height or plumb the depth of the divine deed. The dimensions of Christ's saving work expose the vanity of Israel's pursuit of righteousness through deeds of obedience. Not the horizontal course which a human may run, but the vertical path which God alone can traverse brings righteousness (cf. 9:16, 31). Not one's own 'works of the law', but the incarnation, cross, and resurrection of God's Son form the only way to salvation. God demands 'mere' faith, the confession that the crucified Jesus is the risen Lord.

Summary

As the passages we have examined above indicate, Paul consistently views the law in relation to God's justifying work in Christ.[93] He knows only of one, indivisible law of God, and provides no ground for the traditional bifurcation of the law into moral and ceremonial law.[94] The *whole* law bears witness to Christ. The whole law therefore now stands like John the Baptist in the presence of Christ. It has to yield to the greater one who has arrived. The ministry of death bears witness to the ministry of life. The glory of Moses points to the glory of Christ (2 Cor. 3:7–18). The gift of the law testifies to God's greater gift in Christ (Rom. 10:5–8). In its offer of life the law anticipates what God

---

[93] Even in 1 Tim. 1:8–11, it is likely that Paul has in view the condemning function of the law. Biblically and theologically the *usus politicus* remains significant, although it is obviously secondary.

[94] The requirement of circumcision, since it was a demand of God, was no less 'moral' than the rest of the law!

has accomplished in Christ.[95] In its sentence of death it makes known the work of God's Son, incarnate and crucified for us (Gal. 3:13). Precisely because the good law of God is unable to effect the obedience which it requires, it reveals the bondage of the human being to sin and thereby witnesses here and now to the gospel.[96]

For this reason Paul is able to say that the law is done away with, and yet not done away with, but established by justifying faith (2 Cor. 3:7–17; Rom. 3:31).[97] The law is fulfilled in the gospel, in which its demand becomes a reality (cf. Iwand 1964: 4:11–56). The removal of the veil which allows the vision of Christ's glory is the removal of the veil which lies upon the reading of the law (2 Cor. 3:14–18). The knowledge of Christ and the knowledge of the law are inseparable. The law which condemns serves as the necessary counterpart to the gospel, which announces the joy of condemnation overcome: 'Thanks be to God, through Christ Jesus our Lord!' (Rom. 7:25). In this simultaneity of condemnation and justification, the law is taken up in the gospel. Here, and only here, obedience to the law takes place, for in justifying God's judgment upon us, faith acknowledges God as God.

According to Paul, then, the law serves the gospel, and not the reverse. The gospel has been given not for the purpose of empowering believers to meet the demands of the 'written code', but to place them in the presence of God where that 'written code' is no longer needed. Unquestionably, Christians need instruction from the law, since even in them the knowledge of God's will given in creation remains sup-

---

[95] Against Schreiner 1993: 172, Paul does see a 'problem with the law as such'. It is 'weak, on account of the flesh' (Rom. 8:3).

[96] On the present witness of Scripture, see Koch 1986: 322–331.

[97] We cannot here examine in detail the work of Eaton 1995, which despite some of its legitimate concerns is fraught with serious error. His embrace of Agricola's antinomianism gives some indication of its deficiencies. He fails to recognize the character of sin (1) as our refusal to acknowledge God and his judgment upon us; and (2) as a power to which we have been delivered. Consequently he does not see that there can be no gospel without the abiding witness of the law, no knowledge of Christ without the condemnation by the law. Consequently, in the sense that Eaton wishes to deny it, it must be maintained that justification takes place by the *law* alone! Furthermore, he treats believers as if the flesh had departed and only the Spirit is present – a true follower of Agricola. Yet, ironically, he fails to see that the gift of salvation is the Giver himself and true obedience to him. Moreover, to turn the theme of 'inheritance' into reward is an exegetical and theological absurdity. Here is the beginning of the nomism which (as Luther saw) must emerge from antinomianism, a making the gospel into law. Further yet, he falls into the very error against which he reacts: while some Reformed theology has sought assurance in works, Eaton seeks an unassailable faith, free from *Anfechtung*. Both look for a security in this world which God will *not* give us. We have only the certitude of hope, of reaching forward to what lies ahead.

pressed (Rom. 1:19–25; 2:14–16; 3:9–18). It is a mistake, however, to reduce the law to the function of providing norms for Christian living. Our need of instruction is a mark of our continuing fallenness, our desire to do away with God, which cannot be cured by the law. Furthermore, we misunderstand our condition if we suppose that we require a mere infusion of power in order to obey the law – as if we *would* do so if we *could* do so! Our problem is much deeper. Our rebellion against God has its end only in Christ's cross, where we were put to death with him. Correspondingly, Paul speaks in strikingly unqualified terms of the reality of the new life, in which obedience to God's will is immediate and unconditioned. In producing its fruit, the Spirit of God has no need for the law and its prohibitions (Gal. 5:23). As Paul indicates more than once, love, which by its very nature does no harm to the neighbour, is the fulfilment of the law (Gal. 5:14; Rom. 13:8–10).[98] The law bears witness to the righteousness of God revealed in Jesus Christ (Rom. 3:21).

That is not at all to say that Christian obedience occurs spontaneously. The life of faith is a battle against our very selves, a reckoning that we have been crucified with Christ and a refusing to do what we ourselves want (Rom. 8:13; Gal. 5:16–26). Paul by no means supposes that he or his congregations had attained to sinlessness. To arrive there is to arrive at the resurrection from the dead (Phil. 3:10–11). The fallen state and the new creation are both present with us. Yet they are with us in differing ways. The former is ours naturally: in ourselves we remain, like Paul, 'a wretched person' under sin and death (Rom. 7:25). Yet in the reckoning of faith we are dead to sin and alive to God (Rom. 6:11). Although sin is present with us, it is present only as a conquered reality. The life of the age to come is really and necessarily present in the new obedience of faith. Such faith is utterly realistic: it is fixed upon the resurrection from the dead as the point at

---

[98] As we shall see, Paul speaks of 'love' as a reality which arrives with the eschaton. He does not thinks of it as an ideal (which might be misinterpreted to allow immorality or another form of evil). Where the love which Paul describes in 1 Cor. 13 is present, there is no need for the law. Cf. Luther, on Gal. 5:14: '… grace alone is the fulfilment of the law, and words do not fulfil words, but reality fulfils words, and mighty deeds confirm speech' (*LW* 2:249). Note that Paul does not say that 'Christians fulfil the law'. That would be to say that Christians attain perfection in this body and life. The fulfilment of the law is present in them through 'faith which works through love' (Gal. 5:6). Paul also speaks of the Gentile believer who 'keeps the righteous ordinances of the law' (without knowing the law!; Rom. 2:26). Nevertheless, the 'flesh' is still present in such persons (e.g. Gal. 5:16–18; Rom. 8:12–13). The law has a role to play in establishing civil righteousness, but before God it makes us either hypocrites or sinners; *tertium non datur*.

which God's work in Christ will come to its full reality in us. Until that time we have been placed in an ongoing battle, in which by the Spirit we 'put to death the deeds of the body'. Our struggle is not merely with outward forces, but with the continuing reality of our fallen person (Rom. 8:13; cf. Gal. 5:17).[99] In the last analysis, Paul's understanding of the law is quite straightforward. The law continues in the fallen world and in us, condemning sin and witnessing to Christ, even as it has been transcended in Christ in whom the resurrection from the dead has come. These two realities converge in the apostolic proclamation of the gospel.

Paul obviously makes use of injunctions of the law in his letters.[100] He is intensely practical, reckoning with a range of challenges and questions arising from the fallen world in which his congregations lived. Nevertheless, the law *as law* is absent from Paul's moral instruction.[101] This transposition is apparent in the remarkable lack of direct appeal to the law in his letters, particularly where one might expect it, as, for example, in relation to sexual morality or issues relating to slavery.[102] Where Paul names the law in his exhortations it appears in a corroborative role (1 Cor. 9:8–14; 14:34). Whereas the law says, 'Do this and you shall live', Paul proceeds from what God has done in Christ: because in Christ we have died to sin and live to God, we are to present ourselves for service to God (Rom. 10:5; 6:12–13). Paul accordingly understands the entirety of his ministry to his congregations, and not merely initial evangelization, as a ministry of the gospel (see Rom. 1:15; 15:14–19; 2 Cor. 3:6). His instruction and admonition are a dimension of his gospel without which his gospel is truncated, and vice versa. Naturally, he does not attach to every admonition appearing in his letters a formula rehearsing Christ's work. That would be needlessly repetitive. In all his letters, however, whether in narrower or broader context, his exhortation is invariably based

[99] We misconstrue Paul if we view the Spirit as some infused power. The Spirit represents the new creation, a *whole*, which enters into battle with the fallen human being that we are (Gal. 5:17–26).

[100] On the connections between Paul's instruction and early Judaism see Tomson 1990.

[101] As we have seen, when Paul speaks of 'the law' he has in view the commands given at Sinai, which cannot be detached from their authority to condemn without ceasing to be 'law'. Although there are some valuable insights in the idea that Paul saw the biblical hope of the 'Zion-Tora' (Gese) fulfilled in Christ (see Stuhlmacher 1992: 257), the law for Paul is the law from Sinai.

[102] See e.g. 1 Thess. 4:3–8, where Paul might well have appealed to the Decalogue, or Lev. 18 – 20, or similar passages. Likewise, escaped slaves were not to be returned to their masters according to the law (Deut. 23:15–16). Yet Paul makes no mention of this requirement in returning Onesimus to Philemon.

upon the announcement of the salvation which God has worked in Christ. In short, where imperatives appear in Paul's letters, they appear in the form of gospel, in which the law has been taken up and transcended. In this respect it is necessary to emphasize the first part of Bonhoeffer's dictum, '*Only the one who believes obeys*, and only the one who obeys believes' (1963: 69).

Because the fallen human being does not wish to acknowledge the reality of guilt which the law reveals in the cross of Christ, the law is subject to misuse. This is precisely the charge which Paul brings against his Jewish contemporaries in Romans 9:30 – 10:21 and which colours his argument in 2:1 – 3:20. We should not forget, however, that when Paul treats this problem he addresses congregations of believers in Christ. The abuse of the law – and thereby the abuse of the gospel – is not simply a Jewish failure, as is clear in Paul's pointed letter to the Galatians. His teaching on justification represents churchly instruction, intended to correct Christian disobedience.

Chapter Five

The justification of the ungodly and the obedience of faith

One of the primary distinguishing features of the New Testament over against other Jewish and Hellenistic literature is the fundamental and comprehensive role which it ascribes to faith.[1] According to the Synoptic Gospels, the forgiveness of sins and the healing which are marks of the presence of the kingdom of God are given to faith alone.[2] In John's Gospel believing secures eternal life and makes one a child of God (1:12; 3:15–16; 36, 5:24; 6:35; etc.). According to the letter to the Hebrews, faith brings the age to come into the present, and the believer into the presence of God (4:3; 10:22; 11:1). James presupposes that faith effects salvation, even as he underscores that such faith is never without its works (2:14–26).[3] In all the New Testament writings, faith in Christ and in God's work in him is determinative for the human relationship to God. Paul's intense concern for the fledgling congregation in Thessalonica is characteristic of the New Testament: 'On account of this, since I could no longer bear it, I sent [Timothy] in order to know about your faith, lest somehow the one who tempts might have tempted you, and our labour might be in vain' (1 Thess. 3:5).

This common understanding of the significance and content of faith in the New Testament writings reflects earliest Christianity itself. It goes without saying that the nature of faith was contested in various ways in the first generation of churches: such battles prompted the composition and distribution of the New Testament writings. Indeed, Paul's conflict with those who advocated Judaizing had to do not only

---

[1] Philo is no exception to this judgment, since for him faith represents the goal rather than the basis of spiritual life.

[2] E.g. Mark 2:5; 5:34–36; 6:4–6; 9:23; 10:52; 11:22–24. Likewise, in the book of Acts, faith in Christ itself secures healing and salvation (Acts 3:16; 11:17; Acts 13:39; 48; 14:22; 15:9–11; 16:31–34; 26:18).

[3] We shall consider James and Paul on the topic of justification in our final chapter.

with 'justification', but with the meaning and significance of faith (e.g. Gal. 2:16–21). Nevertheless, that the New Testament authors frequently speak of 'faith' or 'the faith' without further definition or qualification shows that considerable agreement existed among Christians as to the content of that faith. It is especially significant that such absolute usage of the term often appears in letter openings, where one might expect an author to clarify uncertainties or to defend matters under debate.[4] Paul is no exception, generally beginning his letters with reference to the 'faith' which he shares with his addressees, and at various points referring to common traditions which he and they had received.[5] In these occasional confessional statements – which appear on account of difficulties within the congregations – the basic outline of the 'faith' which Paul assumes that his addressees share with him emerges. As we have seen already, the resurrection of the crucified Christ almost always lies at the centre of interest in such passages, a focus which again is common to the New Testament writings.[6] It is more than understandable that the resurrection would take a central position in the faith of the earliest church. If Jesus had not been raised, there could have been no credible proclamation of him as Messiah. At the same time, it is clear that the interest of New Testament writers is not limited to the facticity of Christ's resurrection. Their larger concern lies in the saving significance of that resurrection, a concern which, we have seen, appears frequently in Paul's use of the language of righteousness.[7]

Faith as God's work through the gospel

In accord with the other New Testament writings, and as we have seen at various points in the preceding chapters, for Paul 'faith' is not a mere human disposition or a general sense of dependence upon God. It rather is directed to God's promise to Abraham which has come to fulfilment in Christ (Gal. 3:6–8; Rom. 4:20–21). Faith, by which God

[4] E.g. Heb. 3:12 (cf. 2:1; 3:1); Jas. 1:3; 1 Pet. 1:5–7; 2 Pet. 1:1; Jude 5.

[5] Rom. 1:5, 8, 12; 1 Cor. 1:21; 2 Cor. 1:24; Gal. 1:23; Phil. 1:25; etc.

[6] E.g. 1 Thess. 1:9–10; 4:13–18; 1 Cor. 15:1–3; Phil. 2:6–11. Luke's interest in the resurrection in Acts is well known (see e.g. Acts 2:24–36; 4:33; 5:31). Likewise for the author of Hebrews, the exaltation of the Son is of fundamental importance (Heb. 4:14–16; 5:7–10; 7:15–17; etc.). It is surely implied in Jas. 2:1. Only where the reality of the incarnation is in doubt does the focus on the resurrection give way to other concerns, as in 1 John.

[7] This observation is particularly relevant for assessing the meaning of the debated expression the 'faith of (Jesus) Christ', which we shall discuss below.

blessed Abraham, has been made manifest and effective for the blessing of the nations in the crucified and risen Christ, just as the Scripture announced beforehand (Gal. 3:8, 23–25). God has set Christ as a 'stone' in Zion; faith in him brings salvation (Rom. 9:33; 10:11). Since faith has its basis and source in the promise and work of God, Paul freely interchanges 'faith' with 'the gospel' or 'Christ'. To 'stand in faith' is equivalent to 'standing in the Lord' or 'in the gospel' (1 Thess. 3:6–8; 1 Cor. 5:1–2; 16:13; 2 Cor. 1:24). To be 'justified by faith' is to be 'justified by Christ's blood' (Rom. 5:1, 9). Again, as we have seen in Romans, Paul ascribes a revelatory function to faith: through it the 'righteousness of God' is revealed in the gospel (Rom. 1:16–17). To unbelievers, whether Jew or Greek, the 'message of the cross is foolishness'. To 'us' Christ became wisdom, righteousness, sanctification, and redemption (1 Cor. 1:18, 21, 31). The 'hidden wisdom' given by the Spirit of God is given to faith (cf. 1 Cor. 6:5 with 2:6–16). The zeal of the 'Israel' of Paul's day was misdirected, because it was not 'according to knowledge' (Rom. 10:1–3). For Paul, as for John, faith is a sort of 'seeing', an illumination which brings the knowledge of the glory of God in Christ (e.g. 2 Cor. 4:3–6; cf. e.g. John 9:39–41). Indeed, faith makes Christ present in the human being. To be 'in the faith' is to be indwelt by Christ: 'Test yourselves as to whether you are in the faith. Prove yourselves. Or do you not know concerning yourselves that Jesus Christ is in you – unless you are indeed unapproved?' (2 Cor. 13:5; cf. Gal. 2:20). In the same way Paul associates faith with baptism into Christ's death and resurrection (Rom. 6:1–11, cf. 17–18). Those who are 'sons of God' through faith have been 'clothed with Christ' (Gal. 3:26–27). The distinction between believers and unbelievers is that between Christ and 'Beliar' (2 Cor. 6:5).

According to Paul, then, faith is God's work within the human being through the gospel. It represents the new creation, which is called into existence by the word of God alone: 'God, who said, "Let light shine out of darkness", is the one who has shone in our hearts, to give the light which is the knowledge of the glory of God in the person of Jesus Christ' (2 Cor. 4:6; Gen. 1:3). As we noted in connection with Paul's conversion, Paul speaks here of faith as coming into being *ex nihilo*, as light in the darkness of the human heart. It arises, not from any human cleverness or wisdom, but from the proclamation of God's saving work in Christ (Rom. 10:14–17; 1 Cor. 15:1–11). For this reason it rests upon the power of God, and not upon any human wisdom (1 Cor. 1:21; 2:5). The apostles themselves are mere instruments in God's hand, 'servants through whom you believed' (1 Cor. 3:5). Paul speaks not of what he accomplished in effecting 'the obedience of faith' among the Gentiles, but of what Christ accomplished through him (Rom. 15:18; 1 Cor. 15:10–11). The believing reception of the gospel is nothing other than the word of God performing its work (1 Thess. 2:13). Unbelief is a blindness brought about by 'the god of this age' (2 Cor. 4:4).[8] The apostles do not stand above the faith of the congregations but alongside it; faith is *God's* effectual, saving work.[9] Moreover, as the preceding statements make clear, faith involves the recognition that the gospel which is its object is also its source. This may be seen in the way Paul speaks of faith as the form which Christ's cross and resurrection presently take within the human being: 'I have been crucified with Christ. I live, yet no longer I but Christ lives in me. What I now live in the flesh, I live by faith in the Son of God, who loved me and gave himself up for me' (Gal. 2:19b–20). Faith for Paul cannot exist as a mere assent to facts which must be shaped by love in order to be savingly effective. It is rather the reflection of Christ's cross and resurrection within us, which cannot be supplemented but can – and must – only continue and increase.

This twofold relation of the gospel to faith (object and source) supplies the key to understanding Paul's varying descriptions of the relation of the Spirit to faith. At some points he clearly indicates that the Spirit is given through faith or the work of Christ which forms its basis. The Galatians received the Spirit by the 'message of faith' (Gal. 3:2). Because we are 'sons of God' through Christ's redeeming work, God has sent forth the Spirit into our hearts (4:6). On the other hand, he often states or implies that the Spirit initiates our participation in Christ. The Galatians began their course of faith by the Spirit (3:3, cf. verse 5). The conversion of the Thessalonians represented the arrival of the gospel among them 'in power and in the Holy Spirit' (1 Thess. 1:5). No-one can say that 'Jesus is Lord' except by the Holy Spirit (1 Cor. 12:3, see also verse 13; 2 Cor. 3:3).

In no instance, however, does Paul say that the Holy Spirit brings us to faith or that he works faith within us. The absence of such language is not accidental. For Paul, the Spirit does not transform the old, fallen person that we are, but rather 'wages war against the flesh' (Gal. 5:17;

---

[8] Paul in this context uses the most daring language found in the Scriptures to describe Satan. It is obviously a qualified attribution, in more than one way. But it is worth further theological reflection, particularly in reference to Satan's effecting blindness to God and to his glory in Christ.

[9] 2 Cor. 1:24. Cf. Rom. 1:8; Phil. 1:29; Eph. 2:8; Gal. 3:3.

cf. Rom. 8:6–9, 13). The Spirit constitutes the entrance of the new creation, the presence of Christ, 'the last Adam' (1 Cor. 15:45). On this account Paul refers to the one who believes as '*born* according to the Spirit' (Gal. 4:29; cf. Titus 3:5). The Spirit re-creates the human being through the gospel and thereby establishes both his entrance and his dwelling-place within us.[10]

These observations bring us again to the opposition between the 'works of the law' and faith, upon which Paul repeatedly insists. Although for him faith represents obedience to the gospel, it is not a 'work of the law' which proceeds from the human being, but the work of God. Paul develops this qualitative distinction in his typifying wordplay in Romans: 'Where then is boasting? It is excluded. By what kind of law, a law of works? No, but by a law of faith. For we reckon that a person is justified by faith apart from works of the law' (Rom. 3:27–28). Faith excludes 'works' from justification not by a word of prohibition but by its participation in God's justifying deed in Christ. According to the nature of faith, the one who believes cannot boast: where boasting is present, faith is absent. It is in this sense that faith serves a 'norm' or 'law' which proceeds from God's work and bars the work of the human being (cf. Rom. 3:21–26). As we observed in our discussion of Romans, the inadequacy of human works to justify in the presence of God (and at the final judgment) does not at all mean that God's work in the human being is inadequate: just the opposite. Paul therefore is not self-contradictory in his expectation that all human beings, believers and unbelievers alike, will be judged according to works. This observation brings us to our discussion of the 'obedience of faith'.

Faith as obedience to the gospel

Implicit in the decisive role which the New Testament writings ascribe to faith is the understanding that faith represents obedience to God. According to Mark's Gospel, Jesus *called* his hearers to faith in his proclamation of the kingdom of God (1:14–15). In John's Gospel, Jesus names faith in 'the one whom God has sent' as the sole 'work' which God requires of the human being (6:29).[11] In 1 John, the *single* commandment of God incumbent upon us is 'faith in the name of the

---

[10] In this connection Paul speaks of the 'circumcision of the heart by the Spirit' (Rom. 2:29), in which he takes up the biblical promises that God will remake the human being (Deut. 30:6; Jer. 31:33; Ezek. 11:19; Ezek. 36:26).

[11] See also John 3:36, where 'disobedience' stands in contrast to faith.

Son of God' and 'love of one another' (3:23).[12] According to Hebrews, the word of God now spoken in the Son demands nothing other than faith. Unbelief is the fundamental transgression (3:12, 19; 4:2–3; 10:38–39; 11:6; 12:2; 13:7). Luke characterizes the missionary preaching in Acts in the same way, speaking, for example, of the numerous priests in Jerusalem who 'obeyed the faith' (Acts 6:7; see also 2:38, 44; 16:31).

Paul is in agreement with the rest of the New Testament in this matter. According to his instruction of the Galatian churches, 'in Christ Jesus' faith alone is 'effective' (5:6). He informs the young Philippian congregation that should his imprisonment end in death, it would be a 'drink offering upon the sacrifice and priestly service' of their faith (2:17). Unbelief is a refusal to 'obey the gospel', a failure to submit to the 'righteousness of God' revealed in Jesus Christ (Rom. 10:16; 2 Thess. 1:8; Rom. 10:3). Coming to faith represents 'obedience from the heart' to the teaching of the gospel (Rom. 6:17). The personified 'righteousness of faith' voices Moses' prohibition of pride: 'Do not say in your heart, "Who shall ascend into heaven?"' (Rom. 10:6; Deut. 9:4). All that does not proceed from faith is sin (Rom. 14:23). The saving event is distributed to human beings solely by the means of faith: God has purposed Christ as a propitiation *through faith* in his blood (i.e. Christ's death on the cross; Rom. 3:25).[13] Obviously, Paul does not suppose that faith adds something to Christ's death. He also speaks of 'justification by Christ's blood' (Rom. 5:9). Nevertheless, it is only through faith that Christ's death is effective as an atonement. Interpreters have sometimes been hesitant to allow faith the indispensable role which Paul accords it in Romans 3:25, perhaps in part because they conceive it merely as a human act.[14] But this is to misinterpret Paul, for whom faith cannot be reduced to assent,

---

[12] This faith and love therefore represent aspects of a single reality.

[13] Interpreters have generally chosen to read *en tō haimati* with *hilastērion*. It is most natural, however, to read the phrases in the order in which they stand in the text. Although Paul does not speak of 'faith in Christ's blood' elsewhere, he does speak of 'faith in Christ' (Gal. 3:26; Eph. 1:15), and will shortly speak of being justified *en tō haimati autou* ('by the blood of Christ'; Rom. 5:9). His unusual phrasing, in which Christ's death is momentarily singled out as the object of faith, is understandable given the confessional form of the passage. Paul has already spoken distinctly of Christ's justifying resurrection (i.e. 'the redemption which is in Christ Jesus'; Rom. 3:24). He now speaks of Christ's justifying death.

[14] Longenecker 1993: 479 supposes that is problematic to speak of the faith of the Christian here. Käsemann 1980: 98 speaks of Paul making a 'rough interpolation' in order to relate faith to salvation; so also, Dunn 1988: 1:172–173. Rightly, however, Moo 1996: 236–237.

decision, or any other form of psychology.[15] The necessity of faith does not in the least diminish the centrality of Christ in salvation. It signals just the opposite. By its very nature, the gospel demands faith – and nothing else – from the human being, a faith which itself is the work of God in Christ.

This conception of faith as obedience stands at the centre of Paul's interest in his letter to Rome. At both the opening and the closing of the letter, he describes the purpose of his gospel and the aim of his apostleship as the securing of 'the obedience of faith' among all the Gentiles (1:5; 16:25–27). Through Paul, Christ has effected the 'obedience of the Gentiles' from 'Jerusalem as far as Illyricum' (15:17–19). As we have seen, Paul even goes so far as to speak of 'the law of faith', a demand which transcends 'the law of works' (3:27).[16]

We must be careful to avoid several misunderstandings of the expression 'obedience of faith' which have appeared in recent interpretation of Paul.[17] In formulating his message in this way, Paul is not taking up a concept familiar within early Judaism and stripping it of its otherwise nationalistic implications.[18] That is to say, he is not polemically engaged with his early Jewish contemporaries in Romans, but seeks to communicate his gospel to a circle of congregations which he had not founded.[19] When he speaks of 'the obedience of faith', he

---

[15] See Schlatter 1905: 260, who makes a similar judgment about the apostolic witness as whole.

[16] His following affirmation that justification takes place by faith and not by the works of the law confirms that he is here according faith this status, and not speaking a kind of reading of the law (cf. Rom. 3:21).

[17] I am thinking in particular of Garlington 1991 and 1994.

[18] This is the thesis of Garlington 1991; 1994: 10–31, who seeks to join the two concepts semantically, arguing that 'faith' and 'obedience' were 'virtually synonymous' for Paul. Paul, in contrast, joins faith with obedience on account of the object of faith, namely the promise of God fulfilled in Christ. Garlington also speaks of obedience as *resulting* from faith (e.g. 1994: 10–31), with the result that confusion reigns throughout his work. One cannot have it both ways. The Greek terms for 'obedience' involved (*hypakoē, hypakouein, hypēkoos*), despite their semantic breadth, cannot be said to be synonymous with 'faith' in the biblical tradition. They bear the general sense of 'responding in subjection', thereby carrying connotations of 'hearing' or of response to a person. These associations do not in themselves entail the notion of 'faith' or 'believing' (e.g. Rom. 6:12, 16; Eph. 6:1, 5; Mark 1:27; 1 Pet. 3:6; Gen. 41:40). We can scarcely suppose that Paul uses *hypakoē* in the sense of 'faith' in Rom. 1:5 and 16:27, since that reduces the expression *hypakoē tēs pisteōs* to a redundancy. See Schneider 1993: 394–395. Likewise, *šm'* does not necessarily mean 'to believe' or 'to obey': see Rüterswörden 1995.

[19] Against Garlington 1991: 233–268. The rhetorical engagement with a Jewish dialogue partner in Rom. 2:17–29 does not alter this judgment in the least. Paul does not bring an indictment against Judaism in this passage, only against hypocrisy.

appeals to the demand for faith in Christ which was characteristic of earliest Christianity and clarifies its significance. It is important to recall, too, that the 'faith' of which Paul speaks is not abstract. As elsewhere in his letters and in the New Testament, the absolute usage presupposes faith in Jesus Christ, crucified and risen. It is *this* faith which God requires as obedience, according to Paul. Its discontinuity with early Judaism consists not merely in an exclusion of nationalism from justification, but in its exclusion of the works of the human being, works which are necessarily measured against the law. Paul could not speak as his Jewish contemporaries did of dependence on God for salvation through conformity to the law, because he had come to believe that this ideal is an illusion which leads only to hypocrisy.[20] The law, Paul affirms, is not of faith (Gal. 3:12; cf. Rom. 4:15). In the crucified Messiah, he came to recognize the biblical witness that Jew and Gentile alike are subjected to sin's power.[21]

Paul does not call upon his congregations to 'believe': the imperative of the verb *pisteuein* is absent from his letters. In all but a few instances he treats his addressees as those who already believe and belong to God as 'holy ones'.[22] His letters rather are given to clarifying the nature of faith and the demand which it places upon us. As a prime example, it is instructive to recall Paul's description of Abraham's faith in Romans 4:12–25. He speaks of faith as 'Abraham's footsteps' in which we are to follow, characterizing it from the outset of this passage as an act of obedience (verse 12).[23] In sharp contrast with Jewish

---

[20] See e.g. Sir. 32:24; 33:3; *4 Ezra* 7:24. It is surprising that Garlington does not seriously engage the work of Schlatter 1905, who saw quite clearly the distinction between Paul and his Jewish contemporaries in this regard.

[21] The fundamental weakness in Garlington's work lies in his failure to come to grips with the judgment of God upon fallen humanity in Paul's thought. For this reason he embraces the anthropological optimism of early Judaism (Garlington 1991). In his reading of Paul, Adam bequeaths his descendants 'a disadvantage', namely, the absence of the Spirit, but not guilt (1994: 84–95). 'Righteousness' is 'not sinless perfection or anything approaching it' but 'responsible covenant-behavior' (Garlington 1994: 163). Romans 7 accordingly becomes a narrative of struggle, rather than the recognition of the power of sin. In Garlington's reading, this chapter of Romans offers the following paltry comfort: 'notwithstanding our many failures, there is no condemnation as long [as] we desire to remain within the covenant bond, true to Christ the Lord' (1994: 163). Our 'wretchedness' is no longer our just condemnation, but our temporary lack of power to do what we otherwise would. The human being is basically free and good, but weak. What need is there then for the cross?

[22] Only in the Corinthian correspondence does he sometimes speak to his addressees as if they were unbelievers (e.g. 2 Cor. 6:1–2).

[23] The commentaries generally have overlooked the significance of Paul's language, which is probably intended to make an emphatic statement to Jewish Christians that faith

tradition, Paul focuses his attention entirely upon God's word of promise to Abraham in Genesis 15:1–6. The subsequent testing of Abraham's faith does not come into view, central though it is to the letter to the Hebrews, to James and to Jewish tradition. The word of promise stands in contradiction to all of Abraham's circumstances as a 'hope against hope' (verse 18). After a century of life, his body is effectively dead and Sarah's womb is barren (verse 19). Abraham is driven outside himself by the word of promise to the God who raises the dead and who by his word alone calls into existence that which is not (verse 17). That word, and nothing in or with Abraham, made him strong in faith. He therefore gave glory to God, in contrast with all idolatry and human fallenness (verse 20; 1:23; 3:23), so that, as Paul says, 'it was reckoned to him as righteousness' (verse 23). With this statement Paul returns to the locus with which he began, Genesis 15:6 (verse 3), underscoring the paradoxical convergence of grace and obedience in faith. Abraham's faith simultaneously effects the justification of one who is ungodly and constitutes the obedience which God demands. It is no mere intellectual assent, but an 'act' in which God is acknowledged as God.

Clearly, then, although faith has a cognitive aspect, based as it is upon the promise of God fulfilled in Christ, the whole person is involved in believing. We have seen this already in our discussion of Romans 6. Knowing that one has been joined to Christ's death and resurrection, and that this event is decisive, one must 'reckon oneself dead to sin, but alive to God in Christ Jesus'. Where this 'reckoning' is present, disobedience is overcome (verses 11–13). Apart from it, sin remains and rules, no matter how impressive one's outward deeds might be. The well-known paradoxical relation between the 'indicative' and the 'imperative' which is present in all of Paul's exhortations has its basis in faith. Unfortunately, the phrase has become so overused that most interpreters no longer recognize its content. It does not merely have to do with the chronological priority of God's saving work over the response of the human being. The exodus and Sinai are not paradoxically related to one another. The connection between them is decidedly not equivalent to that of the Pauline 'indicative' and 'imperative'.[24] Paul's exhortations have their basis in and proceed from the resurrection of the incarnate Son of God

---

alone is obedience. The expression 'to follow in the footsteps' has rabbinic parallels. See Käsemann 1980: 116.

[24] See the classic essay of Bultmann 1982 (1924).

in whom the demands which God lays upon us have already come to reality: 'Clean out the old leaven, that you may be a new lump of dough, just as you are unleavened. For, indeed, Christ our Passover has been sacrificed!' (1 Cor. 5:7).

Obedience to imperatives such as these is a matter of faith and hope, in which we grasp Christ's saving work. It is important to see that such faith in Christ carries self-judgment with it. In faith God comes to his justice in his claim against us (Rom. 3:21–26). The Spirit wages war against 'the flesh' and puts to death the deeds of 'the body' (Gal. 5:17–23; Rom. 8:13). All that we are in Christ triumphs over all that we are in ourselves. For this reason, growth and progress for Paul are strictly a matter of the increase of faith, a firmer grasp of that which is already given (see Phil. 1:25, 27; 1 Thess. 3:10; 2 Thess. 1:10). In this way faith is inseparable from hope and *joy* – an important matter which we cannot explore further here (2 Cor. 1:23–24; Rom. 14:17, 23; 15:13; Phil. 1:25).

In accord with its basis and object in Christ, faith expresses itself in the world in the form of love for the neighbour. Only 'faith working through love' has force in Christ Jesus (Gal. 5:6).[25] Faith meets the demand of the law in 'love', not as an idea or theological conception, but as a reality in the world:

> For the [commandments] 'Do not commit adultery', 'Do not murder', 'Do not steal', 'Do not covet', and if there is any other commandment, it is summarized in this word: 'You shall love your neighbour as yourself.' Love does not do evil to the neighbour. Love therefore is the fulfilment of the law (Rom. 13:9–10; see also Gal. 5:13–15).

The prohibitions of the law against doing evil to one's neighbour are fulfilled in love, which by its very nature does no harm to the neighbour. Paul does not offer here a mere ethical criterion by which to judge the course of one's action. He is rather speaking of the presence of Christ, in whom love is effective. As he urges his readers in this context, we are to 'put on the Lord Jesus Christ, and make no provision for the flesh' (Rom. 13:14; cf. Gal. 2:20; 2 Cor. 10:3). Accordingly, love has its source in faith, not merely as gratitude for grace received,

---

[25] This topic deserves far more attention than we can give it here, particularly since it figures largely in the theology of the Reformation. For this very reason, we cannot pass over it, even though we cannot here treat it at length.

but in the Christ who is present within it. From this perspective, Paul's treatment of faith and love in 1 Corinthians 13 becomes understandable. Faith does not have intrinsic value for Paul, but exists as a reflection of Christ and his work. Considered in itself, even a faith which is sufficient to move mountains is nothing (1 Cor. 13:2). Love is greater than faith and hope, since it incarnates the eschatological life which faith apprehends and which hope anticipates will come to its fullness. Paul does not contemplate love as an ideal in 1 Corinthians 13, but speaks of it as a reality in Christ. For this reason he does not here define love, but describes its manifold expressions. The 'love' of which he speaks in the most stirring and sublime terms is a gift from God, a gift which the Corinthians are to seek above all others since it abides for ever (verse 13). The triad of faith, hope and love therefore represents differing aspects of the one reality of Christ's saving presence (cf. 1 Thess. 1:3). If faith is considered as an isolated 'gift' operative in the world, love far exceeds faith. Considered in relation to God, however, faith has a priority over love, since it is by faith alone that the divine reality of love is given to us in Christ (Gal. 5:6). Love is the earthly and visible side of the faith which grasps the heavenly and unseen reality of the righteousness of God in Christ. To use Paul's words again, 'faith works through love'.[26]

The faith of Christ

Paul speaks of the 'faith of Jesus Christ' in varying terms eight times in his letters, primarily in Galatians and Romans (Gal. 2:16 twice; 3:22; Rom. 3:22, 26; Phil. 3:9; Eph. 3:12). Although interpreters have traditionally understood the genitive as signifying the object of faith in such instances, that is, 'faith in Christ', a considerable number of scholars now advocate reading the genitive as expressing the subject of faith, 'Christ's faith'.[27] Moreover, since the Greek term *pistis* can bear the meaning 'faithfulness', it is argued that Paul has in view 'Christ's faithfulness' or at least includes this idea in his reference. Paul speaks of 'Christ's faith(fulness)' as Christ's obedience to God on behalf of humanity in his death on the cross, in which humanity is included and represented: it is the faithfulness of Jesus which saves us. And it does so in such a manner that those who belong to him participate in that

---

[26] See, again Gal. 5:6, and, indeed the entirety of Paul's argument in Galatians.

[27] For a recent bibliography of the growing number of works on this question, see Hays 1997: 36.

faithfulness in their own lives. In this way a connection is properly established between the saving death of Christ and the obedience demanded of the Christian, or so it is claimed (see Hays 1997: 55–57; 1983: 247–266; Wallis 1995: 175–221). Advocates of this interpretation argue, in fact, that the traditional reading of the expression as 'faith in Christ' betrays an individualistic stance which is unrepresentative of Paul and of the biblical message (Hays 1997: 39).

We must note at the outset that the usage and understanding of 'faith' in earliest Christianity stands at some distance from this proposal. As we have seen, the New Testament authors without exception speak of believing in Jesus Christ as the means by which God grants salvation. Only five texts in the New Testament speak of the 'faithfulness of Christ' using the adjective *pistos*, a paucity which stands in stark contrast to the approximately 400 (both implicit and direct) references to faith in Christ in the New Testament. And despite recent attempts to demonstrate otherwise, the topic of 'Christ's faith' (i.e. his believing) is essentially missing from the New Testament.[28] While the three passages outside of Paul's letters which use the expression 'the faith (*pistis*) of Christ' are debatable, in the end it appears that they do not signify Jesus' believing. At least one fundamental reason for this silence is apparent: in the New Testament 'faith' is based upon the work of God *in* Christ. Despite their clear affirmations of Jesus' humanity, the New Testament authors did not speak of *Jesus'* believing in God, since he himself was the object of faith.

The usage of 'faith of Christ' which appears in James 2:1 is instructive in this regard.[29] James speaks of 'having the faith of our Lord of glory, Jesus Christ'. When we take into account James's strict monotheism (2:19), it is quite remarkable that he gives Jesus the title 'Lord'. The description carries overtones of Jesus' deity and sets Christ apart from 'the prophets who spoke in the name of the Lord', and who serve James as models of 'patience and suffering' (5:10–11). Moreover, since James's statement concerning 'the faith of Christ' prepares for his subsequent discussion of the character of saving faith, it is very unlikely that he has in view 'Christ's believing', since he could hardly suppose that the Lord of glory was in need of a faith which saved him in the same way that the ungodly are (see 2:14–26).

That is not to say that the theme of 'Jesus' faithfulness' is lacking in

---

[28] The examples which Wallis 1995 brings forward from the Synoptics, James and Revelation are hardly convincing.

[29] We shall discuss the other two passages, Rev. 2:13 and 14:12, below.

the New Testament. Both Hebrews and Revelation understand salvation to involve our participation in the faithfulness of Christ. In both instances, however, our sharing in that 'faithfulness' appears only as a part of a larger saving reality, an outworking of the atonement which Christ made for us. This distinction is of importance in assessing current claims about Paul's usage, in which 'the faith(fulness) of Christ' assumes a comprehensive character.

In Hebrews, those who belong to Jesus share in his obedience in suffering, but not in his high-priestly act of atonement for sin (2:17; 3:2). We participate in him as 'sons', but we do not thereby become 'high priests'. That honour belongs to Christ alone, who secured the forgiveness of sins in the 'offering of his body once for all' (5:1–10; 2:10–18; 12:1–11).[30] Faith, in Hebrews, arises from and is directed toward the word of God addressed to us in Christ (1:1–2; 4:12–16). We are to fix our attention on him, as the one in whom the saving purpose of God for humanity has been carried to completion (3:14; 2:5–9). He is the 'leader and perfecter of faith', not as a mere example, but as the one in whom the promise of God has come to fulfilment (12:1; cf. 11:39–40). Faith is the present 'substance' of participation in him, a participation which goes well beyond 'faithfulness', since it includes lordship over all things (3:14; 2:5–9). In this focus upon the exaltation of Christ, the letter to the Hebrews is representative of the rest of the New Testament, in which the saving significance of Christ's resurrection is at the centre of interest.

In Revelation, Christ appears as 'the witness, the faithful one', who has borne witness to God, and now calls his followers to do so (15:5; 3:14; cf. 19:11). Indeed, the exalted Christ now has his faithful ones who bear witness to *him*, including the martyr Antipas at Pergamum (2:10, 13; 17:14). There is an obvious sense, therefore, in which believers are called to share in Jesus' faithfulness. At the same time, 'the faith of Jesus' which the faithful Antipas did not deny is faith which 'holds fast his name'. It therefore seems apparent that faith *in* Jesus is in some way contemplated here, since Jesus subsequently warns the churches to 'hold what you have' in the face of other teachings such as those of the Nicolaitans (2:13, 15).[31] Likewise in 14:12, 'the faith of Jesus', which the saints keep, has to do with faith in Jesus, as is clear from the parallel passage in 12:17, which speaks of

---

[30] Although the one who is 'Son' is also addressed as God, 'Son' remains a messianic term and therefore signifies Jesus' humanity. Deity is *predicated* of the Son in Hebrews. In reference to the cross as a sacrifice see Heb. 9:11 – 10:18.

[31] See also Rev. 2:19, where 'faith' is set alongside 'works', 'love', and 'service'.

those who 'have the witness of Jesus', and which in turn refers to the 'witness to Jesus'.[32] This faith in Jesus is directed to the resurrected and glorified Christ, who as the lamb of God shed his blood to redeem a people for God. The genitive usage may well convey the idea that Jesus is the source of faith, and that faith is found exclusively in him, as we shall see is the case in Paul's letters. Yet in Revelation as in Hebrews, participation in Christ's faithfulness cannot be understood apart from faith in his unique, saving death and resurrection (1:5–6; 5:1–14).

As we have observed already, Paul generally presupposes that his addressees share his understanding that faith has its object in God's work in Christ, a stance which is common to the letters of the New Testament. Of course, his frequent absolute usage of the term 'faith' in this sense does not in itself decide the interpretation of the disputed genitives. He does, after all, speak of the 'faithfulness of God' using the term *pistis* (Rom. 3:3). Nevertheless, it strongly suggests that when Paul speaks of 'the faith of Christ' he is speaking of faith which has Christ as its object, particularly since he nowhere speaks of Christ's faithfulness in clear terms.[33]

Several aspects of this observation deserve further development. Those who advocate reading the expression 'the faith of Christ' in its various appearances as 'Christ's faith(fulness)' understand Paul to say that God justifies us or grants us his promise of blessing through the faithfulness of Jesus Christ.[34] It is obviously right to speak of Jesus' obedience accomplishing our redemption, as Paul himself does in Romans 5:18–19. Nevertheless, there are various important reasons for rejecting the thought that it saves simply as a human act. In the first place, Paul, with the rest of the New Testament, understands the resurrection of the crucified Christ as the focal point of faith.[35] Christ's death is salvific only in conjunction with his resurrection (e.g. Rom. 5:9; Gal. 1:4).[36] As Keck observes (1989: 445), Paul never speaks of

---

[32] On the latter see Rev. 1:2–3; 11:7; 19:10; 22:16, 18, 20. Correspondingly 14:12 shows that the parallel in 13:10 speaks of 'the faith of the saints' and not of their faithfulness.

[33] He never applies the adjective *pistos* in the sense of 'faithfulness' to Christ, even though he uses it of God and human beings: 1 Cor. 1:9; 1 Thess. 5:24; 1 Cor. 4:2.

[34] See again Gal. 2:16; 3:22; Rom. 3:22, 26; Phil. 3:9; Eph. 3:12.

[35] This emphasis does not at all imply that Christ's death assumes a secondary role. Just the opposite is the case: Christ's 'death to sin' comes to its saving goal in his 'life to God' (Rom. 6:10).

[36] As we have seen, this is also true of Rom. 5:19, which speaks of the eschatological instatement of the many on account of Christ's obedience.

the gospel of Jesus, only of the gospel of *Christ*, an expression in which his resurrection and exaltation come into view. Consequently, to read Paul as speaking of our salvation being worked through 'Jesus' faithfulness' is to give Christ's death a significance which is unparalleled in Paul's letters.[37] This point takes added force when we consider that when Paul speaks of 'the faith of Christ' he usually describes it as mediating justification or righteousness. As we have seen, it is the resurrection of Christ in particular which Paul associates with our justification (Gal. 2:16; Rom. 3:20, 22, 26; Phil. 3:9).[38]

This defect reveals the deeper problem inherent in this reading, namely, that it makes Jesus' obedience the expression of a moral ideal at the expense of its atoning significance.[39] Although the sacrificial character of Jesus' death often is acknowledged in such interpretations, it stands strangely detached from the act of obedience on the cross. Jesus in his faith(fulness) accomplishes for (and within) humanity the obedience which God requires. In this reading the justification of God in his contention with fallen and condemned humanity is rendered peripheral or even excluded.[40] It is difficult, moreover, to imagine how Jesus' obedience to death might be considered representative or vicarious, apart from its atoning significance (against Hays 1983: 248). And once Jesus' obedience to death is viewed simply as his life of faith, it becomes an ideal which another human being, such as Abraham, might more or less embody. For Richard Hays, for example, there would be nothing 'intrinsically illogical' in Paul's affirming the sufficiency of Abraham's faith apart from the death of Christ, even though that is not how 'the story runs' for Paul (see Hays 1983: 205–

---

[37] Hays 1983: 207–209 understands, of course, that life is granted through the Messiah's death. In his reading, however, life becomes something that Christ 'attains' or 'receives' for us, rather than an integral part of the saving event itself.

[38] Likewise, the arrival of the promise (Gal. 3:22), participation in Christ's life (Gal. 2:20), and access to God (Eph. 3:12) are inherently bound up with Christ's resurrection.

[39] Zahl 1996: 73 notes the proximity of Hays's thought to that of Ernst Käsemann in his interpretation of the cross. Once this moralizing interpretation of Christ's death has been adopted, it is only a short step to the Pelagian view that Christ's obedience is a mere example or pattern which we are to follow.

[40] Hays 1983: 173 understands God's righteousness as his 'covenant faithfulness' which effects the obedience of humanity. Jesus' faithfulness therefore demonstrates that faithfulness. We have seen already that Paul's usage of 'God's righteousness', like biblical usage generally, has to do not with 'covenant faithfulness' but with God's ruling and judging creation. In the crucial text of Rom. 3:21–26, Paul speaks not only of the justification of sinners, but of the justification of God.

206, 226).[41] Although Hays affirms that God was uniquely at work in Jesus' death, and that Jesus vicariously bore the sins of others, he does not recognize that this aspect of Jesus' obedience renders it qualitatively different from that of any other person.[42] In this reading, Jesus appears as the ideal human being who did what the rest of humanity ought to have done, but was unable to do.[43] The Christology of this proposal is essentially Nestorian. For Paul, in contrast, dying itself was a matter of obedience for Jesus, inevitable though it is for the rest of humanity.[44] In his 'giving himself for our sins', his obedience itself bore a unique character: he died as the incarnate Son sent from the Father, the second and last Adam in whom humanity is redeemed and re-created (Gal. 1:4; 2:20; 4:4; Rom. 8:3; 1 Cor. 15:45–49).

Correspondingly, the new line of interpretation fails to do justice to the simultaneity of faith in Christ with faith in God in Paul's thought. Those who believe in Christ believe in the God who raised him from the dead (e.g. Rom. 4:25; Gal. 1:6–8). Although there is much more that could be said on this topic, here we simply wish to observe that once Jesus' faith(fulness) toward God is viewed simply as a morally ideal act, an essential feature of Paul's gospel is lost or at best appears extraneous. For him, God was 'in' Christ's action, thereby 'reconciling the world to himself' (2 Cor. 5:19). We have noted this difficulty already, in the way in which Christ's resurrection becomes an outflow of the saving event, rather than being integral to it in this reading of Paul. Likewise, 'faith' necessarily takes on a general character in this interpretation, since rather than being directed to God's work in Christ, it now consists in Jesus' obedience to God. Even though Hays (1983: 250) speaks of our participating in Jesus' faith, and not merely following Jesus' example, his construal nevertheless entails believing

---

[41] It is very difficult to reconcile this reading of Paul with his characterization of Abraham's faith as working 'the justification of the ungodly' (Rom. 4:5). The thought of Galatians is no different. The whole of 'the present age' is evil (Gal. 1:4). Only the promised son, Isaac, bore God's blessing (4:21–31).

[42] For this reason, too, Hays never fully comes to grips with Paul's understanding that Jesus' obedient death took place 'under the law', insisting, as he does, that redemption takes place by 'Jesus' faith apart from law'. Hays 1983: 206–209; cf. Gal. 4:4.

[43] Hays 1997: 39–40 describes his interpretation as 'Christological', as opposed to the traditional reading, which he labels 'anthropological'. But this is an essentially Nestorian Christology. One therefore may reverse the charge: Hays's reading reduces Christology to anthropology.

[44] This theme is integral to Rom. 5:12–21. Through the 'transgression of the one the many died', but not Christ, whose death rather was a 'gift' to the many (Rom. 5:15). See also Phil. 2:8; 2 Cor. 8:9.

with Jesus, but not in Jesus.[45] According to Hays (1997: 45–46, 56), to say that faith in Christ has saving efficacy (or, for that matter, that it constitutes obedience) threatens to make faith a 'bizarre sort of work'. But this is to fail to see that for Paul, in the critical sense faith is decidedly not a 'work'; that is, it is not the deed or accomplishment of fallen human beings, but the work of God within us through the gospel (e.g. Rom. 4:5). Furthermore, once one excludes faith as the means of participation in Christ's work, we are left wondering precisely how the saving effect of the cross is supposed to be mediated. The door is left open to interpreting the cross in merely exemplary terms.

Much of the argument concerning the meaning of the expression 'the faith of Christ' has quite understandably centred upon grammatical considerations or analysis of limited contexts in Paul's letters.[46] While such work is necessary, it has not proved to be decisive in this instance. Obviously the central issue at stake here is Paul's choice of the genitive form with the noun, 'faith *of Christ*', which he made over against various prepositional phrases which were increasingly used with *pistis* in Hellenistic Greek to express the object of the verbal idea.[47] Several pertinent aspects of the contexts in which this expression appears help in sorting out its meaning. First, Paul always speaks of 'the faith of Christ' in connection with the gift of salvation, and usually in association with justification (Gal. 2:16, 20; 3:22; Rom. 3:22, 26; Phil. 3:9; Eph. 3:12). Second, the passages in which the expression appears invariably have to do with the revelation of God's saving purpose in Jesus Christ, usually in contrast with the will of God as it is expressed in the law, as for example in Romans 3:21–22: 'Now apart from the law, the righteousness of God has been manifested ... the righteousness of God through "the faith of Jesus Christ"'. In other words, the fulfilment of promise is always in view when Paul speaks of 'the faith of Christ'. The antithetical parallelism which Paul creates between 'the works of the law' and 'the faith of Jesus Christ' in Galatians 2:16 likewise plays upon this distinction between the law and the gospel, even if here a misunderstanding of the law also comes into

---

[45] Hays's thought bears an uncanny resemblance to that of Albrecht Ritschl. Cf. Schäfer 1965: 74–75. Indeed, for some who hold this view, 'faith(fulness)' is essentially reduced to an imitation of Jesus' faith: the Pelagian complement of Nestorian Christology (Williams 1987: 439).

[46] Hays 1983 is the exception in this regard.

[47] Pace Hultgren 1980, the noun *pistis* appears with *eis*, *en* and *pros* in Paul's letters, revealing that Paul had ways of expressing the object of faith other than the genitive relation (Rom. 3:25; Eph 1:13, 15; Col. 2:5; Philem. 5; 1 Thess. 1:8). The verbal usage with prepositions must be taken into account as well.

view (see Dunn 1998: 381). Third, as we have noted, much of Paul's usage of the noun is absolute. He speaks of 'the faith' without further qualification, under the assumption that his addressees know the content of that faith, namely, God's saving work in Christ's cross and resurrection.[48] When we take into account these factors and recall that prepositional phrases were available to Paul, it seems very likely that he uses the genitive relation to express the basis of faith and therewith its character. He might have expressed this idea by speaking of 'faith from (*ek*) Christ', but the semantically broader genitive relation serves to define faith in a way that the mere designation of its source does not.[49] We have to do here with a 'qualifying' genitive, which is roughly parallel to Paul's usage of the genitive in 'the word of Christ', 'the gospel of Christ', 'the truth of Christ', 'the law of Christ' and the like.[50] In speaking of 'the faith of Christ', Paul points to the cross and resurrection as the ground of faith, the decisive act of God in which 'faith' has come into the world as a reality and demand. He sets forth Christ as the exclusive, all-determining source of faith. In fact, his striking statement in Galatians that 'faith has *arrived*' appears precisely in conjunction with his use of the expression 'the faith of Christ' (3:22–23, 25). As we have observed, Paul contrasts 'the faith of Christ' with the law in the same way, and connects it with the revelation of righteousness and salvation. Those who have argued for reading the expression as a subjective genitive have rightly sensed that in these contexts Paul is concerned to affirm that faith itself is the work of God. They have failed to see, however, that Paul speaks of Christ's cross *and* resurrection as the 'place' in which God has effected faith.

[48] As we have seen, Paul describes that content at various points in his letters, including the object(s) of the verb *pisteuein*: e.g. Rom. 4:24; 10:9–10; 1 Cor. 1:21–23; 15:11, 17; 2 Cor. 4:13–14; 1 Thess. 1:8–10.

[49] The same may be true in Col. 2:12, where Paul speaks of being raised with Christ in baptism through 'the faith which is of the working of God, who raised him from the dead'.

[50] Rom. 10:17; 2 Cor. 2:12; 11:10; Gal. 6:2; etc. In a slightly different sense, Hultgren 1980: 257 speaks of 'Christic faith'. This reading is not incompatible with the observations of Harrisville 1994: 233–241, that the early Fathers do not use *pistis Christou* as a subjective genitive. It is worth reviewing the examples he cites to consider whether they too, might have a genitive of source or origin in view. The expression represents a parallel to Paul's reference to the 'faith of Abraham', which in a different sense serves as the source of all subsequent faith. As the one who first believed in the promise of God, Abraham is the father of us all (Rom. 4:16–17).

Faith and justification

Paul speaks with particular frequency of 'justification' as the saving benefit given to faith. He occasionally employs other terms: salvation (Rom. 9:33; 10:9–10; 13:11; 1 Cor. 1:21; 15:2; Eph. 2:8), grace (Rom. 5:2), the promise (Rom. 4:13, 16; Gal. 3:22), the Spirit (Gal. 3:2, 5, 14), access to God (Eph. 3:12), Christ himself (Eph. 3:17). But the connection between faith and justification is prominent, and stands in contrast with the 'holiness' word-group in Paul's letters.[51] We have here Paul's 'grammar of righteousness': over against the righteousness of the law which comes by works stands the righteousness of faith which arises from the promise of God fulfilled in Christ. Faith has its place in this 'grammar', since it is not a generalized trust in God, but derives from the divine promise to Abraham. That is to say, the justifying work of God takes the same form within us in faith as it does outside of us in the cross and resurrection. This form has two fundamental aspects, which we have noted already. On the one hand, 'faith' involves our recognition of the absolute gratuity of our justification. We believe in 'the one who justifies the ungodly', as Abraham did (Rom. 4:5). Faith itself comes to us as a gift from God: 'faith is from the proclamation, and proclamation is from the message of Christ' (Rom. 10:17). On the other hand, 'faith' is a matter of obedience, in which we are brought to nothing in our own estimation, and justify God in his contention with us. The life of the believer likewise conforms to this pattern, since we share in both the sufferings of Christ and the comfort given through him. In this way we are made to trust in God alone, and to give thanks to him alone. In faith God comes to be God in us. This, and nothing less, is obedience.

Justification by faith and judgment according to works

We may now return to Paul's understanding of final judgment and its relation to the message of justification. We recall that in Romans 2:1–16, in a strikingly straightforward manner, Paul declares that justification is contingent upon obedience, and specifically upon 'doing the law' (verse 13). Mere knowledge of God's will is insufficient to save, since only the 'doers of the law will be justified'. Yet shortly

---

[51] Rom. 1:17; 3:26, 28, 30; 4:5, 9, 11, 13; 5:1; 10:4, 6, 10; Gal. 2:16; 3:8, 11, 24; 5:5; Phil. 3:9.

afterwards he goes on to maintain that justification takes place by faith 'apart from the works of the law' (verse 28). Interpreters have offered a wide range of solutions to this difficulty. Some simply claim that Paul is inconsistent. But it is hardly likely that an experienced teacher and missionary, who so confidently set forth his gospel in this letter, could stumble so badly. Nor is there any evidence that a later gloss has been added to Paul's letter here, as others have claimed. Sometimes, particularly among Protestant interpreters, it is argued that Paul presents a hypothetical case here, or perhaps the view of Judaizing opponents. But this reading is hardly likely, since Paul directly connects this 'justification by works' to the coming judgment of God which he proclaimed as part of his gospel (2:16). Often Protestants attempt to resolve the difficulty by arguing that Paul speaks of the 'works' functioning as evidence of faith at the final judgment. Although this proposal is theologically unobjectionable, and finds support elsewhere in the New Testament, Paul never speaks in this manner.[52] Moreover, the distinction between 'faith' and 'obedience' which this reading presupposes represents a serious reduction of Paul's thought, as is apparent from our preceding discussion. Often, particularly in Roman Catholicism, a distinction is made between 'initial' justification and 'final' justification: a beginning transformation (which 'justification' is understood to include) must grow until final acceptance unto salvation. Clearly the temporal distinction between present justification and that which takes place at the final judgment is valid. Paul speaks of our 'now being justified' and yet awaiting deliverance from God's wrath (e.g. Rom. 5:9). As we have seen, however, Paul regards our present justification as an accomplished reality, a real and full vindication, not as a gradual transformation which has begun within us. Consequently, he juxtaposes two 'wholes': a full and complete justification in the present, which does not do away with final judgment.

Although this paradox deserves lengthier discussion than we can give it here, we may at least draw together some of its dimensions which we have touched upon in the preceding chapters. 'Works' cannot justify because they do not meet the demand of the law or its purpose. The law addresses the human being as an outward demand, 'do this and you will live' (Lev. 18:5). Although it is 'holy, righteous, and good', it has no power to change the human being, who is condemned and given over to sin. Some, like Paul, may achieve outward conformity to the

---

[52] The letter of James does, of course: Jas. 2:18–19.

demands of the law. Yet true love for God and neighbour is not possible for us as fallen human beings. To seek justification from 'works (of the law)' is to reject the reality about us that the law reveals, to refuse to submit to God in his contention with us. In Christ our condemnation has been effected, and the life of the age to come which the law offers has come to reality. Those who believe share in Christ, who, risen from the dead, has transcended the law and sin. Christ is present in faith, which therefore is necessarily active in love. This love is not a human ideal, but a reality. It does not, and cannot, 'rejoice in unrighteousness, but it rejoices together with the truth' (1 Cor. 13:6). In this love which 'does no harm to the neighbour' the law is fulfilled. Its 'righteous requirements' are carried out by those who are no longer under it, but rather already know the life which it offers. We hardly need to mention again that Paul does not imagine that the new creation has now come in its fullness, or that his congregations had already arrived at the resurrection from the dead. Nevertheless, 'the newness of life' of the age to come is really present here and now in the form of faith and love. Indeed, as children of God, those who believe have been placed on God's side in his contention with the world. They yet shall judge the world and even the angels themselves. Of course, they themselves are still subject to judgment. As we noted in our discussion of the law, in this context our works manifest our persons: *we* shall be manifest before the judgment seat of Christ in order that our deeds might receive recompense (2 Cor. 5:10). When our lives as a whole are taken into account and the secrets of our hearts are manifest, our works will reveal our persons (Rom. 2:12–16). Paul speaks of the singular *work* of a person receiving judgment: either selfishness and dis-obedience to the truth, or perseverance in seeking 'glory, honour, and immortality' (Rom. 2:7–8). For Paul, hope takes its place alongside faith and love in salvation! Although we in ourselves are sinners, Christ – the new person – is present within faith, performing his works. On account of faith in him alone we shall stand at the final judgment. Paul speaks in precisely this manner to the Corinthian congregation (2 Cor. 13:5). Conversely, as he indicates in his ethical instruction to the Roman church, 'all that does not proceed from faith is sin' (Rom. 14:23).

We cannot enter into a treatment of Christian assurance here, except to indicate that for Paul 'assurance' cannot arise from a present assessment of our works. Paul himself refused to pass judgment upon himself 'before the Day', and forbade the Corinthians to do so as well (1 Cor. 4:4–5). In himself he knew that he was under condemnation by the law (Rom. 7:14–25). What he was in Christ is yet to be revealed: not the one who commends himself is approved, but the one whom the Lord commends (2 Cor. 10:18). In fact, Paul does not speak of 'assurance' in psychological terms, but in an active sense, as 'boasting'. This boasting, as we have seen, is found solely in Christ and in faith in him (Rom. 5:1–11). By virtue of its inseparability from hope and love, faith entails constant motion, a 'forgetting what lies behind, and reaching forward to what lies ahead' (Phil. 3:13–14). It is this 'certitude' of hope and not a present 'security' which belongs to the believer, according to Paul.

Chapter Six

The justification of ungodly Israel and the nations

The promise to which all faith is directed includes both Jew and Gentile, both the 'one of the law' and the 'one of Abraham's [uncircumcised] faith' (Rom. 4:16). Moreover, the gospel in which the 'righteousness of God' is revealed gives priority to the Jew, even if it is a priority without prerogative (1:16; cf. 2:9–10). Although there is no advantage in being Jewish, the Jew paradoxically has 'much advantage in every way' (3:9, 1–2). From the outset of Romans, Paul speaks of the gospel for the Gentiles in terms of 'resurrection of the seed of David' (1:3). Justification is therefore inseparable from the election of Israel.[1] And the election of Israel is bound up with God's dealings with the nations. The promissory word of God has created and carries both their histories. Of course, the communities of Adam and Christ encompass Jew and Gentile: in the first, they are swallowed up by the power of sin and death; in the second, they are transcended by the fulfilment of promise and the arrival of life (5:12–21). Nevertheless, in the wake of the entrance of the promise into history Paul knows no undifferentiated universalism: the 'one who believes' does so either as a Jew or as a Gentile. The relationship between them is as fundamental to the present order as the created distinction between man and woman.[2]

As is apparent from these brief allusions to the text of Romans, the first chapters of the letter anticipate Paul's discussion of Israel in chapters 9 – 11. This is especially apparent in chapters 3 and 4, where Paul discusses Israel's benefits and the promise to Abraham. Chapters 9 – 11 therefore cannot be treated as a mere afterthought or appendage

[1] On this topic see especially Sänger 1994: 80–197.

[2] Of course Paul knows of other distinctions, such as 'slave and free' and 'Greek and barbarian', but he never accords them such significance. Donaldson 1997a: 162 fails to see that for Paul it is not the law, but the promise to Abraham, which creates 'Jew' and 'Gentile'.

to chapters 1 – 8, as expositors long have been tempted to do. Paul's teaching on justification has its indispensable counterpart in the outworkings of God's election of Israel. Those who believe in Christ lay hold of the promise of God to Abraham, by which Israel itself came into existence (4:24–25). That word of God to Israel, which must run its saving course by effecting judgment on the nation, is Paul's theme in these chapters. The lack of a grammatical connection at 9:1 to Paul's preceding, exalted profession of assurance expresses the theology of promise which governs the message of these chapters as a whole. God 'gives life to the dead, and calls into being that which is not' (4:17). The same is true of the powerful expression of sorrow with which Paul opens these chapters (9:1–3). The affections which he discloses are not mere human responses, but the outworkings of God's word and Spirit in the apostle (see also 10:1–2; 11:33–36). Israel's rejection of the gospel is part of the course which the promise of God must follow in coming to its fulfilment. All other construals of chapters 9 – 11 must be rejected. Paul is not wrestling with a cognitive dissonance brought about by an unexpected course of events. Nor is he assuring his largely Gentile audience of the faithfulness of God in the face of apparent failure. His intent is to discomfort and warn them. They now share in the promise which belongs to Israel, grafted like branches into a tree where others have been broken off: 'if God did not spare the natural branches, neither shall he spare you' (11:21). Their history, too, is comprehended by the word of God. In them as well, God wills to be recognized as God, 'from whom, through whom, and to whom are all things' (11:36). Paul's topic in these chapters is not the trustworthiness of Scripture, but the God who hides himself in Israel's failure in order that he might redeem and save. The breaks and paradoxes which mark Romans 9 – 11 are part of its theology, which we shall now consider.[3]

Israel as the creation of God's promise (Rom. 9:1–13)

As a creation of the promise of God, Israel presently lives under judgment and – although it does not recognize it – in hope of the salvation yet to come. The nation presently is under condemnation so

---

[3] In my view the chapters fall into the following three sections. Paul begins with the creation of Israel (9:1–13). As a counterpart, in the central section he deals with the divine rejection of Israel and its failure to submit to the word of God which has come to fulfilment in Christ (9:14 – 10:21). He then returns to where he left off, describing the salvation of Israel by the promise of God alone (11:1–36).

that it may receive redemption. Differences between them notwithstanding, Israel lives by the same promise as those who believe in Christ. It is therefore subject as they are to the simultaneity of sin and righteousness, rejection and reconciliation. Israel and those called by the gospel have a common hope, and travel the same path to the fulfilment of that hope, where they shall be joined together in Christ.

In the first portion of his argument Paul recounts the formation of Israel as *creatura verbi Dei* (verses 1–13). Despite his grief over Israel's rejection of the gospel, Paul knows that the word of God has not failed. His sorrow therefore has its limit (verse 6). As his subsequent argument shows, the benefits of election he names belong to Israel in the form of promise (verses 4–5).[4] The 'sonship' granted to Israel in its redemption from Egypt foreshadows the adoption to sonship at the 'redemption of the body' (8:23).[5] The glory of God which followed Israel in the wilderness had as its 'goal' the glory of God which will be manifest in the resurrection of the dead (5:2; 6:4; 8:18, 21; 9:23).[6] The giving of the law anticipated the sending of Christ (10:6-8). Israel's worship in the wilderness pointed forward to the gathering of the Gentiles and their priestly service to God (12:1–2; 15:16). Over against the fathers to whom the promises were given stands the Christ in whom they are fulfilled. In other words, Israel's history itself is promissory. Consequently, the gifts granted to Israel do not come to fulfilment in accord with fallen humanity ('according to the flesh'; *kata sarka*), but in opposition to it (9:3, 5, 8; 11:14; cf. Gal. 4:21–31). The nation exists only as it is determined by the word of God which created it. Not all of Israel is 'Israel' (9:6). Not all of Abraham's 'seed' are children of God. The 'calling' of seed takes place according to the pattern found in Isaac, who was born of the word of promise (verses 7–9). The 'children of the flesh' are excluded.

The saving word of God is therefore also unconditioned by human works. Before Jacob and Esau were born and had done good or evil, the divine word set apart Jacob for blessing and dominion over his brother (10–13). The promise of God performs its saving work in absolute freedom, and with the Spirit wages war against the flesh.

---

[4] The 'covenants' and 'the promises' which appear in the list of these benefits represent summary statements, comprehending the whole.

[5] Paul speaks of 'sonship' as a present possession in Galatians, since he has in view the participation of believers in the risen Christ (Gal. 3:26–29; 4:5–7).

[6] See too, the discussion of 2 Cor. 3:1–18 in chapter 4 above.

God's righteousness and Israel's rejection (Rom. 9:14 – 10:21)

The freedom of the Creator is displayed in his work within the world. The promise constitutes 'an election' (Paul here uses the term to refer to God's saving action in history, not his eternal counsel), which necessarily has reprobation as its counterpart (9:5; 11:5; cf. Thess. 1:4). The granting of mercy is always accompanied by hardening. With the 'calling' of Isaac comes the expulsion of Ishmael (9:7).[7] With the blessing of Jacob comes the rejection of Esau (9:12–13).[8] With the deliverance of Israel comes judgment upon Pharaoh and his people (9:17). The calling of Jew and Gentile by the gospel brings the hardening of Israel (9:24; cf. 11:28). The world in which God elects and saves contends against him, so that judgment is necessarily present alongside salvation. The Creator, who forms light and creates darkness, makes peace and creates harm, shows himself as such in his works (Is. 45:7). In these unsearchable judgments and unfathomable ways, God comes to be known as God and therefore as Saviour.

Paul concludes his instruction concerning the exclusion of 'Israel according to the flesh' from the promise by anticipating a challenge from the human being: 'What shall we say then? There is no unrighteousness with God, is there? By no means! For to Moses he says, "I will be merciful to whom I will be merciful, and show compassion to whom I will show compassion"' (9:14–15; Exod. 33:19).[9]

At one level, Paul answers the question he raises by pointing to the faithfulness of God to his word. God is not unrighteous in his dealings with Israel, since from the outset he has announced his freedom in choosing the objects of his mercy. At another, deeper level, Paul here rejects the right of the human being to call God to account. 'God's righteousness' has to do with the right of God to be God, whose action is not subject to human judgment or conditions. Divine mercy is 'not of the one who wills, or of the one who runs, but of the God who grants mercy' (9:16).

In his immediate response, Paul turns to the example of Pharaoh, whom God raised up as an instrument by which to display his power

---

[7] The divine utterance to which Paul appeals is found in the context of Ishmael's rejection (Gen. 21:12).

[8] Paul cites Gen. 25:23; Mal. 1:2–3.

[9] The passage therefore parallels Rom. 3:5–8, where Paul voices the human objection to the divine word of judgment.

(verse 17). He thereby reminds his readers that Israel's birth as a nation itself was accompanied by the triumph of God over human might and wisdom. God 'hardens' whom he will, turning evil back in upon itself, as he did with Pharaoh (verse 18; see esp. Exod. 14:4, 8, 17). Such 'hardening' serves God's saving purposes, since in thereby 'displaying his power', he 'makes known his name in all the earth'. In this act of judgment and mercy God is recognized as God (verse 17).[10]

This freedom of God appears unjust to those who make themselves God's equals. 'If no-one is able to resist the divine purpose, God ought not find fault with us', so Paul's imaginary interlocutor responds (verse 19). The human being therewith declares the divine contention null and void, treating God as nothing more than the large-scale projection of the human being.[11] Paul has now reached the centre of the debate. The creature openly disputes the right of the Creator. Now, therefore, the interrogator becomes the interrogated as Paul echoes the divine contention with Israel found in the book of Isaiah: 'On the contrary, O human, who are you to answer back to God? That which is formed shall not say to the one who forms it, "Why do you make me thus?", shall it?' (verse 20; cf. Is. 29:15–16; 45:9; 64:7).

This human rebellion against God is nothing more than the empty and absurd attempt of pottery to take the place of the potter. Just as the potter has the right to make from the same lump of clay both a vessel 'for honour' and one 'for dishonour' (Rom. 9:21), God has the legitimate power (*exousia*) to have mercy and to harden, to save and to destroy.[12] Although he is more than ready to display his wrath and power, he patiently endures 'vessels of wrath prepared for destruction' in order that he might make his glory known to 'vessels of mercy, prepared for glory' (verses 22–23). The Creator who is free has purposed to have ungrounded, unfathomable mercy. He will make himself known as God to these persons whom he has chosen.

With this final statement Paul returns to the issue at hand, which he has already summarized briefly: mercy is not 'of the one who wills or of the one who runs, but of the God who has mercy' (verse 16). Paul's phrasing reveals that the question he has voiced concerning God's

---

[10] The scope of God's saving purposes comes into view here: divine 'hardening' brings mercy, not merely for Israel, but ultimately also for the nations.

[11] As others have noted, Feuerbach's analysis of human religion contains considerable truth.

[12] Paul alludes to Jer. 18:1–6, while retaining the use of the *topos* of God as potter as it appears in Isaiah. His usage also reflects something of the development of the theme as it appears in Wis. Sol. 15:7.

righteousness is not merely intellectual. It comprehends the life, will and action of the human being. His reference to 'willing' and 'doing' reflects his earlier description of the human condition in Romans 7. Our 'willing' has been delivered over to the power of sin, and our 'doing' is death. He likewise here anticipates the conclusions he draws concerning Israel's futile 'running' after the law by the way of works (verse 31).[13] Israel stumbled over Christ, 'the stone of stumbling and rock of offence', which God placed in its path. The one who believes in that stone shall not be put to shame (verses 32–33). Mercy itself brings judgment: Israel failed because it sought to 'establish its own righteousness'. It did not submit to 'the righteousness of God' found in Christ, who is the goal of the law which Israel pursued (10:3–4). That law, holy though it is, offers a merely human righteousness based on deeds of obedience (verse 5). It has been transcended by a higher righteousness of God revealed and given to the one who believes. This 'righteousness of faith' dismisses our attempt to attain a righteousness of our own, by which we deny God's judgment upon us and right over us. It demands that we listen to its witness to the righteousness found in Christ incarnate, crucified and risen for us (verses 6–8). The human questioning of the Creator's freedom receives its 'answer', not in mere words, but in God's deed in Christ, where it is exposed as rebellion and silenced with mercy. God's sovereign word does not pass us by on its way to fulfilment, but meets us and calls us to account in Jesus Christ.

As we have seen already in our discussion of 'boasting', the human challenge to the Creator bears an earthly dimension, a claim to status and superiority over others. Israel's pursuit of the law 'on the basis of works' carried with it the assumption that it was set apart from the nations on this basis, and not by the promise alone (cf. 4:13–15). This claim has been manifest as empty in a dramatic reversal: the Gentiles who did not pursue righteousness arrived at it (9:30–33). God has shown quite concretely that mercy is 'not of the one who wills or runs' (9:16). Israel must surrender its own outward and inadequate righteousness achieved through the law, in order to possess the 'righteousness of God' revealed in Christ (10:2–3). In accord with the prophetic word, however, Israel has failed to believe the gospel which has now gone forth to the nations (10:14–21). It has been reduced to nothing, in order that God might yet save it.

---

[13] See the discussion of this topic in chapter 4 above. Such 'works' conform to the law, but the persons who perform them do not. Paul here obviously presupposes Israel's confidence – 'boasting' he would say – in its works, by which it hides from God's judgment. Indeed, it is this human confidence which challenges God's right.

Based as it is on the 'word of God', Paul's argument throughout these chapters rests on a startlingly direct appeal to Scripture: the words of promise and judgment which the prophets announced have now come to pass. In interpreting the Scriptures in this way, he does not set aside Israel's past experience. He rather indicates that it has been taken up in the hour of fulfilment which has now arrived. Paradigmatic though they are, God's dealings with the patriarchs lie in an earlier age (9:6–13). The same distinction appears in Paul's appeal to the prophet Elijah, in whose day God left a remnant just as he has 'in the present time' (11:5). Similarly, that which Moses 'says at the first' has now taken place (10:19). As we observed above, Israel's history itself is promissory and prophetic.

This immediate usage of biblical texts appears in Romans 9 the moment Paul turns to speak of the gospel. With striking freedom, he appropriates the words addressed to Israel by the prophet Hosea to describe the present calling of a people from among Jews and Gentiles: 'I shall call "Not My People", "My People" and "Not Beloved", "Beloved". And it shall be that in the place where it was said to them, "You are not my people", they shall be called sons of the living God' (9:26; Hos. 1:10 [Hebrew 2:1]). As we have noted, in this context Paul's attention is fixed on Israel's failure to believe the gospel of which the prophetic announcements of judgment speak. The hour of judgment has come upon the nation. It has been reduced to a remnant by the Lord's execution of his word on the earth (9:27–29).[14] Israel has refused to believe the 'good news' according to the witness of Isaiah (10:15–16; Is. 52:7; 53:1). The provocation to jealousy by 'another people', which Moses foretold is now taking place (10:19; Deut. 32:21). Those who did not seek God have now found him, even as God 'stretches out his hands' to a disobedient and contrary people (10:20–21; Is. 65:1–2). David's curse upon his enemies has now come into effect for them. Israel's table-fellowship has become a cause for their own stumbling: 'their eyes have been blinded and their backs bent' (11:9–10; Ps. 68:23–24 [Hebrew 69:23–24]).

While the biblical announcements of disaster which Paul cites cluster around Israel's exile, he does not exclusively rely on such texts, but draws on a broader stream of biblical thought.[15] The focal point and criterion of his use of Scripture is the gospel of Christ. Just as all the

---

[14] In Rom. 9:27–28 Paul cites Is. 10:22, to which he adds echoes from Hos. 2:1, Is. 28:22, and Dan. 5:28. In Rom. 9:29 he cites Is. 1:9.

[15] See Rom. 10:19 (Deut. 32:21); 11:3–6 (1 Kgs. 19:1–21); 11:9 (Ps. 69:22–23).

promises of God are fulfilled in him, so too are all the judgments of God. Now the moment has come, in which God has executed his word 'finally and decisively on the earth' (9:28). Christ crucified and risen is the 'stone of stumbling' which God has placed in Zion (9:33). The prophets' announcement of exile represents the pinnacle, or perhaps we should say the nadir, of the biblical witness to him. A series of themes found in the prophets in connection with divine judgment and exile reappears in Paul's description of Israel's failure: the entire people is guilty;[16] they are incapable of doing good;[17] God himself has hardened them (11:8; Is. 29:10; cf. 6:9–13). Through the divine word of judgment which has come to pass, Israel no longer exists as a nation. It has been brought to 'the null point'.[18] The path of Israel's election runs through death and nothingness in order that it may know God as the justifier of the ungodly.[19]

The triumph of God in Israel's redemption (Rom. 11:1–36)

For Paul, as for the prophets, the end of Israel is not the end, but the way to a new beginning: 'God has not rejected his people, whom he foreknew' (11:1–2).[20] God's dealings with Israel follow the pattern of judgment and mercy announced by the prophets: 'Should the number of the sons of Israel be as the sands of the sea, only the remnant shall be saved' (9:27; Is. 10:22).[21] 'Unless the Lord of hosts left behind a seed for us, we would have become as Sodom, and we would have been like Gomorrah' (9:29; Is. 1:9).

As in the former divine judgments, there has come to be 'therefore in the same way also' a remnant 'in the present time' (11:4–5). This 'remnant', then, embodies the judgment of God, and not merely

[16] Rom. 9:21; Is. 65:2. Cf. e.g. Is. 1:1–4; 6:5; Jer. 5:1; 6:13; Ezek. 2:3–7.

[17] Cf. e.g. Deut. 9:6; 29:4; 31:24–29; Hos. 5:4; Jer. 6:10; 13:23; 17:1–2.

[18] Rom. 9:27–29; 11:7–8; Is. 10:22; 1:9. Cf. e.g. Hos. 1:6–10, to which Paul appeals in another sense, and yet implicitly applies to Israel. See also Amos 8:2; Zeph. 1:1–6; Is. 6:11–12; Jer. 16:1–21.

[19] On this theme and the broader theology of justification found in the Old Testament, which deserves more discussion than we can give it here, see Reventlow 1971: 41–65; Schmidt 1981; Hofius 1989; Zimmerli 1976; Levin 1999.

[20] Paul makes the statement twice. As his reference to his heritage shows, 'the people' of which Paul speaks can be none other than the nation of Israel. He echoes perhaps 1 Sam. 12:22 or Ps. 94:14; cf. Jer. 31:37.

[21] Like the LXX, Paul exchanges 'the remnant shall be saved' for 'the remnant shall return' (*šeʾār yāšûḇ*).

eschatological salvation as one recent interpreter has urged.[22] It does not come into being in the return from exile, but in its very beginning in the disasters God brings on the nation (against Wright 1996: 232). It serves as a sign of hope in the midst of judgment.[23] Moreover, it certainly does not represent a continuing stream of faithful Israelites, as another interpreter has suggested.[24] The remnant rather signifies the fulfilment of divine judgment upon the nation, and *thereby* points to the salvation of Israel yet to come.

Overtones of judgment are apparent in the term 'remnant' (*leimma*) itself. The word generally signifies objects or persons who have been delivered out of destruction, disaster or battle.[25] The biblical usage is concentrated in the prophets, especially Isaiah, where the 'remnant' represents those whom God preserves in the judgments he brings upon Israel and Jerusalem, judgments which culminate in the exile of the entire nation. In these contexts the word takes on a number of significant theological associations. The remnant emerges from total destruction, solely by the work of God the Creator.[26] Its deliverance comes through the prophetic word, in which it believes and for which it waits (e.g. Is. 28:16–17; 7:9; 8:16–18). As we have observed already, the 'remnant' holds the promise of Israel's restoration. In it God creates the nation anew: the return of the remnant from exile is equivalent to the deliverance of Israel from Egypt.[27] Through God's saving intervention it again becomes his 'holy' possession, as it did in the exodus (Is. 4:2–6; 6:13; cf. e.g. Deut. 7:6). That is not to say that the remnant is righteous in itself. It fully shares in the guilt of the nation, as does the prophet around whose message the remnant is

---

[22] Against Wright 1996: 232, who leaves the biblical theme of the remnant decidedly undeveloped in his work.

[23] E.g. 2 Kgs. 19:30–31; Mic. 5:7; Ezek. 11:13–21; Ezra 9:8.

[24] Against Hafemann 1997: 368–369, n. 74. Paul could never say that 'there had always been a remnant of faithful people … who had fulfilled the covenant stipulations'. He knows nothing but the justification of the ungodly. All else is contrary to his gospel.

[25] We may think of Noah in the ark (Gen. 7:23), the twelve patriarchs in Egypt (Gen. 45:7), or Jerusalem in the face of the Assyrian invasion (2 Kgs. 19:4). The idea is represented by various terms in the biblical literature, especially the substantives *šeʾērît* and *šeʾār* in Hebrew, which are translated in the LXX mostly with verbal forms of *kataleipein* or *hypoleipein*, but also with corresponding substantival forms. Although the theme may appear in other contexts (e.g. Acts 15:16–18; Amos 9:11–15), the terms appear in the New Testament only in Rom. 9:27–29; 11:4–5. See Schrenk & Herntrich 1966.

[26] See Is. 10:20–23, to which Paul appeals in Rom. 9:27–28: the remnant returns out of the complete end which God effects (*kālâ*). Cf. Is. 1:8–9; 6:13; 10:20–23; 28:16; Mic. 2:13–13; 4:6–7; 5:7; Jer. 6:9.

[27] See Is. 10:20–27; 11:11–16; Jer. 23:1–8; Amos 9:11–15. Cf. Hos. 2:14–23.

formed:[28] 'Woe to me, for I am destroyed! For I am a person of unclean lips, and dwell in the midst of a people of unclean lips. For my eyes have seen the King, the Lord of Hosts' (Is. 6:5).[29]

God, and God alone, makes atonement for the guilt of the prophet and the remnant with him, although the nation itself is rejected, hardened, and given over to destruction (Is. 6:6–13). It is little wonder that Paul appeals to Habbakuk 2:4 in introducing his gospel in Romans 1:17. The 'righteous one who lives by faith' belongs to the remnant which waited in the hope of the prophetic vision of deliverance (see Hab. 2:1–3). The remnant consists of the ungodly who are justified by faith alone.

Already in the story of Elijah, Paul sees an adumbration of the later judgment which was to come upon Israel, elaborating the significance of the remnant on the basis of this text. His attention rests on the divine utterance to Elijah: 'I have left behind (*katelipon*) for myself seven thousand, who did not bend the knee to Baal' (11:4).

The translation of the verb *katelipon* as 'left behind' is to be preferred to either the NRSV ('kept') or the NIV ('reserved'), not only because this meaning corresponds to the usual sense of the word, but also because it provides the connection to the idea of the remnant in Paul's following statement.[30] With this term Paul takes up a wordplay which is present in the biblical text. In the wake of Israel's persecution of the prophets, Elijah complains, 'I alone am left' (*hypeleiphthein*). God makes known to him that the situation is exactly the reverse of the way it appears – this is how the Creator works in the fallen world! Israel has not destroyed all the worshippers of Yahweh but one, Yahweh has done away with all of Israel but a few: he has 'left' (*katelipon*) seven thousand for himself (11:3–4). God remains God despite Israel's idolatry and Elijah's despair.

At this juncture, Paul has introduced a small but significant alteration in the text. He has replaced the futuristic, imperfective verbal form of the Hebrew passage ('I shall leave in Israel seven thousand'), with a Greek aorist which in context signals past time ('I left seven thousand').[31] While the Hebrew text predicts the destruction of all

---

[28] See Is. 50:20; Mic. 7:18; Ezek. 9:1–11. On the unity of the prophet and the remnant, see Is. 8:16–18.

[29] If the niph'al *niḏmêṯi* is to be rendered 'destroyed' as seems likely (cf. Is. 15:1), Isaiah's experience itself anticipates the divine judgment coming on Jerusalem.

[30] See e.g. Gen. 2:24 (LXX); 2 Cor. 4:9; Eph. 5:31; 1 Thess. 3:1; 2 Tim. 4:10; 2 Tim. 4:16. The verb is a regular part of 'remnant' vocabulary, and cognate with other such terms: e.g. Rom. 9:27;9:29; Is. 4:11–12 (LXX); 6:12–13. See Schrenk & Herntrich 1966.

[31] The LXX connects the sparing of the seven thousand with the prior mention of

Israel save the seven thousand, Paul speaks of this destruction and deliverance as an accomplished reality (see 1 Kgs. 19:15–18). Consequently, the 'not bending the knee to Baal', which appears as a condition of salvation in the Hebrew text, may be read, and almost certainly should be read, as the content or result of divine deliverance in Romans.[32] In confirmation of this reading, we may note a further variation from the Hebrew. According to Romans 11:4, the divine oracle says, 'I have left behind *for myself* seven thousand.' Paul brings into view God's purpose of creating a people for himself in the sparing of the seven thousand, a purpose which itself consists in deliverance from idolatry. This interpretation receives further support from the unusual Septuagintal rendering of Psalm 69:23–24 of which Paul makes use in Romans 11:9–10. Where the Hebrew reads 'let their loins continually tremble', Paul has the Septuagintal substitution 'let their back continually be bent', which is without parallel in the Scriptures. He probably uses it to recall his earlier reference to the 'bending of the knee to Baal', thereby completing his application of the psalm's curse to Israel's rejection of the gospel (11:4). Just as Israel's 'eyes have been darkened' so as not to see the gospel, so its 'back has been bent' in servitude to idolatry.[33] The refusal to bend the knee to Baal therefore implicitly represents the content of divine deliverance and not its basis. A final and decisive support for this interpretation comes from the immediately following verse (5), where Paul connects the divine sparing of the seven thousand with the remnant which has come about 'in the present'. The seven thousand correspond to the 'remnant' which has come into existence 'by grace, not from works' (verse 5). Indeed, Paul himself, the former persecutor of the church, is the prime representative of this remnant. The refusal of the seven thousand to bend the knee to Baal represents the deliverance of a remnant, that is, the justification of the ungodly.

For Paul, as for the prophets before him, even though the remnant emerges from Israel, it is *not* the former nation but a new creation of God's word. It is 'an election of grace' which has arisen from God's hidden and unfathomable purposes: 'What then? That which Israel seeks, it did not attain. The election attained it; the rest were hardened' (verse 7). Grace operates at the 'null point' of God's judgment, there –

Elijah's final task of anointing replacements. It is he who will leave seven thousand in Israel.

[32] Undoubtedly Paul is aware of the sense of the Hebrew text; he simply chooses to view the divine action from a broader perspective.

[33] See Rom. 11:8, where Paul cites Is. 29:10, adapting it to Deut. 29:4.

and only there – creating a people *ex nihilo*. God raises up children for Abraham from the stones themselves, so to speak. Israel's boasting is therewith made empty: grace is given apart from works, otherwise 'grace is no longer grace' (verses 5–6). The continuity of God's promises is maintained 'in the flesh', but not 'according to the flesh'.

In this connection, it cannot escape our notice that Paul here characterizes Israel's rejection of the gospel as idolatry. The hostility and persecution which Paul and other Jewish believers faced from their own people are reflected in Elijah's complaint, 'they have killed your prophets and overturned your altars'.[34] Israel's exclusive table-fellowship has become a snare by which they are entrapped and enslaved to idolatry. As in the Deuteronomic pronouncements, God has given his people over to serve other gods (Deut. 4:28; 28:36; Jer. 16:13). Ironically, this idolatry now consists in Israel's seeking to establish its righteousness through the law. As we have seen, it is not the accomplishment of good works that Paul finds objectionable but the opinion attached to them, that Israel thereby could be righteous. Prior to and apart from all such works, the human being must give God justice, acknowledging the divine claim that we are 'liars', that is, idolaters. Otherwise our works become the means of hiding our idolatry, from God, from others, and from ourselves. Indeed, as lost and condemned creatures, we have been plunged into this blindness of idolatry, a blindness which is removed only in the crucified and risen Christ. Everything outside of faith is idolatry.

The remnant, then, is the sign that in wrath God has remembered mercy. Precisely as the evidence of divine judgment it represents the promise of Israel's coming salvation. Paul himself has repeatedly intimated this emergence of mercy from judgment at various points in his earlier argument. In introducing his citation of Isaiah 10:22 he describes Isaiah as 'crying out on behalf of Israel' (9:27). The prophet, like Paul himself, fervently appeals to God for the nation. The announcement that a mere remnant will be saved obviously expresses divine judgment, yet with this introduction it takes on a different tone. The prophet's prayer for Israel - not the remnant – faintly suggests that the remnant is not the end of the story. The same is true of Paul's preceding use of Hosea 1:10 [Hebrew 2:1] to refer to believing Jews and Gentiles. In its original context, the text refers to the nation of Israel, of course. There, in a section of the verse which Paul leaves uncited, God assures the prophet that 'the number of the sons of Israel

---

[34] Cf. Rom. 15:30–33; 1 Thess. 2:14–16; Gal. 4:29; 6:11–17.

shall be like the sands of the sea'. This wording appears in Paul's immediately following citation of Isaiah 10:22, which therefore serves of a reminder of the promise Paul omitted ('even if the sons of Israel should be as the sand of the sea ...'). In other words, Paul subtly points to the salvation of Israel even while depicting Israel's judgment. A similar connection between judgment and mercy appears in 10:19, where Paul applies the Song of Moses to Israel's failure to believe the gospel: 'I shall provoke you to jealousy by a non-people, by a people without understanding I shall antagonize you' (10:19).

This 'provocation to jealousy' is not entirely negative, for by it Paul seeks to save some of his kinspeople (11:11, 14).[35] Furthermore, we should not think that in speaking of a 'non-people' Paul has in view the Gentiles, that is, 'the peoples', to which he always refers in the plural. He rather recalls his earlier citation of Hosea 1:10.[36] The 'non-people' is the new people of God, Jews and Gentiles together, which has been created by the word of God. His characterization of it as 'a people without understanding' is not a description of Gentiles alone, but of the ungodly who have been called by the gospel, Jew and Gentile alike. It is not a 'Gentile church' which provokes Israel: Paul knows of no such entity. It is rather the gathering in of Gentiles along with Israel to worship the one God through Jesus Christ which is to make Israel jealous.[37] This 'non-people' marks the entrance of the eschaton into the present, a sign of hope for Israel and all creation (15:7–13). Consequently, Paul's following citation of Isaiah 65:1–2 also portends Israel's salvation, as is suggested by his bifurcated application of the passage to the church (of Jews and Gentiles) and to Israel. Paul's introduction to the first verse shows that he is continuing his description of Israel's provocation to jealousy: 'And Isaiah becomes bold and says, "I was found by those who did not seek me. I became manifest to those who did not enquire after me"' (10:20). Here again Paul speaks, not of Gentiles alone, but of all those who believe in the crucified and risen Christ and find God in him. He is concerned not with ethnicity, but with the manifestation of human unrighteousness by the righteousness of God. In the face of Israel's attempt to establish its own righteousness, God has justified the ungodly. For this reason Isaiah 65:2, which pronounces judgment on Israel, contains Israel's hope: 'I have stretched out my hands all the day to a disobedient and

---

[35] On this theme see Bell 1994.

[36] Of course, following the texts, he shifts from *laos* (Hos. 1:10) to *ethnos* (Deut. 32:21).

[37] Paul subsequently speaks of the 'engrafting' of the Gentiles (Rom. 11:17, 19).

argumentative people' (10:21). Precisely because Israel has been shown to be such a people, the divine announcement of Isaiah 65:1 ('I was found by those who did not seek me ...') holds the promise of salvation for it. The remnant which Paul describes in 11:1–10 found God apart from seeking him. It therefore represents hope for the nation.

The hope of which the remnant is a sign remains yet unseen: one does not hope for what one sees. Paul does not reduce the salvation of the nation to the salvation of the remnant, nor does he expect the conversion of a remnant to lead to the salvation of the nation. He operates with a 'realism of hope' according to which mission to his fellow Jews is necessary, even if it is bound to be limited in its results. By effecting the gathering in of the Gentiles and setting forth its meaning for biblical hope (i.e. 'glorifying his ministry'), Paul seeks to save *some* of his 'flesh' (11:13).[38] He is not under the illusion that he might effect the conversion of the nation. Instead, by its very nature as the joining of Jews and Gentiles for the worship of the one God through Jesus Christ, the church is to be a sign of hope for Israel and the world (see again 15:7–13). We need not say how far in the course of its history it has fallen from the apostolic standard.

The remnant itself is quite visible, even if the hope to which it points is not. Indeed, it serves as a sign precisely because it is a tangible indication that 'God has not rejected his *people*' (11:2).[39] This language appears twice at the outset of Romans 11, first in the form of a rhetorical question, and again as a denial, which Paul emphatically elaborates, 'God has not rejected his people, whom he foreknew' (verses 1–2).[40] The declaration reflects God's assurances to Israel of his unchanging love, and anticipates Paul's closing affirmation that the nation remains 'beloved on account of the fathers' (11:28).[41] The 'remnant' is a sign of the salvation of the people of Israel. Paul's usage allows no allegorizing. The 'Israelites' are those of whose remnant Paul is a member, as one 'of the seed of Abraham, of the tribe of Benjamin' (11:1). His very use of the honorific title 'Israel' (which predominates in these chapters) underscores the enduring validity of the divine promise to the nation.[42] The limitation of the election to the

[38] We may think in particular of the offering which he has collected for the saints in Jerusalem (Rom. 15:25–29).

[39] Note *people*, and not merely the remnant, which Paul clearly distinguishes from the nation.

[40] 'Foreknowledge' of persons signifies their being made the objects of love and care, i.e., their election. Cf. Rom. 8:29.

[41] See Deut. 4:31; 31:6, 8; Ps. 94:12–15; 1 Sam. 12:22; Is. 54:7–8.

[42] Even where he speaks of judgment on the nation in these chapters, Paul elects to

'children of promise' in no way changes its ethnic character (9:6–9). Israel, which has transgressed and has been defeated in its contention with God, will yet be brought to its eschatological 'fullness' (11:12). Although it has been rejected, it shall yet be accepted, an acceptance which means nothing less for the world than the resurrection of the dead (11:15). Despite their present rejection, the 'branches' remain 'holy', God's possession and objects of his care (verse 16). True, the Gentiles now have been included. They have been engrafted as branches into 'the rich root of the olive tree', but they have not supplanted the root of which Israel constitutes the 'natural branches' (*kata physin*; verses 17, 21).[43] Their engrafting took place 'contrary to nature' (*para physin*; verse 24). Although Israel was broken off for unbelief, God is able to engraft them into their *own* olive tree. 'Nature' (*physis*) here serves as an obvious parallel to 'flesh' (*sarx*): Israel's salvation constitutes a continuity of nature, but not a continuity in nature. The remnant is the outward and visible promise of the justification of the ungodly nation.

As we have noted, the remnant is promissory because it marks the fulfilment of the divine word upon Israel, a word which brings judgment as well as mercy. Paul does not transpose the biblical order of salvation in speaking of the 'fullness' of the Gentiles entering in prior to Israel's salvation.[44] His opening affirmation that salvation is 'for the Jew first, and also for the Greek' remains central to his gospel (1:16). He rather sees the fulfilment of promise in the risen Christ, the seed of Abraham and David.[45] The entrance of the 'fullness' of the Gentiles into the people of God (embodied in Christ and the remnant) signals the presence of the kingdom of God in this fallen world. It is an 'eschatological event' in the strictest sense, as the term 'fullness' itself suggests.[46] Paul's 'priestly service' of the gospel among the Gentiles

---

speak of 'Israel' (9:27, 31; 10:19, 21; 11:2, 25). Only where he speaks of response to the gospel does he speak of 'Jews' (9:24; 10:12). He uses the title 'Jacob' only in reference to the re-creation of the nation at Christ's coming (11:26; cf. 9:13).

[43] In speaking of the 'root', Paul has in view the patriarchs as objects of the divine promise. Cf. Is. 17:6; Jer. 11:16; Hos. 14:5–7; Hab. 3:17.

[44] Against Munck 1959. See Is. 2:1–4 (Mic. 4:1–4); Amos 9:11–15.

[45] Rom. 1:3; 4:25. The 'Israel of God' to which Paul refers in Gal. 6:15–16 is the eschatological Israel, the new creation in which neither circumcision nor uncircumcision counts, which corresponds to the Israel of promise (Gal. 4:28; Rom. 9:6–9).

[46] One of the fundamental flaws in Donaldson 1997a is that he fails to appreciate that for Paul the eschaton entered the world in the resurrection of Christ (see e.g. 1997a: 173, 243). His thesis collapses here: Paul does not regard believing Gentiles as proselytes who have joined the nation of Israel. Believing Jew and Gentile alike have entered into the Israel of promise which has come to reality in Christ. It is precisely the

and the common worship of Jews and Gentiles which arises from it are a cause for hope because they signal the entrance of the eschaton into the world in Christ (15:7–21).[47] Although the hour of promise remains, the hour of fulfilment has come.

Therefore the idea that the church has now replaced Israel as the object of promise is foreign to Paul. Indeed, Paul wants his Gentile readers to know 'this mystery', this once-hidden truth of Scripture now revealed: a hardening in part has come upon Israel, until 'fullness of the Gentiles' enters in. In this strange way (*houtōs*), by its present hardening, *all* Israel shall be saved (11:25).[48] The nation is presently consigned to disobedience, in order that it may know justification by the Redeemer who shall come 'from Zion' to 'remove ungodliness from Jacob' (verse 26). He shall effect the new covenant of which Jeremiah spoke, taking away their sins (verse 27).[49] The passage from Isaiah which Paul cites calls the nation 'Jacob', a striking deviation from his use of 'Israel' in these chapters. The nation has been brought back to its beginning, to the time of its contention with God, in order that it might be created anew (Gen. 32:27–28).[50] It is not without accident that Paul speaks of God's receiving Israel to himself as 'life from the dead' (verse 15). The promise of God to Abraham comes to its fulfilment in the resurrection of the dead and of Israel (cf. Ezek. 37:1–14).

Paul knows only this certitude of hope, and not any security for Israel according to the flesh. He does not suppose that all Jews from all times will be saved. This is evident both in his lament of their failure to believe and in his striving to save 'some' of them (9:1–5; 11:14). Contemporary Israel therefore may not content itself with saying, 'We are the children of Abraham.' It is called to believe in the 'stone of offence', who shall appear from Zion as Israel's redeemer. The eschatological Israel, which will be created by the fulfilment of promise, will believe in the crucified and risen Christ. Like the apostle Paul and the doubting Thomas before him, this Israel will believe not because it hears the gospel, but because it sees the risen Lord at his

---

joining of Jew and Gentile (qua Gentile) in worship which is a sign of hope.

[47] Paul cites Ps. 18:49; Deut. 32:43; Ps. 117:1; Is. 11:10.

[48] *Houtōs* serves its usual role as an adverb of manner.

[49] Paul here freely conflates Is. 59:20 and Jer. 31:33–34, partly employing the LXX renderings of these texts and borrowing other biblical language (cf. Ps. 14:7; Is. 27:9). He is concerned to communicate the meaning of the Scripture, not to provide a word-for-word citation of particular texts. For this reason he interprets Is. 59:20 in terms of the justification of the ungodly.

[50] Is. 59:20 reflects the same idea, since it speaks of the return of God to Zion.

coming. Nevertheless, it will believe. It will come to share in the faith by which the 'Gentile branches' now stand, and by this means be engrafted into its 'own olive tree' (11:19–24).

The conclusion of Romans 11 rises to a crescendo of praise which equals that of Romans 8 and which is inseparable from it. The God who triumphs and saves in the gospel is the God who will triumph and save in Israel, in fulfilment of one and the same promise. God will be known as the one true God, whose judgments and ways are beyond exploring: 'From him, through him, and unto him are all things. To him be the glory for ever. Amen' (11:36). There can be no salvation apart from this triumph of God in his contention with humanity. He has 'imprisoned all within disobedience, that he might be merciful to all' (11:32). In these chapters it becomes manifest that our very existence within history – our being as well as our doing – is encompassed by the word of God's judgment and mercy: 'For just as you were once disobedient to God, and now have been given mercy in their disobedience, so also they are now disobedient in the mercy given you, that also they might now be given mercy' (11:31–32).[51]

Israel and the nations are the tools by which God the Creator establishes the ungodliness of all, and so justifies the ungodly. They are not merely occasional or transitional realities of the first century, but the ineradicable effect of the word of God within this fallen order. The promise of God to Israel projects Christ's cross and resurrection across its history, stripping it of its idolatry and rendering it 'godless' in order to save it.[52] And in God's unsearchable wisdom, this promise has accomplished the same for the nations. Abandoned to their disobedience for a time, they have now encountered mercy in the gospel in which the promise has been fulfilled. We cannot overlook the sharp warning against pride which Paul delivers to the predominantly Gentile church in Rome (11:13–24).[53] Gentiles who have believed must not suppose that they are wise or understanding (11:25; 12:16). They have come to share in the promise which belongs to another, and which will be fulfilled for another quite apart from them. In a concrete

[51] The textually difficult *nyn* in Rom. 11:31b, which is probably to be retained as the *lectio difficilior*, expresses both the finality of the present hour and the simultaneity of sin and grace.

[52] On this topic see Käsemann 1971: 60–78; Schmitt 1984.

[53] The figure of Elijah, whom the divine oracle corrects, may anticipate Paul's admonition of the Gentiles. Could it be that Paul regards him as a Gentile on the basis of 1 Kgs. 17:1, where he is introduced as 'from the sojourners of Gilead' (*mittōšabe gilʿād*, MT)? In any case, he appears in stark contrast to Isaiah (Rom. 9:27) and to the apostle (Rom. 9:3; 10:1).

manner, God will show that their salvation lies outside them, in his own free mercy. They stand by faith alone and will enjoy God's kindness to them only so long as they grasp it as nothing other than unfathomable *kindness* (11:20–22). In Israel and the nations, God will show himself to be the righteous God, who justifies the ungodly.

Israel's exile in Romans 9 – 11

We recall that according to a current reading of Paul, he saw the end of Israel's exile and the beginning of Israel's return to Zion in Jesus' cross and resurrection. In the first chapter we raised questions concerning this view from the perspective of early Jewish sources. Romans 9 – 11 brings us back to this topic, since Paul himself here cites biblical texts which have to do with Israel's exile. His perspective, however, is nearly the opposite of the 'exilic' interpretation of him. As we have seen, he views Israel's history itself as prophetic. Christ is the centre and key to understanding God's dealings with the nation, for in him they have been 'fulfilled' in an eschatological recapitulation.[54]

We need only briefly mention the texts we have just examined. A remnant of Jewish believers in Christ has come about in the present effectuation of God's word in Christ (9:28; 11:1). Israel's rejection of Jesus is the 'stumbling against the stone of offence', which leads to exile (9:33). The believing community of Jews and Gentiles represents 'a provocation to jealousy by a nation which is not'. That is to say, it signifies the exile (10:19). The servitude to which Israel is now subjected is its failure to believe the gospel (11:7–9). The image of the exile stands behind the figure of the olive-tree branches, 'who' were broken off because of their unbelief (11:20). It is on account of the gospel, not of some past failure, that God now treats the Jewish people as enemies (11:28). Paul finds the 'mystery' of Israel's final salvation in biblical texts which speak of the end of exile and the establishing of the new covenant (Is. 59:20; Ps. 14:7; Jer. 31:33–34). In short, Paul sees the Deuteronomic sequence of apostasy, exile and return in Israel's present rejection of Jesus as Messiah and its salvation at his appearing. We recall, too, that Paul is capable of viewing Christ's cross as the proleptic moment of 'exile' for the world (1 Cor. 1:19).

---

[54] That is not to say that Paul does not use the 'exilic' motif in his letters. See 2 Cor. 6:1, 14 – 7:1, where it is bound up with Christ's resurrection and the final entrance of the eschaton in a typical Pauline paradox. Paul employs the theme here in speaking to Gentile believers. See Webb 1993.

That is again to say that Paul's understanding of the nation is determined by Christ, and not by any assessment of its outward condition. He is perfectly aware that the earlier exile continues, as his allusion to Israel's disobedience in the Diaspora in Romans 2:24 shows (cf. Is. 52:5; Ezek. 36:20). Yet, as in Galatians, he presupposes that from a human perspective Israel is vigorous and numerous, 'like the sands of the sea' (Rom. 9:27). Israel's attempt to establish its own righteousness in its pursuit of the law and its exclusive table-fellowship suggest a confident nation, proud of its religious heritage. This *securitas* is incompatible with Paul's view of exile, in which the nation is removed, and the remnant which remains is made to face its guilt and rebellion. Paul did not come to see Israel's condition in this light apart from faith in Christ.

The claim that Christ is the present end of Israel's exile misrepresents Paul by pushing Israel's exile into the past. The cross does not sweep away human guilt; it confronts us with it, so that it may be judged. Israel was not desirous of the good and merely too weak to attain it. It is in open rebellion against its Creator and can receive mercy only from the hand of its Judge. Its 'reduction to nothing' is no more a matter of the past than its current refusal to believe in the crucified Messiah. The continuing remnant, which is truly a miracle of God given much of the behaviour of Gentile Christians, is a sign of the salvation which is yet to come for Israel.

Chapter Seven

Justification in Paul, the New Testament witness and beyond

Paul's theology of justification can be properly summarized only by considering its implications for the preaching, confession and life of the church. Here we can draw only some basic conclusions, which require much further application in living itself. Two fundamental issues are at stake here: the unity of the New Testament and its message, and the unity of the church and its message.

Justification as verdict and vindication

My description of Paul's understanding of justification approaches the views of Adolf Schlatter, Ernst Käsemann, and especially Peter Stuhlmacher. At the same time, the interpretation of Paul which I am presenting here differs from their writings on this topic, or at least adds new emphases. Consequently, it is necessary to draw out some of the distinctions I would wish to maintain, and to clarify the relation ship of these views to traditional Protestant understandings of justification.

We have seen that God's saving righteousness and his righteous wrath stand in a synthetic relation, rather than a strictly antithetical one. That is to say, there can be no justification of the sinner which is not simultaneously a justification of God in his wrath against the sinner: the revelation of the saving righteousness of God is based upon the righteousness of God's wrath which is revealed against all idolatry and hypocrisy (Rom. 1:18, 29, 32; 2:5, 8, 13). 'Justification' for Paul is therefore fundamentally a forensic event precisely in its earthly, saving character (cf. Stuhlmacher 1995: xxiv). In interpreting Paul's view of retributive justice and saving righteous as interdependent in this manner, I stand at some distance from Schlatter, Käsemann and Stuhlmacher. Although God's role as judge unmistakably appears in their work, it is in some measure understated

171

in their understanding of 'God's righteousness'.[1]

Furthermore, there is no reason to suppose that Paul adopts a sort of 'meta-concept' of justification, in which he somehow combines the ideas of gift and power.[2] It is merely the case that, as in the biblical tradition, the two ideas of verdict and vindication belong together for him. When Paul speaks of a 'righteousness of God' given to faith in Christ, he has in view both God's justifying verdict and its result (Rom. 1:17; 3:21–22). He nevertheless knows the difference between the justifying verdict and the vindicating action, as is clear, for example, in Romans 5:1–11, where he speaks of 'justification' as present peace with God. There is no need to seek a 'meta-concept' which might encompass the ideas of 'gift and power'. We need only recognize that for Paul 'verdict' and 'vindication' belong together in God's ruling and judging the world, and are presently separated only under the paradox of faith.

Consequently, Paul *does* know of a distinction between 'declaratory' and 'effective' (or 'transformatory') righteousness (Stuhlmacher 1992: 334–335). It is entirely correct and important to stress, as Stuhlmacher does, that God's justifying work in Christ brings with it the entrance of the new creation into the fallen world, in the form of the gift of the Spirit (see esp. Stuhlmacher 1967: 1–35). Indeed, Paul speaks of 'justification by the Spirit' (1 Cor. 6:11; 1 Tim. 3:16; cf. Rom. 1:4). Nevertheless, for him 'justification' is something more than the giving of the Spirit. That gift proceeds from the justifying verdict which God has rendered in Christ: 'Because you are sons, God has sent forth the Spirit of his Son into our hearts' (Gal. 4:6; cf. Rom. 8:16; Stuhlmacher 1966: 101).

Furthermore, the Spirit constitutes the anticipatory granting of the *whole* of salvation, not merely a part of it. It is the gift of the resurrection in its proleptic form: 'Although the body is death on account of sin, the Spirit is life, on account of righteousness' (Rom. 8:10, cf. verse 11; Gal. 5:5). For this reason, the presence of Spirit is nothing other than 'Christ' in the believer (8:10). We therefore cannot rightly speak of justification as a 'process of becoming new' (Stuhlmacher 1986: 72–73). For Paul the work of the Spirit is 'a whole', which is not yet wholly present.[3]

---

[1] Cf. Stuhlmacher 1992: 327–341; Schlatter 1977: 437–451. Schlatter 1935: 36–38 speaks of a 'righteousness of God' which destroys sin, but not one which destroys the sinner.

[2] For further discussion of this matter see Seifrid 1992a: 37–46.

[3] Although Rom. 5:19 and Phil. 1:11 are debatable in this regard, in my view Paul

We have found reason to place even greater emphasis upon the fundamental place Christ's cross and resurrection hold in Paul's thought than is apparent in Käsemann's line of thought.[4] According to his proposal, in speaking of 'the righteousness of God' Paul borrows the language of certain segments of Judaism of his day in the idea of God's saving righteousness as charged with eschatological expectation (Käsemann 1969). Paul's message is that this transforming power has broken into the world in Christ. Stuhlmacher (1986) has developed and broadened Käsemann's thesis, thereby linking Paul to the early believing community and to Jesus himself. We certainly do not wish to contest a connection between Paul and Jesus, the earliest church or early Judaism! Neverthless, it cannot escape our notice that Paul does not appeal to a traditional understanding of God's righteousness in Romans as a reminder to his readers. Moreover, as we have noted elsewhere, Paul can hardly presuppose that they were familiar with a conception of God's righteousness as 'gift and power' (see Seifrid 1992a: 37–46). If he had done so, he certainly would not have needed to clarify the nature of grace in Romans 6 by expounding the believer's death with Christ to sin. To anyone who knew of God's righteousness as a 'transforming power', that discussion is unnecessary. Paul sets forth the 'new obedience' in Romans 6 by returning to Christ's cross and resurrection. The same is true of his treatment of the law in Romans 7 and of life in the Spirit in Romans 8. While his theology of justification reappears in varying forms in these chapters, it is always centred in Christ's incarnation, cross and resurrection. It is *in* the crucified and risen Christ that the righteousness of God has been manifest, not in us. It is not a diffuse power within the world, but has its locus in Christ and in the gospel which makes him known.[5]

At the same time, we must stress that in calling attention to the inseparability of 'declaratory' and 'effective' justification in Paul's thought, Schlatter, Käsemann, and especially Stuhlmacher have brought an important reminder of Paul's 'Christ-centred' theology of justification. It is fair to say that something of the 'Christ-centred' understanding of justification which Luther and Calvin grasped was

---

speaks in both instances of the granting of righteousness as a whole.

[4] See Zahl 1996 for a balanced assessment of Käsemann's work.

[5] There is no place in Paul's thought for interpreting justification in terms of liberation theology as does Tamez 1993, who makes human beings good and 'structures' of society evil, and according to whom 'justice' will be effected by liberated human beings! Käsemann's lack of precision in speaking of the righteousness of God as a power opens the door to this interpretation, although he never could have followed it.

lost in subsequent Protestant thought, where justification came to be defined in terms of the believer and not in terms of Christ. It is worth observing that Paul never speaks of Christ's righteousness as imputed to believers, as became standard in Protestantism.[6] Protestants draw the language of 'imputation' from Paul's use of Genesis 15:6 in Galatians 3:6 and Romans 4:3, where it is said that God 'imputed' (or 'reckoned') the faith of Abraham as righteousness.[7] In contrast, when Paul speaks of Christ's justifying work his language is direct and holistic: we are justified by the redemption which is 'in Christ Jesus' (Rom. 3:24); his resurrection is our justification (4:25); through Christ we receive 'the gift of righteousness' the 'justification which is life' (5:17, 18); Christ himself is our righteousness (1 Cor. 1:30); we become the righteousness of God in him (2 Cor. 5:21). The justifying verdict which has been rendered on us in Christ can be distinguished, but not separated from the resurrection from the dead. Our justification in Christ demands that we wait for the 'hope of righteousness' (Gal. 5:4).[8]

The common Protestant formulation of justification as the 'non-imputation of sin and the imputation of Christ's righteousness' is understandable as a way of setting forth justification as a forensic reality, in distinction from the Tridentine claim that an infused, imparted or inherent righteousness had to be added to the grace of forgiveness. It nevertheless treats the justifying verdict of God as an immediate and isolated gift. The justification of the believer is thereby separated from the justification of God in his wrath against us. Salvation is then portioned out, so that one possesses it piecemeal. It is held together as a series of *ideas* (justification, sanctification, glorification), rather than being grasped – by faith – as the comprehensive *act* of God in Christ. The insistence that the sanctification of the believer always accompanies justification does not fully overcome this deficiency. Indeed, Protestant confessions sometimes take on the appearance of unreality at this point because they speak of believers in themselves.[9] Once one shifts away from

[6] This formulation apparently derives from Melanchthon. See McGrath 1998: 207–213.

[7] We recall that this language allows Paul to speak of justification as simultaneously a gift and the recompense of 'the obedience of faith'.

[8] For a sample of Luther's thought, see 'The Two Kinds of Righteousness' (*LW* 31: 297–306).

[9] E.g. the Heidelberg Catechism, Answer to Question 60: 'God ... imputes to me the perfect satisfaction, righteousness, and holiness of Christ, as if I had never committed nor had any sin, and had myself accomplished all the obedience which Christ has fulfilled for me ...'

Paul's frame of reference in Christ to one located in the believer, the continuing demand of faith, hope and love is obscured.

By virtue of their extrinsic character and finality, Christ's cross and resurrection exclude the notions of an inherent righteousness and progress in justification which Protestant divines were concerned to avoid. As a result, there is no need to multiply entities within 'justification', as Protestant orthodoxy did when it added the imputation of Christ's righteousness to the forgiveness of sins. When Paul speaks of 'justification' as the forgiveness of sins, he has in view the whole of justification, the resurrection from the dead, not merely an erasure of our failures which must be supplemented by an 'imputed' righteousness (Rom. 4:6–8, 25). Likewise, the further distinction which some Protestants made between the imputation of Christ's active righteousness (in fulfilling the law) and his passive obedience (in dying on the cross) is unnecessary and misleading. This view, too, arose from a failure to grasp that Christ's work represents the prolepsis of the final judgment and the entrance of the age to come.[10] His 'passive obedience' was the fulfilment of the law which condemned us! In Christ and in hope, the triumph over sin and death is ours here and now. Yet it is not ours: we possess it only in faith. In this way, and only in this way, the grace of God and the demand for obedience meet. In reducing 'justification' to a present possession of 'Christ's imputed righteousness', Protestant divines inadvertently bruised the nerve which runs between justification and obedience.

It is not so much *wrong* to use the expression 'the imputed righteousness of Christ' as it is *deficient*. Paul, after all, speaks of the forgiveness of sins, of reconciliation to God, the gift of the Spirit, 'salvation' and so on. But his teaching on justification is more comprehensive than any of these, and provides the framework in which they are to be understood. Even where he speaks of 'salvation' and not justification, the essential elements of the latter appear alongside the former. If we fail to capture the sense of the whole, the pieces themselves lose their significance. It is better to say with Paul that our righteousness is found, not in us, but in Christ crucified and risen.[11] The Westminster Confession (and that of my own institution) puts the matter nicely when it speaks of 'receiving and resting on [Christ] and his righteousness by faith'.

---

[10] See the comparison of John Owen and John Wesley in Clifford 1990: 177–197.

[11] Note that our righteousness is found in the crucified and risen Christ, in whom God's verdict on us (and vindication of us) is found. We ought not fall into the error of Osiander!

In raising the foregoing criticism, we are touching upon problems which attend Protestant placement of justification within in an 'order of salvation' (*ordo salutis*).[12] According to Paul, 'justification' has to do with Christ's cross and resurrection for us – the whole of salvation – and therefore cannot be reduced to an event which takes place for the individual at the beginning of the Christian life. The problem deepens when 'justification' is made to follow 'regeneration', a sequence which was constructed in order to allow for the response of faith prior to the justification of the individual. In this case, the limitation of the justifying event to the act of faith threatens to diminish the significance of the cross.[13] If 'justification' occurs *only* upon my believing (or being regenerated), we must conclude that the cross creates the precondition for justification, but not its reality. Indeed, when faith (or regeneration) is given this independent role, the cross appears as an arbitrary means by which God has chosen to justify humanity. Paul, in contrast, locates justification wholly in Christ – and yet makes justification contingent upon faith (see 2 Cor. 5:21; cf. Rom. 3:22, 25). Christ's cross and resurrection are the whole of justification, but that justification must be 'distributed' through preaching and faith: God reconciled the world to himself through Christ, and yet has committed the 'word of reconciliation' to the apostles (2 Cor. 5:19). As we have seen, faith for Paul is nothing more than 'hearing' the good news, the reception of that already accomplished and given, a mirror-reflection of the word of promise (Gal. 3:1–5; Rom. 10:14–17). Consequently, if we reduce the dimensions of 'justification' to an 'order of salvation' constructed around the human being we distort Paul's message.

It is not the 'order' itself which is objectionable. Paul himself places 'justification' in an order of saving events: 'And whom he predestined, these also he called. And whom he called, these also he justified. And whom he justified, these also he glorified' (Rom. 8:30). Here, however,

---

[12] On this topic see Dantine 1968: 21–36 and Gaffin 1978: 135–143, who offers reflections similar to mine on the topic of Christ's resurrection.

[13] The same must be said for N. T. Wright's recent scheme in which he regards justification as an analytical judgment of God deriving from regeneration. God declares the state of affairs which he sees, namely precisely who (by the work of the Spirit) are 'the true people of God', who will be vindicated at the Last Day. One wonders why Wright proposes that such persons must be granted the forgiveness of sins. In any event, 'faith' plays a secondary role in Wright's view. It is not an act of obedience of the sinner before God, but a badge of 'membership' in the covenant community. The priority which Wright gives to regeneration brings his system especially close to the theology of some late seventeenth-century Anglican divines, who shared his misunderstanding that the reformational understanding of justification made faith into a 'work'. See Wright 1997: 113–133; McGrath 1998: 237–240, 292–298.

we find a sequence of divine acts rather than operations within the individual. Paul's 'order of salvation' retains a call to faith and hope lacking in the usual Protestant schemes, because it proceeds from God and his work.[14] For Paul, God's justifying work *extra nos* in Christ determines all that we are and shall be.

Justification in the witness of the New Testament

Paul's understanding of the justifying work of God in Christ is no isolated phenomenon within the biblical witness, but part of its fabric. Although we have touched upon the roots of Paul's gospel in the Old Testament understanding of God's righteousness, the law, and the promise to Abraham, these themes deserve far more treatment than we have been able to give them here. We must also leave the relationship between Paul's message and the broader witness of the New Testament largely unexplored, including its understanding of the law. It would be inappropriate, however, to conclude this study without at least pointing to some of these rich theological connections.[15]

Obviously, Jesus' pronouncements of forgiveness, his fellowship with sinners and his calling them to discipleship anticipated the gospel which Paul later preached. His announcement of the kingdom of God parallels Paul's declaration of the revelation of the 'righteousness of God'. In fact the terms criss-cross one another: Paul speaks of the kingdom of God as the presence of righteousness (Rom. 14:17), just as Matthew testifies to Jesus' witness to the coming 'righteousness of God' (Matt. 6:33)[16]. Furthermore, in the Gospels the good news brings not only salvation but judgment. The two are inseparable, just as they are for Paul. The infant Jesus is appointed for the rise and fall of many within Israel (Luke 1:51–53). The cities which saw Jesus' miracles and did not believe will face a stricter judgment (Matt. 11:20–24). In those who do not respond to Jesus' parables, the divine hardening of the heart of which Isaiah spoke comes to fulfilment (Mark 4:10–12).

At various points Luke presents Jesus' message in terms of the justification of the ungodly, including a pair of parables which parallel

---

[14] Other statements, such as 1 Cor. 6:11, which might appear to suggest an *ordo salutis* much more probably represent differing perspectives on the same saving reality.

[15] On this topic see Stuhlmacher 1986; 1992. The second volume of Stuhlmacher's *Biblical Theology of the New Testament* is in the press as I write. See also Carson (ed.) 1992, although its essays differ considerably from this study.

[16] It is in this framework that the Sermon on the Mount is to be understood. See Stuhlmacher 1992: 66–84.

the essence of Paul's thought. The importunate widow who awaits her justification (i.e. vindication) from an unrighteous judge serves as a model for believers who are to wait in faith for the coming of the Son of Man (Luke 18:1–8). The tax collector who as a mere sinner asks God for mercy returns to his home from the temple justified (Luke 18:9–14). The justification of the ungodly as a present pronouncement stands alongside justification as future vindication, for which one must wait. Likewise, in one of his reports of Paul's missionary preaching in Acts, Luke describes justification as given in Christ on account of his resurrection. It consists in the forgiveness of sins and deliverance which could not take place through the law of Moses (Acts 13:37–39).[17]

According to John's Gospel, the hour of judgment has come upon the world in Jesus (e.g. 3:19; 12:31). In him the false righteousness of the world has been judged, its self-justification, which measures all things by outward standards and visible glory (7:18, 24). The Spirit who has been sent to the disciples acts as God's advocate in his contention with the world, bringing the charge of sin (16:8–9). In Jesus' departure to the Father, 'righteousness' has entered the world by the Spirit and in the faith of the disciples of the unseen Lord (16:10). In the cross and resurrection the 'ruler of the world' has been condemned and stripped of his power (16:10; cf. Rev. 12:10–12). The Son of God gave his 'flesh' for the ungodly world, so that the life of the resurrection is present in him and his word (e.g. 6:51; 5:24–29; 11:25). All who see and believe in him possess that life (e.g. 3:16; 6:40). Faith in the Son is the one 'work' which God demands of the human being (6:29). It is necessarily accompanied by love, the new commandment which Jesus leaves with his disciples (13:34–35). The presence of the eschaton brings the reality of love. The first epistle of John, I suggest, speaks of this reality in terms of 'righteousness', that is, the saving righteousness of the age to come, which is present already in the children of God (1:9; 2:1, 29; 3:7, 10, 12).

In the letter to the Hebrews, 'sanctification' appears as the equivalent of 'justification' in the letters of Paul (Denney 1951: 126). The author does not speak of it as a process, but as a 'whole' in which believers already share through the high-priestly work of Christ, who has entered into God's presence on our behalf (e.g. 3:1; 10:10, 14, 19).[18] Our

---

[17] Cf. 1 Pet. 3:21, in which Christ's resurrection is said to be the basis of the good conscience of the believer.

[18] On the theme of 'sanctification' in the New Testament see Peterson 1995.

pilgrimage to our heavenly home has its basis in our arrival there already through Christ (10:19–23; 12:18–24). As in Paul, the imperative paradoxically flows out of the indicative.

Faith, works, and justification according to James

Even from the period of the early church, the relationship between Paul's understanding of justification and that of James has been regarded as a test of the unity of the New Testament. It naturally played an important role in the period of the Reformation. Luther expressed doubts about the value of the epistle, and in one of his utterances at table wagered his doctoral biretta than no-one could reconcile them satisfactorily.[19] On the other hand, the Council of Trent appealed to James 2:24 to help establish that 'the righteousness which has been received is preserved and increased by good works' (Canon 24).[20]

In the critical text, 2:14–26, James is concerned to correct a false understanding of 'faith' which endangered the churches of his day. He does not, however, aim at correcting mere monotheism, as some have argued.[21] He writes to brothers, who have rightly grasped the source, object and end of faith. He assumes that they share his conviction that faith comes from the risen Christ, the Lord of glory (2:1). This faith saves (verse 14). It is the very substance of salvation, its 'body' according to James' closing metaphor (verse 26).

The problem rather is that the brothers then — and we now — are tempted to suppose that faith can be present without works. If someone 'says that he has faith' but has no works, such 'faith' can hardly be expected to save him (2:14). James concedes the title 'faith' to the idle assent which he combats, but only barely, as his opening language shows. It is 'faith' in name only, a denatured entity which has neither the character nor the effect of the reality. It is dead, inoperative, inanimate, a corpse rather than a living thing (verses 17, 20, 26). In exposing this error, James employs a parable: 'If a brother or sister should be without clothing and lacks the nourishment needed for the day, and someone of you should say to them, "Go in peace, be warmed

[19] WA TR 3, 253.

[20] Cf. chapter 10 and Canon 32. The following discussion is indebted in its main line, and at numerous points to Laato 1997.

[21] The demons 'believe' that God is one and shudder, because they have no works (Jas. 2:19). Indeed, in the narrative of Joshua, it is Rahab's monotheistic faith which saves her (Jos. 2:8–14).

and be filled", and you do not give them the things necessary for the body, what use is that?' (verses 15–16). The empty comfort of the needy brother or sister with mere words corresponds to saying that one has faith without having any works. Words accomplish nothing. The failure to assist the fellow believer is a mirror which reflects the ineffectiveness and unreality of the 'faith' to which such a person lays claim. Just as that one does not help the needy brother or sister, his 'faith' shall not save him in the least.

Faith which properly deserves the name has works. Mere assent is not faith, but unbelief hiding under a pseudonym. It is not necessary to add works to faith: faith produces its own works, or it is not faith. Works therefore are not only evidence of faith; they are integral to it.[22] According to James, faith 'worked with' Abraham's works, not adjunctively but concursively, accomplishing them just as the body with the spirit performs deeds.[23] When, therefore, James speaks of faith 'being perfected' by Abraham's works, he does not mean that works supplied something alongside faith, which faith inherently lacks (2:22). Rather, faith came to its own perfection by means of works. He understands Genesis 15:6 in prophetic terms: the sacrifice of Isaac was the fulfilment of the Scripture which announced Abraham's faith in God (verse 23). Faith has a course to run, deeds which it must do in the world. As James makes clear at the very outset of his letter, faith necessarily undergoes testing so that those who believe may come to perfection (1:2–4).

Consequently, James freely draws the conclusion that the justification of Abraham and Rahab was based upon works, as it is likewise for all others (2:21, 24, 25).[24] His formulation is important: he does not say that they were justified 'by faith and works', but that they were justified by works alone! Justification ultimately must be by works, because works are faith's perfection. James's concluding

---

[22] The interlocutor of Jas. 2:18–19 is best understood as James speaking anonymously as another. He uses this form because it is improper for him to vindicate himself or place himself in the role of judge of another person (cf. Jas. 4:11–12). Because it is he who has been speaking in another's voice, his reversion to his own person follows without notice (Jas. 2:20).

[23] The verb *synergō* bears the sense of concursive action, as in Rom. 8:28 and 1 Cor. 6:2, and as is confirmed by James's subsequent illustration of faith as the body and of works as the spirit (Jas. 2:26).

[24] On James's understanding of the law, see Laato 1997: 47–61. I would only add that in my view James does not regard the (eschatological) 'law of freedom' (Jas. 1:25; 2:12) and the 'kingdom law' (2:8) as the continuation of the law which condemns us as transgressors, but as the transcendence of it (2:11, cf. 12–13).

illustration of the body and the spirit sheds light on his way of speaking (2:26). If people perform acts of kindness, one might say either that their 'body' performs these acts or that their 'spirit' performs them, depending on one's perspective. When speaking of the basis or substance of salvation, James speaks of faith, which he calls 'the body'. When, however, he views salvation in its completeness and perfection he speaks of the works which justify, 'the spirit' which makes the body something more than a corpse. He certainly does not suppose that works in themselves justify, despite his bold language. In terms of his imagery that would be like a disembodied spirit, an idea which he does not even contemplate. Justification is by works alone, but the works that justify are never alone. They are an outworking of faith, which is present with them: 'You see that a person is justified by works, and not by faith alone' (2:24). This point becomes especially clear in James's example of Rahab, whom he explicitly calls 'the harlot'. She obviously was not justified on account of her occupation, but on account of the works in which her faith was present. James as well as Paul understands justification as the justification of the ungodly.

The faith which justifies arises from the saving word of God.[25] The promise made to Abraham lies behind the Genesis narrative (Jas. 2:23). The spies whom Rahab received were 'messengers', who implicitly brought the announcement of coming judgment (verse 25). Furthermore, the justification which Abraham and Rahab experienced took place at the point of crisis. In accord with Jewish tradition, James speaks as if Abraham completed the act of sacrifice, 'offering up Isaac upon the altar' (verse 21; cf. Heb. 11:17–19). Rahab was delivered from the destruction of Jericho, when she 'received the messengers and sent them out by another way' (verse 24). These points of crisis arose from God's contention with the world. This is most apparent in the conquest of Jericho, in which divine judgment falls on the inhabitants of the land. But it is also present in James' appeal to Abraham, who in being justified came to be called 'a friend of God', and therefore an enemy of the world (verse 23; cf. 4:4; 5:1–6). The experiences of justification by Abraham and Rahab were prolepses of the day of judgment, which now stands immediately before the church (5:9).

It is already apparent that in speaking of justification James has in view the saving act of God, his rectification of creation. As we have noted, in being justified Abraham becomes the friend of God (2:23). It

---

[25] On the broader implications of this theme in James, see Laato 1997: 47–61.

probably is not going too far to say that the 'resurrection' of Isaac lies in the background as well.[26] Rahab's justification was deliverance from death. 'Justification' is the establishment of the 'righteousness of God', the right order of creation which takes place only by the saving word of God (cf. 1:19–21). As in Paul's thought, however, this justification is not a mere 'saving deed', but a vindicating act on behalf of the one who has believed. In Abraham's justification, the reckoning of his faith as righteousness came to fulfilment (2:23; Gen. 15:6). Rahab was delivered from destruction because she was already 'justified' by receiving the messengers and sending them forth in safety. James speaks of justification as the vindication that follows the divine verdict, in accord with Paul and their common biblical precedents.

In this light, James and Paul vary in their understanding of justification only in their emphases. Both understand that salvation is by faith, of which the risen Christ is the source and basis. Both understand that our justification at the last judgment will be based upon works. Both understand that these works belong to faith, and that they are God's works, not our own.[27] Both understand that this justification at the last judgment will be a justification of the ungodly. Both understand justification as the triumph of God over the world. Both understand justification as God's verdict which issues in his vindicating action. Both understand that the final judgment is proleptically present here and now in the justification of those who believe. They differ only in that James is concerned to describe the character of saving faith itself, and not its source and basis. Paul elaborates the theme that James presupposes: the crucified and risen Christ who dwells in faith and is its object. While Paul speaks of Christ's cross and resurrection as the prolepsis of the final judgment, James speaks of the past vindications of believers as prolepses of that same event. He finds examples of this justification of believers in Abraham and Rahab, just as he elsewhere appeals to the 'prophets who spoke in the name of the Lord' as models of patience and final blessing (5:10–11). The two cohere in that they both understand that Christ is the word of God which at once saves us and calls us to obedience.

Paul and James formulate their statements on justification differently from each other. They fight their battles in different ways, even though their battles are not entirely dissimilar. We need not think that laxity in

---

[26] The author of Hebrews explicitly speaks of it, of course (Heb. 11:19).

[27] Even for James, these are qualitatively different from human works, by which we might hide our ungodliness in boasting.

faith and a lack of love were problems for Paul's congregations alone. James's addressees might have profited from the Corinthian correspondence, just as the Corinthian congregation might have done well to read James's letter. The differences between the two are largely due to the cultural distance between synagogues of Jewish believers near Palestine and the Hellenistic congregation in Corinth. It is not necessary to suppose that James is responding to Paul or to a distortion of Paul in his appeal to the figure of Abraham. All Jewish believers had to come to grips with the significance of the patriarch for Christian faith.

Luther's suspicions concerning James therefore turn out to be unjustified. And Trent's appeal to James is clearly without support. The idea that good works 'increase righteousness' or add anything to faith would have been entirely foreign to him. James and Paul are not of one voice on the matter of justification, but they are in harmony.

Justification and Protestant–Roman Catholic dialogues

A number of ecumenical dialogues between Roman Catholics and various Protestant bodies have taken place in recent years. While it is beyond our scope to assess these developments at length, it is appropriate to comment briefly on some of the discussions concerning justification. Generally statements which have emerged from these dialogues have been characterized either by a lack of clarity, or by the willingness to treat Protestant and Roman Catholic positions as complementary, but not exclusive, perspectives on salvation (see McGrath 1998: 387–395). I have expressed my dissatisfaction with one such statement on this account, which I shall not repeat (Seifrid 1999). It seems more appropriate here to apply the conclusions of this study to the disagreement on justification between Protestants and Rome, in the hope that the basic issues at stake will stand out more clearly.

We have seen that Paul's understanding of justification is an expression of the contention which exists between God the Creator and the world. The biblical background differs from the modern courtroom in which an impartial judge presides, in that it presupposes a two-party dispute. One party is to be demonstrated to be in the right, the other in the wrong. The one does not take place without the other. The justification of God means the condemnation of the human being. In Christ's cross and resurrection God has been shown to be in the right, and we have been condemned. Christ was the God-Human, in whom both parties to the contention receive their justice. In him the verdict in

God's favour against the world is ours. He took our death that we might have his life. We died with him in order that we might live with him. Moreover, the event which took place in Christ is final and incapable of revision, a prolepsis of the day of judgment. This forensic setting means that Paul's thought excludes any idea of an infused, imparted or inherent righteousness, which treats the human being as one in need of healing or repair. Justification is a matter of death and life, wrath and vindication.[28]

God has been vindicated in the resurrection of the crucified Christ. In him the 'righteousness of God' has been manifest. In him the promise of a new creation has come to fulfilment. Although that promise awaits fulfilment in the world, it creates faith here and now through the gospel. And faith is obedience, in which God comes to be God in us: God is given his right and we are given Christ's righteousness. Faith is the opening through which the resurrection is projected into the present order. In it death to sin and life to God are ours, even though they are yet to come. Our righteousness therefore is not properly ours, but an alien righteousness given us in Christ: 'I live, yet no longer I, but Christ lives in me' (Gal. 2:20). Consequently, there can be no talk of merit in any form. The 'work of faith' and the works which faith produces are God's and not our own. They are the *new* creation which is already present in Christ. Our justification in Christ carries us forward to meet our justification before God and the world at the final judgment. The 'whole justification' outside of us in Christ will then become the 'whole justification' in us: we shall be raised from the dead. Our righteousness does not increase as we traverse this path, which, we must remember, leads through death. There is only the progression of the already completed work of God, like the movement of the sun from the faintest light of early dawn to the blazing glory of midday. Presently, we stand at the twilight of the beginning day, with our backs in darkness even as we are in the light.[29] That is to say, we are simultaneously righteous and sinners. The old reality has been defeated in Christ, but it is still present with us. In ourselves, we are yet the 'wretched persons' of Romans 7 condemned by the law and given over to death. Our justification according to works at the final judgment will be the justification of the ungodly. In the present world, our graves will testify to our continuing godlessness — indeed, there we shall be properly God-less — 'the body is dead on account of sin'

---

[28] On this theme, see Forde 1982.
[29] See Luther, WA 2, 586, 9–11, on Gal. 5:17.

(Rom. 8:10a). Our final separation from sin has taken place in Christ, but it must yet come to reality in us. Nevertheless, the Spirit is life on account of righteousness (verse 10b)! The dawning of the day is upon us, and those who believe necessarily walk into that dawn in obedience. Through the Spirit we wait for the hope of righteousness by faith which is active in love. Already the light of day, the life of the eschaton, is present with us (Gal. 5:5–6, 14).

It is this final point, the *simul justus et peccator*, which has proved the most difficult to overcome in ecumenical dialogue.[30] Differing judgments of this summary statement reveal differing understandings of the human being, which turn out to be the heart of the matter. If with Roman Catholic theology we presuppose that there is some sort of 'remainder' within the human creature which is not comprehended by our being sinners, we must necessarily conceive of salvation as our healing or transformation. Righteousness must then in some manner be infused, radiated or otherwise communicated to us. If, on the other hand, we see ourselves in the cross and resurrection of the Son of God, a radically different picture emerges. Then there is no 'remainder' within us, only the judgment of God in which we are reduced to nothingness and death. Our righteousness and life are not our own, but that of Christ. In the end, the debate concerning justification is determined by the cross. We shall either allow the cross to tell us who we are, or we shall interpret the cross in light of some prior understanding of our own. In other words, either we shall allow God to be our Creator, or we shall create ourselves.

Christian preaching of the gospel

We live within a society which is characterized by both moralism and moral chaos. This juxtaposition should not surprise us, since moralism is the way we fallen human beings seek to hide ourselves from God. We and our churches are not immune to either danger. Very often, I am afraid, all that is heard from our pulpits is a series of admonitions as to what we ought to do. These may produce the appearance of righteousness, but they cannot bring Christ to the human heart. Worse yet, when we preach in this way we implicitly point to ourselves as examples of the Spirit and power, as if the secret of piety were to be found in our persons, programmes, or wisdom. We have to learn what it means to preach Christ crucified and risen from the Scriptures. I

---

[30] See the excellent survey by the Roman Catholic O'Callaghan, 1997.

count myself a mere beginner in this and have no special advice, only the appeal that we seek to preach the gospel in its fullness. Such preaching cannot mean that we cease to preach the law, although we have to learn how to preach it rightly. The Spirit of God, not human manipulation, brings the confession of sin *and* the knowledge of Christ. Obviously, we must insist on the reality of coming judgment. And we must understand that whatever outward resistance there might be, the will of God expressed in the law has an echo in the human heart where it is recognized as the good will of the Creator. Above all else, our preaching must go beyond the call to 'do this and you will live' to the announcement that 'it is finished'. I do not at all mean this in the sense of 'cheap grace'. Such preaching will not mean that we cease to insist on God's claim on all that we have and are, but that we realize that this demand is filled only in Christ and in faith. Undoubtedly this will mean that we become theologians who are made such not merely by reading and study, but 'by living, rather, by dying and being damned'.[31] And this God will give us in differing measures and in differing ways.

---

[31] 'Vivendo immo moriendo et damnando fit theologus, non intelligendo, legendo aut speculando.' Luther, WA 5, 163, 28–30 (*Operationes in Psalmos,* 1519–1521; Ps. 5:12).

Bibliography

Assmann, Jan (1990), *Ma'at: Gerechtigkeit und Unsterblichkeit im Alten Agypten*. Munchen: C. H. Beck.

Avemarie, Friedrich (1996a), *Tora und Leben: Untersuchungen zur Heilsbedeutung der Tora in der frühen rabbinischen Literatur*. Texte und Studien zum Antiken Judentum 55. Tübingen: Mohr (Siebeck).

————(1996b), 'Bund als Gabe und Recht', in Friedrich Avemarie and Hermann Lichtenberger (eds.), *Bund und Tora: Zur theologischen Begriffsgeschichte in alttestamentlicher, frühjüdischer und urchristlicher Tradition*, 163–216. Tübingen: Mohr (Siebeck).

————(1999), 'Erwählung und Vergeltung: Zur optionalen Struktur rabbinischer Soteriologie'. *New Testament Studies* 45: 108–126.

Badenas, Robert (1985), *Christ the End of the Law: Romans 10.4 in Pauline Perspective. Journal for the Study of the New Testament* Supplements 10. Sheffield: JSOT.

Banks, Robert J. (1978), 'Romans 7:25a: an eschatological thanksgiving?'. *Australian Biblical Review* 26: 34–42.

Bassler, Jouette (1982), *Divine Impartiality: Paul and a Theological Axiom*. Society of Biblical Literature Dissertation Series 59. Chico, CA: Scholars.

Bell, Richard H. (1994), *Provoked to Jealousy: The Origin and Purpose of the Jealousy Motif in Romans 9 – 11*. Wissenschaftliche Untersuchungen zum Neuen Testament. Second Series 63. Tübingen: Mohr (Siebeck).

Bellah, Robert N., & Richard Madsen, William M. Sullivan, Ann Swidler, Steven M. Tipton (1985), *Habits of the Heart: Individualism and Commitment in American Life*. New York: Harper and Row.

Blocher, Henri (1999), *Original Sin: Illuminating the Riddle*. New Studies in Biblical Theology. Leicester: Apollos; Grand Rapids: Eerdmans.

Bockmuehl, Markus N. A. (1990), *Revelation and Mystery in Ancient Judaism and Pauline Christianity*. Wissenschaftliche Untersuchungen zum Neuen Testament. Second Series 36. Tübingen: Mohr (Siebeck).

Bonhoeffer, Dietrich (1954), *Life Together*. ET New York: Harper and Brothers (German original 1939).

————(1963), *The Cost of Discipleship*. ET New York: Macmillan (German original 1937).

Bovati, Pietro (1994), *Re-Establishing Justice: Legal Terms, Concepts and Procedures in the Hebrew Bible*. *Journal for the Study of the Old Testament* Supplements 105. Sheffield: JSOT.

Brecht, Martin (1985), *Martin Luther: His Road to Reformation, 1483–1521*. ET Minneapolis: Fortress (German original 1981).

Bultmann, Rudolf (1951), *Theology of the New Testament*. Scribner Studies in Contemporary Theology. New York: Scribner's (German original 1948).

————(1982), 'Das Problem der Ethik bei Paulus', in K. H. Rengstorf (ed.), *Das Paulusbild in der neueren deutschen Forschung*, 179–199. Wege der Forschung 24. Darmstadt: Wissenschaftliche Buchgesellschaft (1st edn 1924).

————(1990), '*kauchaomai, ktl.*', in Gerhard Kittel (ed.), *Theologisches Wörterbuch zum Neuen Testament* 3:646–654. Stuttgart: Kohlhammer (1st edn 1933).

Campbell, Douglas (1994), 'Romans 1:17 – a *crux interpretum* for the *pistis Christou* debate'. *Journal of Biblical Literature* 113: 265–285.

Carson, D. A. (ed). (1992), *Right with God: Justification in the Bible and the World*. Grand Rapids: Baker; Carlisle: Paternoster.

Clifford, Alan C. (1990), *Atonement and Justification: English Evangelical Theology 1640–1790 – An Evaluation*. Oxford: Clarendon.

Corley, Bruce (1997), 'Interpreting Paul's conversion – then and now', in Richard N. Longenecker (ed.), *The Road from Damascus: The Impact of Paul's Conversion on his Life, Thought, and Ministry*, 1–17. Grand Rapids: Eerdmans.

Cranfield, C. E. B. (1975, 1979), *A Critical and Exegetical Commentary on the Epistle to the Romans*. International Critical Commentary. 2 vols. Edinburgh: T. & T. Clark.

Cremer, Hermann (1900), *Die paulinische Rechtfertigungslehre im Zusammenhange ihrer geschichtlichen Voraussetzungen*. Gütersloh: s.n.

Dantine, Wilhelm (1968), *The Justification of the Ungodly*. ET St Louis, MO: Concordia (German original 1959).

Denney, James (1951), *The Death of Christ*. London: Tyndale.

Dodd, C. H. (1935), *The Bible and the Greeks*. London: Hodder and Stoughton.

Donaldson, Terence (1997a), *Paul and the Gentiles: Remapping the Apostle's Convictional World*. Minneapolis: Fortress.

————(1997b), 'Israelite, convert, apostle to the Gentiles: the origin of Paul's mission', in Richard N. Longenecker (ed.), *The Road from Damascus: The Impact of Paul's Conversion on his Life, Thought, and Ministry*, 62–84. Grand Rapids: Eerdmans.

Drane, John W. (1975), *Paul: Libertine or Legalist? A Study in the Theology of the Major Pauline Epistles*. London: SPCK.

Dunn, James D. G. (1980), *Christology in the Making*. Philadelphia: Westminster.

————(1983), 'The New Perspective on Paul'. *Bulletin of the John Rylands Library* 65: 95–122.

————(1988), *Romans*. Word Biblical Commentary 38. 2 vols. Dallas, TX: Word.

————(1990), *Jesus, Paul, and the Law: Studies in Mark and Galatians*. London: SPCK.

————(1992), 'Yet once more – "The works of the law": a response'. *Journal for the Study of the New Testament* 46: 99–117.

————(1993), *The Epistle to the Galatians*. Black's New Testament Commentaries. Peabody, MA: Hendrickson.

————(1997), '4QMMT and Galatians'. *New Testament Studies* 43: 147–153.

————(1997), 'Paul's conversion – a light to twentieth-century disputes', in Jostein Ådna, Scott Hafemann, and Otfried Hofius (eds.), *Evangelium, Schriftauslegung, Kirche: Festschrift für Peter Stuhlmacher zum 65. Geburtstag*, 77–93. Göttingen: Vandenhoeck & Ruprecht.

————(1998), *The Theology of Paul the Apostle*. Grand Rapids: Eerdmans, 1998.

Dunn, James D. G., and Alan M. Suggate (1994), *The Justice of God: A Fresh Look at the Old Doctrine of Justification by Faith*. Grand Rapids: Eerdmans.

Eaton, Michael (1995), *No Condemnation: A New Theology of Assurance*. Downers Grove: IVP.

Eckstein, Hans-Joachim (1983), *Der Begriff Syneidesis bei Paulus*. Wissenschaftliche Untersuchungen zum Neuen Testament. Second Series 10. Tübingen: Mohr (Siebeck).

————(1996), *Verheißung und Gesetz: Eine exegetische Untersuchung zu Galater 2,15 – 4,7*. Wissenschaftliche Untersuchungen zum Neuen Testament 86. Tübingen: Mohr (Siebeck).

Feldman, Louis H. (1997), 'The concept of exile in Josephus', in James M. Scott (ed.), *Exile: Old Testament, Jewish, and Christian Conceptions*, 145–172. Leiden: Brill.

Fitzmyer, Joseph A. (1993), *Romans: A New Translation with*

Introduction and Commentary. Anchor Bible 33. New York: Doubleday.

Forde, Gerhard O. (1982), *Justification by Faith: A Matter of Death and Life*. Philadelphia: Fortress.

Fredriksen, Paula (1986), 'Paul and Augustine: conversion narratives, orthodox traditions, and the retrospective self'. *Journal of Theological Studies* NS 37: 3–34.

Fuller, Daniel P. (1980), *Gospel and Law: Contrast or Continuum?: The Hermeneutics of Dispensationalism and Covenant Theology*. Grand Rapids: Eerdmans.

Furnish, Victor Paul (1984), *II Corinthians*. Anchor Bible 32A. New York: Doubleday.

Gaffin, Richard B. (1978), *The Centrality of the Resurrection: A Study in Paul's Soteriology*. Baker Biblical Monograph. Grand Rapids: Baker.

Garland, David E. (1985), 'The composition and unity of Philippians: some neglected literary factors'. *Novum Testamentum* 27: 141–173.

Garlington, Don (1991), *The Obedience of Faith*. Wissenschaftliche Untersuchungen zum Neuen Testament. Second Series 38. Tübingen: Mohr (Siebeck).

————(1994), *Faith, Obedience, and Perseverance: Aspects of Paul's Letter to the Romans*. Wissenschaftliche Untersuchungen zum Neuen Testament 79. Tübingen: Mohr (Siebeck).

Gaston, Lloyd (1979), 'Paul and the Torah,' in Alan Davies (ed.), *Antisemitism and the Foundations of Christianity*, 48–71. New York: Paulist.

————(1984), 'Works of the law as a subjective genitive'. *Studies in religion / Sciences religieuses*. 13: 39–46.

Hafemann, Scott J. (1995), *Paul, Moses, and the History of Israel: The Letter/Spirit Contrast and the Argument from Scripture in 2 Corinthians 3*. Wissenschaftliche Untersuchungen zum Neuen Testament 81. Tübingen: Mohr (Siebeck).

————(1997), 'Paul and the exile of Israel in Galatians 3 – 4', in James M. Scott (ed.), *Exile: Old Testament, Jewish, and Christian Conceptions*, 329–371. Journal for the Study of Judaism Supplements 56. Leiden, Brill.

Harrisville, Roy A., III (1994), 'PISTIS CHRISTOU': witness of the Fathers'. *Novum Testamentum* 36: 233–241.

Hays, Richard B. (1983), *The Faith of Jesus Christ*. Society of Biblical Literature Dissertation Series 56. Chico, CA: Scholars.

————(1985), 'Have we found Abraham to be our forefather

according to the flesh?'. *Novum Testamentum* 27: 76–98.

————(1989), *Echoes of Scripture in the Letters of Paul*. New Haven: Yale University Press.

————(1997), 'PISTIS' and Pauline Christology', in E. Elizabeth Johnson and David M. Hay (eds.), *Pauline Theology, 4: Looking Back, Pressing On*, 35–60. Society of Biblical Literature Symposium Series 4. Atlanta, GA: Scholars.

Hengel, M. (1991), *The Pre-Christian Paul*. Philadelphia: Trinity.

Hengel, Martin, & Anna Maria Schwemer (1997), *Paul Between Damascus and Antioch: The Unknown Years*. Louisville, KY: Westminster/John Knox.

Herold, Gerhart (1973), *Zorn und Gerechtigkeit Gottes bei Paulus: Eine Untersuchung zu Röm. 1,16–18*. European University Papers, Series XIII: Theology 14. Bern: Herbert Lang.

Hill, Craig C. (1992), *Hellenists and Hebrews: Reappraising Division within the Earliest Church*. Minneapolis: Fortress.

Hofius, Otfried (1989), '"Rechtfertigung des Gottlosen" als Thema biblischer Theologie', in *Paulusstudien*, 121–147. Wissenschaftliche Untersuchungen zum Neuen Testament 51. Tübingen: Mohr (Siebeck).

Hübner, Hans (1984), *Law in Paul's Thought*. Edinburgh: T. & T. Clark.

Hultgren, Arland J. (1980), 'The *Pistis Christou* formulation in Paul'. *Novum Testamentum* 22: 248–263.

Iwand, Hans Joachim (1991), *Glaubensgerechtigkeit*, in Gerhard Sauter (ed.)., Theologische Bücherei: Systematische Theologie 64. München: Chr. Kaiser (original edn 1980).

Jervis, L. Ann (1991), *The Purpose of Romans: A Comparative Letter Structure Investigation. Journal for the Study of the New Testament* Supplements 55. Sheffield: JSOT Press.

Käsemann, Ernst (1969), 'The "righteousness of God" in Paul', in *New Testament Questions of Today*, 168–182. ET Philadelphia: Fortress (German original 1961).

———— (1971), 'The Spirit and the letter', in *Perspectives on Paul*, 138–166. ET Philadelphia: Fortress (German original 1969).

———— (1980), *Commentary on Romans*. ET Grand Rapids: Eerdmans (German original 1974).

Keck, Leander E. (1989), '"Jesus" in Romans'. *Journal of Biblical Literature* 108: 443–460.

Kim, Seyoon (1982), *The Origin of Paul's Gospel*. Grand Rapids: Eerdmans.

Koch, Dietrich-Alex (1986), *Die Schrift als Zeuge des Evangeliums: Untersuchungen zur Verwendung und zum Verständnis der Schrift bei Paulus*. Beiträge zur historischen Theologie 69. Tübingen: Mohr (Siebeck).

Kutsch, Ernst (1978), *Neues Testament – Neuer Bund? Eine Fehlübersetzung wird korrigiert*. Neukirchen/Vluyn: Neukirchener.

Laato, Timo (1995), *Paul and Judaism: An Anthropological Approach*. South Florida Studies in the History of Judaism 115. ET Atlanta: Scholars (German original 1991).

————(1997), 'Justification according to James: a comparison with Paul'. *Trinity Journal* NS 18: 43–84.

Levin, Christoph (1999), 'Altes Testament und Rechtfertigung'. *Zeitschrift für Theologie und Kirche* 96: 161–176.

Longenecker, Bruce W. (1993), '*Pistis* in Romans 3:25: neglected evidence for the "faithfulness of Christ"?' *New Testament Studies* 39: 478–480.

Longenecker, Richard N. (ed.) (1997), *The Road from Damascus: The Impact of Paul's Conversion on his Life, Thought and Ministry*. Grand Rapids: Eerdmans.

Lull, Timothy F. (ed). (1989), *Martin Luther's Basic Theological Writings*. Minneapolis, Fortress.

Luther, Martin. *LW = Luther's Works*, 55 vols. St Louis: Concordia; Philadelphia: Fortress, 1955–86.

————WA = (Weimarer Ausgabe) *D. Martin Luthers Werke: Kritische Gesamtsausgabe* Weimar: Hermann Böhlaus Nachfolger, 1883– .

————WA TR = *D. Martin Luthers Werke: Tischreden*, 6 vols. Weimar: Hermann Böhlaus Nachtfolger, 1912–21.

McGrath, Alister E. (1998), *Iustitia Dei: A History of the Christian Doctrine of Justification*. Cambridge: Cambridge University Press (original edition 1986).

Marshall, I. Howard (1996), 'Salvation, grace and works in the later writings in the Pauline corpus'. *New Testament Studies* 42: 339–358.

Moo, Douglas J. (1983), '"Law," "works of the law," and legalism in Paul'. *Westminster Theological Journal* 45: 73–100.

———— (1996), *The Epistle to the Romans*. New International Commentary on the New Testament. Grand Rapids: Eerdmans.

Müller, Christian (1964), *Gottes Gerechtigkeit und Gottes Volk: Eine Untersuchung zu Römer 9 – 11*. Forschungen zur Religion und Literatur des Alten und Neuen Testaments 86. Göttingen: Vandenhoeck & Ruprecht.

Munck, Johannes (1959), *Paul and the Salvation of Mankind.* ET Richmond, VA: John Knox (German original 1959).

Neusner, Jacob (1988), *The Mishnah: A New Translation.* New Haven: Yale.

O'Callaghan, Paul (1997), *Fides Christi: The Justification Debate.* Dublin: Four Courts.

Peterson, David (1995), *Possessed by God: A New Testament Theology of Sanctification and Holiness.* Grand Rapids: Eerdmans.

Piper, John (1983), *The Justification of God: An Exegetical and Theological Study of Romans 9:1–23.* Grand Rapids: Baker.

Qimron, Elisha, & John Strugnell (1994), *Qumran Cave 4: V, Miqsat Ma'ase Ha-Torah.* Discoveries in the Judean Desert 10. Oxford: Clarendon.

von Rad, Gerhard (1962, 1965), *Theology of the Old Testament.* 2 vols. ET New York: Harper and Row (German original 1957).

Räisänen, Heikki (1986), *Paul and the Law.* ET Philadelphia: Fortress (German original 1983).

Reumann, John (1982), *Righteousness in the New Testament: "Justification" in the United States Lutheran–Roman Catholic Dialogue.* Joseph Fitzmyer and Jerome Quinn, respondents. Philadelphia: Fortress; Ramsey, NY: Paulist.

Reventlow, Henning Graf (1971), *Rechtfertigung im Horizont des Alten Testaments.* Beiträge zur evangelischen Theologie 58. München: Chr. Kaiser.

de Roche, Michael (1983), 'Yahweh's rîb against Israel: a reassessment of the so-called 'prophetic lawsuit' in the preexilic prophets'. *Journal of Biblical Literature* 102: 563–574.

Rupp, Gordon (1953), *The Righteousness of God: Luther Studies.* London: Hodder and Stoughton.

Rüterswörden, U. (1995), '*šm*'', in *Theologisches Wörterbuch zum Alten Testament,* 8: 255–279. 8 vols. Stuttgart: Kohlhammer.

Sanders, E. P. (1977), *Paul and Palestinian Judaism: A Comparison of Patterns of Religion.* Philadelphia: Fortress.

———(1978), 'On the question of fulfilling the law in Paul and Rabbinic Judaism' in E. Bammel, C. K. Barrett and C. J. D. Davies (eds.), *Donum Gentilicium,* 103–106. Oxford: Clarendon.

———(1982), 'Jesus, Paul, and Judaism', in H. Temporini & W. Haase (eds.), *Aufstieg und Niedergang der römischen Welt,* 25.1: 390–450. Berlin: de Gruyter.

———(1983), *Paul, the Law, and the Jewish People.* Philadelphia: Fortress.

————(1991), *Paul*. Past Masters. Oxford: Oxford University Press.

————(1992), *Judaism: Practice and Belief, 63 BCE – 66 CE*. London: SCM; Philadelphia: Trinity Press International.

Sänger, Dietrich (1994), *Die Verkündigung des Gekreuzigten und Israel: Studien zum Verhältnis von Kirche und Israel bei Paulus und im frühen Christentum*. Wissenschaftliche Untersuchungen zum Neuen Testament 75. Tübingen: Mohr (Siebeck).

Sass, Gerhard (1995), *Leben aus den Verheissungen: traditionsgeschichtliche und biblisch-theologische Untersuchungen zur Rede von Gottes Verheissungen im Frühjudentum und beim Apostel Paulus*. Forschungen zur Religion und Literatur des Alten und Neuen Testaments 164. Göttingen: Vandenhoeck & Ruprecht.

Schäfer, Rolf (1965), 'Die Rechtfertigungslehre bei Ritschl und Kähler'. *Zeitschrift für Theologie und Kirche* 62: 66–85.

Schlatter, Adolf (1905), *Der Glaube im Neuen Testament*. Stuttgart: Vereinsbuchhandlung.

————(1935), *Gottes Gerechtigkeit: ein Kommentar zum Romerbrief*. Stuttgart: Calwer.

————(1977), *Das christliche Dogma*, 3rd edn Stuttgart: Calwer (original edn 1923).

Schmid, Hans Heinrich (1968), *Gerechtigkeit als Weltordnung: Hintergrund und Geschichte des alttestamentlichen Gerechtigkeitsbegriffes*, Beiträge zur historischen Theologie 40. Tübingen: Mohr (Siebeck).

————(1974), *Altorientalische Welt in der alttestamentlichen Theologie*. Zürich: Theologischer Verlag.

Schmidt, Werner H. (1981), '"Rechtfertigung des Gottlosen" in der Botschaft der Propheten', in J. Jeremias & L. Perlitt (eds.), *Die Botschaft und die Boten: Festschrift für Hans Walter Wolff zum 70.sten Geburtstag*, 157–168. Neukirchen: Neukirchener.

Schmitt, Rainer (1984), *Gottesgerechtigkeit – Heilsgeschichte – Israel in der Theolgie des Paulus*. Europäische Hochschulschriften: Theologie 20. Frankfurt: Peter Lang.

Schneider, G. (1993), '*hypakoē, -ēs, hē*; *hypakouō*', in H. Balz & G. Schneider (eds.), *Exegetical Dictionary of the New Testament* 3: 394–395. ET Grand Rapids: Eerdmans.

Schreiner, Thomas R. (1991), '"Works of Law" in Paul'. *Novum Testamentum* 33: 217–244.

————(1993), *The Law and its Fulfilment: A Pauline Theology of the Law*. Grand Rapids: Baker.

Schrenk, G., & V. Herntrich (1966), '*leimma, ktl.* ', in G. Kittel and

G. Friedrich (eds.), *Theological Dictionary of the New Testament*, 4:194–214. ET Grand Rapids: Eerdmans.

Seifrid, Mark A. (1985), 'Paul's approach to the Old Testament in Rom 10:6–8'. *Trinity Journal* NS 6: 3–37.

————(1992a), *Justification by Faith: The Origin and Development of a Central Pauline Theme. Novum Testamentum* Supplements 68. Leiden: Brill.

————(1992b), 'The Subject of Rom 7:14–25'. *Novum Testamentum* 34: 313–333.

————(1998), 'Natural revelation and the purpose of the law in Romans'. *Tyndale Bulletin* 49: 115–129.

————(1999), '"The gift of salvation": its failure to address the crux of justification'. *Journal of the Evangelical Theological Society* 42: 679–688.

Silva, Moisés (1994), *Biblical Words and their Meaning: An Introduction to Lexical Semantics*. Rev. edn. Grand Rapids: Zondervan (1st edn 1983).

Steck, Odil Hannes (1967), *Israel und das Gewaltsame Geschick der Propheten*. Wissenschaftliche Monographien zum Alten und Neuen Testament 23. Neukirchen: Neukirchener.

Steinmetz, David C. (1995), *Luther in Context*. Grand Rapids: Baker.

Stendahl, Krister (1963), 'The Apostle Paul and the introspective conscience of the West'. *Harvard Theological Review* 56: 199–215.

Stuhlmacher, Peter (1966), *Gerechtigkeit Gottes bei Paulus*. 2nd edn. Forschungen zur Religion und Literatur des Alten und Neuen Testaments 87. Göttingen: Vandenhoeck & Ruprecht (1st edn 1965).

————(1967a), 'Erwägungen zum ontologischen Charakter der KAINE KTISIS bei Paulus. *Evangelische Theologie* 27: 1–35.

————(1967b), 'Erwägungen zum Problem von Gegenwart und Zukunft in der paulinischen Eschatologie'. *Zeitschrift für Theologie und Kirche* 64: 423–450.

————(1986), *Reconciliation, Law, and Righteousness: Essays in Biblical Theology*. ET Philadelphia: Fortress (German original 1981).

————(1992), *Biblische Theologie des Neuen Testaments: Grundlegung; Von Jesus zu Paulus*. Gottingen: Vandenhoeck & Ruprecht.

————(1994), *Paul's Letter to the Romans: A Commentary*. ET Louisville, KY: Westminster/John Knox (German original 1989).

————(1995), *How to do Biblical Theology*. Princeton Theological Monographs 38. Pittsburg: Pickwick.

Tamez, Elsa (1993), *The Amnesty of Grace: Justification by Faith from a Latin American Perspective*. ET Nashville: Abingdon (Spanish original 1991).

Thielman, Frank (1993), 'The story of Israel and the theology of Romans 5 – 8', in *Society of Biblical Literature 1993 Seminar Papers*, 227–249. Society of Biblical Literature Seminar Papers 32. Atlanta, GA: Scholars.

————(1994), *Paul and the Law: A Contextual Approach*. Downers Grove: IVP.

Thür, Gerhard, & Peter E. Pieler (1978), 'Gerichtsbarkeit', in *Reallexikon für Antike und Christentum* 10:360–491. Stuttgart: Anton Hiersemann.

Tomson, Peter (1990), *Paul and the Jewish Law: Halakha in the Letters of the Apostle to the Gentiles*. Compendia Rerum Iudaicarum ad Novum Testamentum 3.1. Assen and Maastricht: Van Gorcum; Minneapolis: Fortress.

Walker, William O., Jr (1997), 'Translation and Interpretation of *ean mē* in Galatians 2:16'. *Journal of Biblical Literature* 116: 515–520.

Wallis, Ian G. (1995), *The Faith of Jesus Christ in Early Christian Traditions*. Studiorum Novi Testamenti Societas Monograph Series 84. Cambridge: Cambridge University Press.

Webb, William J. (1993), *Returning Home: New Covenant and Second Exodus as the Context for 2 Corinthians 6.14 – 7.1. Journal for the Study of the New Testament* Supplements 85. Sheffield: JSOT.

Westerholm, Stephen (1988), *Israel's Law and the Church's Faith: Paul and his Recent Interpreters*. Grand Rapids: Eerdmans.

————(1997), *Preface to the Study of Paul*. Grand Rapids: Eerdmans.

Williams, Sam K. (1987), 'Again *Pistis Christou*'. *Catholic Biblical Quarterly* 49: 431–447.

Winger, Michael (1992), *By What Law? The Meaning of Nomos in the Letters of Paul*. Society of Biblical Literature Dissertation Series 128. Atlanta, GA: Scholars.

Wright, N. T. (1992), *The New Testament and the People of God*. Christian Origins and the Question of God 1. Minneapolis: Fortress.

————(1996a), 'The law in Romans 2', in James D. G. Dunn (ed.), *Paul and the Mosaic Law*, 131–150. Wissenschaftliche Untersuchungen zum Neuen Testament 89. Tübingen, Mohr (Siebeck).

————(1996b), *Jesus and the Victory of God*. Christian Origins and the Question of God 2. Minneapolis: Fortress.

————(1997), *What Saint Paul Really Said*. Oxford: Lion; Grand Rapids: Eerdmans.

Zahl, Paul Francis Matthew (1996), *Die Rechtfertigungslehre Ernst Käsemanns*. Calwer Theologische Monographien 13. Stuttgart: Calwer.

Zimmerli, Walther (1976), 'Alttestamentliche Prophetie und Apokalyptik auf dem Wege zur "Rechtfertigung des Gottlosen"', in J. Friedrich, W. Pöhlmann, & P. Stuhlmacher (eds.), *Rechtfertigung: Festschrift für Ernst Käsemann zum 70. Geburtstag*, 575–592. Tübingen: Mohr (Siebeck).

Index of authors

Assmann, J., 40
Avemarie, F., 13–16, 21

Badenas, R., 121
Banks, R., 119
Bassler, J., 53
Beker, J., 93
Bell, R., 163
Bellah, R., 50
Blocher, H., 70
Bockmuehl, M., 37
Bonhoeffer, D., 50, 127
Bovati, P., 43
Brecht, M., 14
Bultmann, R., 19, 104, 137

Calvin, J., 173
Campbell, R., 37
Carson, D. A., 39, 177
Clifford, A., 175
Corley, B., 19
Cranfield, C., 61, 96, 120
Cremer, H., 39, 41, 45

Dantine, W., 176
Denney, J., 178
Dodd, C., 96
Donaldson, T., 18, 20–21, 151, 165
Drane, J., 95
Dunn, J., 14, 18, 20–21, 24, 37–38, 71, 100, 104, 106, 134, 146

Eaton, M., 124

Eckstein, J., 54, 97, 106–107, 108
Emser, J., 98

Feldman, L., 23
Fitzmyer, J., 46, 70
Forde, G., 184
Fredriksen, P., 26
Fuller, D., 95–96, 120
Furnish, V., 98

Gaffin, R., 176
Garland, D., 88
Garlington, D., 102, 135–136
Gaston, L., 100
Gese, H., 126

Hafemann, S., 110–113, 159
Harrisville, R., 146
Hays, R., 46, 68, 98, 107, 110, 114, 139–140, 143–145
Hengel, M., 13
Herntrich, V., 159–160
Herold, G., 47–49
Hill, C., 29
Hofius, O., 158
Hübner, H., 95
Hultgren, A., 145–146

Iwand, H., 117, 120, 124

Jervis, A., 36

Käsemann, E. 72, 84, 98, 114, 135, 137, 143, 167, 171–173

Keck, L., 142
Kim, S., 13, 28
Koch, D.-A., 124
Kutsch, E., 111

Laato, T., 17, 95, 102, 179, 180–181
Levin, C., 40, 158
Longenecker, B., 135
Longenecker, R. N., 13
Lull, T., 76
Luther, M., 14, 46, 76, 98, 117, 125, 173–174, 179, 183–184, 186

McGrath, A., 174, 176, 183
Marshall, I., 92
Melanchthon, P., 90
Moo, D., 38, 66, 71, 96–97, 100, 134
Müller, C., 59
Munck, J., 165

Neusner, J., 24

O'Callaghan, P., 185
Owen, J., 175

Peterson, D., 84, 179
Pieler, P., 59
Piper, J., 45

von Rad, G., 66
Räisänen, H., 95
Reumann, J., 39, 77
Reventlow, H., 39, 158
Ritschl, A., 145
de Roche, M., 43
Rupp, G., 14
Rüterswörden, U., 135

Sanders, E. P., 14–18, 102
Sänger, D., 151
Sass, G., 69, 80
Schäfer, R., 145
Schlatter, A., 37, 39, 46, 48, 73, 135–136, 171–172
Schmid, H., 40–41, 45
Schmidt, W., 158
Schmitt, R., 167
Schneider, G., 135
Schreiner, T., 100–101, 124
Schrenk G., 159–160
Schwemer, A.-M., 13
Seifrid, M., 13, 16, 21, 35, 39, 48, 61, 116, 121, 172–173, 183
Silva, M., 96
Steck, O., 23
Steinmetz, D., 14
Stendahl, K., 14
Stuhlmacher, P., 39, 66, 97, 108, 126, 171–173, 177

Tamez, E., 173
Thielman, F., 22, 25, 70
Thür, G., 59
Tomson, P., 126

Walker, W., 106
Wallis, I., 140
Webb, W., 168
Wesley, J., 175
Westerholm, S., 39, 95–96, 98, 100
Williams, S., 145
Winger, M., 96
Wright, N. T., 22, 25, 39, 59, 159, 176

Zahl, P., 143, 173
Zahn, T., 70
Zimmerli, W., 158

Index of subjects

Abraham, 20–21, 23, 26, 38,
40, 55, 67–69, 70, 72, 79–
81, 83, 90, 100, 104, 107–
108, 109, 111, 114, 130–
131, 136–137, 144, 146–
147, 151–153, 162, 164–
166, 174, 177, 180–183
Adam, 50, 62, 70–71, 76, 116,
118, 133, 136, 144, 151
atonement, 15–16, 31, 66–67,
102, 134, 141, 160

blamelessness, 13, 25, 27
blessing, 20, 53, 68–69, 80–
81, 83–84, 88, 96, 105,
107, 111, 117, 131, 142,
144, 153–154, 182
boasting, 13, 67–70, 76, 85–
86, 91–93, 100, 103–104,
133, 150, 156, 162, 182
body, 51, 69, 72–73, 79, 81,
83, 96–97, 101, 115, 118,
125–126, 137–138, 141,
153, 172, 179–181, 185
boundary-markers, 18, 100

church, 13, 26–30, 32–33, 35–
36, 84, 93, 114, 130, 149,
161, 163–164, 166–167,
171, 173, 179, 181
circumcision, 13, 18, 20, 26–
27, 55, 58, 63, 68–69, 79,
89, 93, 98–101, 105–106,
122–123, 133, 165
commandment, 55–56, 60, 62–
63, 92, 97–98, 102, 111–
112, 115–119, 121–122,
134, 138, 178
community, 23, 29–30, 33, 50,
102, 104, 151, 168, 173,
176
conscience, 14, 27, 54, 178
covenant, 15–16, 20, 22, 26,
39, 81, 109–113, 136, 143,
159, 166, 169, 176
creation, 18, 21, 28, 39–40,
44–45, 50–51, 67, 69, 74,
77, 81, 86–88, 91–92, 99,
104, 108, 112, 124–126,
131, 133, 143, 149, 152,
161, 163, 165, 172, 182,
184–185
Creator, 17, 44, 49–51, 54, 58,
62, 65, 68–69, 83, 87–88,
103, 123, 154, 155–156,
159–160, 167, 169, 183,
185–186
creature, 49–51, 54, 58, 155,
185
cross, 18–22, 31, 38, 49, 52,
61, 63–66, 72, 76, 84–85,
91, 104, 107, 118, 120,
123, 125, 127, 131–132,
134, 136, 140–141, 143,
145–147, 167–169, 173,
175–176, 178, 182–183,
185
crucifixion, 17, 29–33, 46–47,
65–67, 71–73, 75–76, 78,
82–83, 85–86, 123–125,

130–132, 136, 142, 156,
158, 162–163, 167, 169,
173, 175, 182, 184–185
curse, 20, 22–23, 30, 80–81,
96, 101–102, 105, 107–
108, 122, 157, 161

dead, 28, 46–47, 65, 68–71,
73–77, 82–83, 86, 90, 92,
99, 119–120, 123, 125–
126, 137, 144, 146, 149,
152–153, 165–166, 174–
175, 179, 184–185
death, 22, 30–31, 33, 46–49,
51, 62–63, 65–66, 70–75,
77–80, 83, 86–87, 90, 92,
95–97, 106–107, 109, 112–
123, 125–126, 131, 134,
137–138, 140, 142–144,
151, 156, 158, 172–173,
175, 182, 184–185
demand, 16–17, 26, 33, 37–38,
46, 56, 71, 97, 100–103,
105, 120, 123, 135–136,
138, 146, 148, 175, 186

election, 14–17, 26, 105, 151–
154, 158, 161–162, 164–
165
Elijah, 57, 157, 160–162, 167
eschatology, 20, 46, 55, 70,
72, 74, 78, 81, 82, 84, 92,
118, 139, 143, 159, 165,
167–168, 173, 180
ethics, 19, 21, 33, 75, 91, 138,
149
ethnicity, 18–20, 26–27, 50–
52, 55, 64, 67–68, 85, 99–
100, 106, 163, 165
exile, 18, 21–25, 57, 85–86,
122, 157–159, 168–169
existential, 19–21, 33

faith of Christ, 64, 82, 90,
106–107, 139–143, 145–
146
flesh, fleshly, 13, 28, 33, 55,
60, 68, 73, 82–83, 85, 89,
91, 99, 103, 109, 110, 111,
114–115, 117, 119, 123–
125, 132–133, 138–139,
153–154, 162, 164–166,
178
forgiveness, 15–16, 31, 65, 68,
73, 92–93, 129, 141, 174–
178
fulfilment, 14, 17, 21, 23, 35,
37–38, 47, 50, 55, 63, 66–
70, 74, 79–81, 83, 87, 107–
109, 118–121, 124–126,
131, 135, 137–138, 141,
145, 147, 149, 151–153,
156–159, 165–168, 174–
175, 177, 180, 182, 184

Gentiles (nations), 16–18, 20,
22, 28, 35–39, 45–46, 48–
49, 50–56, 58–59, 61, 64,
67–70, 76, 78–81, 84–85,
89, 91–93, 100, 104, 106–
107, 120, 122, 125, 131–
132, 135–136, 151–157,
162–169
glory, 18, 24, 28, 31, 33, 45,
49, 64, 66, 70, 75–76, 81,
89, 91, 101, 108, 112–114,
123–124, 131–132, 137,
140–141, 149, 153, 155,
167, 174, 178–179, 184
gospel, 13, 20, 22, 28, 31, 35–
38, 45–48, 50–52, 55–57,
62, 68, 73, 78–80, 82, 84,
88, 91–93, 96–98, 104,
109–114, 120–121, 124,
126–127, 129–135, 143–

146, 148, 151–163, 165–
168, 173, 177–178, 184–
186

grace, 14, 18, 23, 28, 32, 36,
57, 64–65, 70, 72, 87–88,
91–92, 95, 99–100, 105,
114–115, 120, 125, 137,
139, 147, 161–162, 167,
173–175, 186

guilt, 14–15, 18, 22–23, 25,
27, 33, 42–43, 60–63, 66,
105, 109, 115, 119–120,
127, 136, 159–160, 169

heart, 21, 27–28, 32, 42, 51–
55, 60, 62, 74, 98–99, 101,
103–104, 110–111, 118,
122–123, 131, 133–134,
177, 185–186

holiness (and sanctification),
13, 38–39, 78, 84–85, 88,
91, 95, 100, 117, 121, 131–
132, 136, 147–148, 156,
159, 165, 174, 178–179

hope, 13, 21, 29, 39, 41, 46,
67, 69–70, 72, 75, 77–78,
82–83, 90–91, 104, 124,
126, 137–139, 149–150,
152–153, 159–160, 163–
166, 174–175, 177, 183,
185

idolatry, 48–51, 54, 56, 58, 60,
64, 100, 111, 118, 137,
160–162, 167, 171

imperative, 37, 73, 136–138,
179

individual, 20, 50, 64, 70, 97,
101, 115, 176, 177

individualism, 50

Israel, 13–18, 20, 22–30, 33,
35, 38–41, 46–47, 50, 52,

55–58, 60, 63, 68–70, 85,
93, 96, 98, 100, 106, 112–
114, 120–123, 131, 151–
169, 177

Jerusalem, 16, 22–25, 29, 35,
79, 81, 87, 88, 109, 134–
135, 159–160, 164

Jesus, 13, 20, 22, 25, 28–33,
36–37, 43, 50, 59, 63–71,
73–75, 77, 81, 83–88, 90–
92, 97, 99, 102–103, 109,
117–118, 123–125, 130–
146, 156, 163–164, 168–
169, 173–174, 177–178

Judaism, 13–22, 26–29, 39,
102, 117, 126, 135–136,
173

Judaizing, 89, 93, 106, 109,
130, 148

judgment, 15, 17, 21, 25, 29–
30, 39–62, 66, 69–70, 74,
77, 81, 84–85, 90–91, 97,
101, 104, 106, 112, 114,
119, 122, 124, 129, 133,
135–136, 138, 147–149,
152, 154–171, 175–178,
180–186

legalism, 89, 96

life, 13–16, 19, 25–27, 37–38,
46–48, 51, 63, 67, 70–78,
81, 83, 86–87, 89, 91–92,
96–99, 101–102, 105–108,
112–125, 129, 137, 139,
142–143, 147, 149, 151–
152, 156, 166, 171–174,
176, 178, 184–185

love, 13, 33, 38, 60, 70, 75–
76, 91, 102–104, 110, 117,
122, 125, 132, 134, 138–
139, 142, 149–150, 164,

175, 178, 183, 185

mercy, 15, 17, 23, 32, 42, 45,
  57–58, 66, 91, 103, 111,
  154–156, 158, 162–169,
  178
morality, 51, 63, 68, 73, 78,
  95, 111, 118, 123, 126,
  143, 185
Moses, 17, 21, 28–29, 54–55,
  96–100, 109, 112–114,
  121–123, 134, 154, 157,
  163, 178
mystery, 37, 73, 91, 166, 168

nation, 13, 17–18, 22–23, 25–
  26, 29, 33, 122, 152–153,
  155, 157–169
nationalism, 17–18, 20–21,
  25–26, 33, 40, 53, 85, 96,
  99–104, 135–136
nature, 51, 53, 106, 112, 119,
  125, 129, 133, 135–136,
  138, 164–165, 173
new creation, 18, 21, 28, 45,
  74, 77, 81, 86–88, 91–92,
  99, 104, 112, 125–126,
  131, 133, 149, 161, 165,
  172, 184

obedience, 14–17, 21, 26–27,
  29, 33, 36–38, 53–56, 63,
  69–75, 78, 80, 83, 90, 92,
  95–96, 98–108, 111, 118–
  125, 129, 132–148, 156,
  173–176, 182, 184–185
obedience of faith, 36–37, 125,
  129, 132–136, 174

piety, 13, 16–18, 20, 23, 26,
  33, 79, 89–91, 102, 117,
  186

promise, 14, 16–18, 20–22,
  37–39, 41, 46–47, 50, 53,
  55–56, 66–71, 74, 79–83,
  86–87, 93, 98, 105, 107–
  111, 114, 121–122, 130–
  131, 133, 135, 137, 141–
  147, 151–159, 162–168,
  176–177, 181, 184
prophet, 29, 57, 157, 159–160,
  162–163
prophetic, 20, 29, 38, 45–46,
  95, 111, 121, 156–157,
  159–160, 168, 180

recompense, 14–15, 50, 90,
  97, 101, 149, 174
reconciliation, 70, 79, 153,
  175–176
redemption, 24, 64–65, 69–70,
  79, 85, 87–88, 108, 119,
  131, 134, 142, 144, 153,
  158, 174
remnant, 23, 57, 100, 157–
  165, 168–169
repentance, 14–15, 29, 65
resurrection, 17, 21–22, 31,
  38, 46–47, 64–65, 67, 69–
  77, 81–92, 107, 109, 114,
  119–120, 123, 125–126,
  130–134, 137–138, 141–
  153, 165–168, 172–178,
  182–183, 185
revelation, 17, 28, 31, 36–37,
  45–53, 57–58, 62–63, 66,
  69, 97, 121–122, 140–142,
  145–146, 171, 177
righteousness, 13, 21, 26–27,
  29, 35–52, 55, 58, 60–61,
  63–77, 79, 80, 82–83, 85–
  91, 93, 95, 97–100, 103–
  106, 112, 120–125, 130–
  131, 134, 136–137, 139,

143, 145–147, 151, 153–
154, 156, 162–163, 169,
171–179, 182–186
ruling and judging, 40–41, 44,
143, 172

sacrifice, 16, 103, 134, 141,
143, 180–181
salvation, 13–21, 26–27, 29,
35–39, 42, 44–48, 53, 56–
57, 71, 78–80, 84–87, 90,
92, 101, 105, 109, 111,
120, 123–124, 126, 129,
131, 133–136, 140–141,
143, 145–149, 152, 154,
159, 161–169, 172, 174–
177, 179, 181–183, 185
Scripture, 31, 37–38, 46, 57,
59–60, 68, 80, 85, 97, 108–
109, 114, 121, 124, 131,
152, 157, 166, 180
Servant (of God), 31, 42, 47,
75, 87, 106
sin, 14, 17, 21–23, 27, 31, 33,
47, 51, 53, 56–65, 70, 72–
74, 77, 81, 83, 86–88, 95–
97, 99, 103, 105–111, 114–
119, 124–126, 134, 136–
138, 141–142, 147, 149,
151, 153, 156, 167, 172–
175, 178, 184–186
Sinai, 16, 81, 109–113, 126,
137

Spirit, 20, 38, 55, 72, 79, 81,
82, 86, 91, 96–99, 104,
107, 109–110, 112–116,
121, 124–126, 131–133,
136, 138, 147, 149, 152–
153, 172–173, 175–176,
178, 180–181, 185–186

ungodly (godless, sinner), 13,
29, 31, 33, 37, 47–49, 66–
69, 82, 91, 100, 106, 129,
137, 141,144, 147, 151,
158–161, 163, 165–168,
171–172, 176, 178, 181–
182, 185

works, 15, 18–21, 28, 42, 46,
54, 60–61, 63, 67–69, 76,
80, 82, 87, 91–92, 97–106,
118, 120, 123–125, 129,
132–133, 135–136, 139,
142, 146–149, 153–156,
160–162, 179–185
wrath, 42, 45, 48–49, 51–52,
58–59, 61, 63, 65–66, 70,
77–78, 92, 114–115, 120,
148, 155, 162, 171, 174,
184

Zion, 20, 121, 126, 131, 158,
166, 168

Index of Bible references

Old Testament

Genesis
1:3, *131*
2:24, *115*
2:24 (LXX), *160*
3, *118*
3:4, *116*
3:13, *116*
4:1, *62*
7:23, *159*
12:3, *80*
15:1–6, *137*
15:6, *68–69, 80, 174, 180, 182*
15, *111*
21, *109*
21:12, *154*
22:18, *80*
25:23, *154*
32:27–28, *166*
39:9, *42*
41:40 (LXX), *135*
45:7, *159*

Exodus
9:27, *43, 66*
14:4, *45, 155*
14:8, *155*
14:17, *155*
20:18–21, *112*
25:17–22, *66*
33:19, *154*
34:29–35, *112–*
114

Leviticus
12:3, *55*
16:1–34, *66*
18:5, *98, 120–121, 148*
18 – 20, *126*

Numbers
16:19, *45*
24:4 (LXX), *56*
24:16 (LXX), *56*

Deuteronomy
4:1–2, *102*
4:7–8, *122*
4:8, *44*
4:28, *162*
4:31, *164*
5:22–27, *112*
5:28–33, *112*
5:29, *102, 122*
6:1–5, *102*
6:13, *102*
6:18, *122*
6:24, *102, 122*
7:6, *159*
8:6, *102*
8:17, *122*
8:20, *102*
9:4–5, *44*
9:4–7, *122*
9:4, *122, 134*
9:6, *158*

10:12, *102*
10:16, *55, 99*
13:4, *102*
13:18, *102*
17:19, *102*
21:23, *29, 80*
23:15–16, *126*
26:5–9, *24*
26:16–17, *102*
27:1 – 28:68, *122*
27:26, *80, 102*
28:36, *162*
28:58, *102*
28 – 30, *22*
28 – 32, *24*
29:4, *122, 158, 161*
29:25, *111*
30:1–6, *122*
30:4–10, *102*
30:6, *55, 99, 133*
30:11–14, *121–122*
31:6, *164*
31:8, *164*
31:12–13, *102*
31:24–29, *158*
32:4–5, *43*
32:21, *157, 163*
33:2, *108*

Joshua
2:8–14, *179*
7:19–21, *66*
22:5, *102*

Judges
2:16–23, *40*
5:11, *40*
6:7–10, *102*

1 Samuel
2:25, *42*
12:22, *158, 164*
14:47, *41*

2 Samuel
8:15, *41*
12:13, *42*

1 Kings
8:9, *111*
8:21, *111*
10:9, *41*
17:1, *167*
19:1–21, *157*
19:15–18, *161*

2 Kings
10:9, *43*
18:11–12, *102*
19:4, *159*
19:30–31, *159*

2 Chronicles
12:1–6, *66*
12:6, *43*
5:10, *111*

Ezra
9:8, *159*
9:15, *43*

Nehemiah
9:8, *43*
9:33, *43, 66*

Job
5:16, *61*
10:2, *41*

Psalms
5:11–12, *103*
5:12, *186*
7:1–17, *43*
7:3–5, *45*
7:10, *43*
7:12, *43*
9:1–20, *40*
9:4, *39*
11:1–7, *45*
11:5–7, *43*
14:1–2, *60*
14:1–3, *60*
14:7, *166, 168*
20:7, *104*
22:31, *39*
24:5, *39, 41*
31:1, *39*
31:1–2, *68*
34:1–3, *103*
35:24, *39*
36:6–7, *39*
37:33, *41*
40:9–10, *39*
44:4–8, *103*
44:6, *104*
44:11 (LXX), *75*
49:5–6, *104*
50:1–23, *45*
50:6, *43*
51, *42*
51:4, *43*
51:4b, *58*
51:6, *60*
51:10, *42*
51:14, *39, 42*
53:2–4, *60*
63:11, *61*
68:17, *108*
68:23–24
   (Hebrew
   69:23–24),
   157
69:22–23, *157*
69:23–24, *161*
69:27–28, *39*
71:15, *39*
71:16, *39*
71:19, *39*
71:24, *39*
72:1–3, *39, 41*
88:12, *39*
89:5–14, *40*
89:5–18, *43*
89:15–17, *39*
94:12–15, *164*
94:14, *158*
96, *40*
97:1–6, *45*
97:1–12, *40*
97:6, *39*
97:7, *104*
98, *64*
98, *40, 44–45*
98:1–3, *38*
98:2, *39*
98:6, *39*
98:7–9, *40*
98, *64*
99:4, *39*
103:6, *39–40*
107:42, *61*
112:9, *87*
116:5, *39*
116:11, *57–58*
118:19–21, *39*
119:123, *39*
119:140, *39*
129:4, *39*
143:1, *39*

143:1–3a, *42*
143:11, *39*
145:7, *39*

Proverbs
12:2, *41*
13:6, *44*
31:8–9, *41*

Isaiah
1:1–4, *158*
1:8–9, *159*
1:9, *157–158*
1:10–26, *41*
1:17, *43*
1:24–28, *45*
1:27, *43*
2:1–4, *20, 165*
4:2–6, *159*
4:11–12 (LXX),
  160
4:13–15, *43*
5:1–30, *45*
5:24 (LXX), *56*
6:5, *158, 160*
6:6–13, *160*
6:9–13, *158*
6:11–12, *158*
6:12–13 (LXX),
  160
6:13, *159*
7:9, *159*
8:16–18, *159–
  160*
9:1–6, *41*
9:1–21, *45*
9:7, *39*
9:17, *44*
10:20–23, *159*
10:20–27, *159*
10:22, *43, 157–
  158, 162–163*

11:3–5, *43*
11:4, *39*
11:11–16, *159*
15:1, *160*
17:6, *165*
27:9, *166*
28:13 (LXX), *56*
28:16, *121, 159*
28:16–17, *159*
28:17, *43*
28:22, *157*
29:10, *158, 161*
29:14, *85*
29:15–16, *155*
30:27 (LXX), *56*
32:16, *39*
33:5, *39*
40 – 48, *58*
40 – 66, *58, 75*
40:1–31, *47*
40:5, *45*
41:10, *39*
41:21–29, *45*
41:25–29, *47*
41:26, *66*
41:26 (LXX), *58*
42:3 (LXX), *58*
42:8, *45*
42:10–13, *40*
42:21, *39*
43:6–11, *86*
43:9–10, *58*
43:14–21, *86*
44:26 (LXX), *58*
45:7, *154*
45:8, *39*
45:9, *155*
45:18–25, *45*
45:19 (LXX), *58*
45:21, *39*
45:23, *39, 59*
45:24, *39*

46:13, *39*
48:1–12, *45*
48:18, *39*
49:1, *28*
49:7–9, *75*
49:8, *87*
49:13, *40*
50:1, *60*
50:9, *41*
50:20, *160*
51:1–23, *45*
51:4–8, *39, 86*
51:4–11, *40*
51:5, *39*
51:6, *39, 43–44*
51:8, *39*
52:5, *169*
52:7, *157*
53:1, *157*
53:11, *31*
54:1–17, *75*
54:7–8, *164*
54:14, *39*
54:17, *39*
55:10, *87*
55:11, *87*
56:1, *39*
58:1–14, *41*
58:8, *39*
59:9, *39*
59:16–17, *39*
59:20, *166, 168*
60:17, *39*
61:1–4, *47*
61:10–11, *39*
62:1, *39*
63:1, *39*
64:7, *155*
65:1, *164*
65:1–2, *157, 163*
65:2, *158, 163*
65:17–25, *86*

Jeremiah
1:4–12, 28, *111*
1:5, *28*
4:4, 55, 99, *111*
5:1, *158*
6:9, *159*
6:10, *158*
6:13, *158*
7:22–23, *111*
7:23, *111*
9:22, *85*
9:23, *85–86*
9:23–24, *40, 103*
9:25–26, *55*
11:1–8, *102*
11:16, *165*
13:23, *158*
16:1–21, *158*
16:13, *162*
17:1, *110*
17:1–2, *158*
18:1–6, *155*
22:3, *41*
23:1–8, *159*
23:5–6, *41*
31:31–34, *53,
    110–111*
31:32, 111
31:33, *133*
31:33–34, *166,
    168*
31:37, *158*
38:32 (LXX), *102*

Lamentations
1:18, *43, 66*

Ezekiel
2:3–7, *158*
5:6, *44*
9:1–11, *160*
11:13–21, *159*

36:20, *169*
36:26, *110, 133*
37:1–14, *166*

Daniel
5:28, *157*
6:13 (LXX), *92*
9:4, *102*
9:7, *43*
9:9–14, *102*
9:14, *43*
9:16, 43, *66*

Hosea
1:6–10, *158*
1:10, *163*
1:10 (Hebrew
    2:1), 157, 162
2:14–23, *159*
5:4, *158*
14:5–7, *165*

Amos
5:1–27, *41*
8:2, *158*
9:11–15, *159*
9:11–15, *165*

Micah
2:13–13, *159*
4:1–4, *165*
4:1–5, *20*
4:6–7, *159*
5:7, *159*
7:18, *160*

Habbakuk
2:1–3, *160*
2:1–4, *38*
2:4, 37, *46–48,
    80, 160*
2:5–20, *38*

3:17, *165*

Zephaniah
1:1–6, *158*

Malachi
1:2–3, *154*
1:4, *44*

New Testament

Matthew
3:9, *26*
5 – 7, *177*
5:25–26, *59*
6:33, *177*
7:1–5, *52*
10:5–6, *20*
11:20–24, *177*
15:1–20, *103*
15:24, *20*
16:22, *30*
19:16–22, *103*
23:23, *103*

Mark
1:14–15, *133*
1:27, *135*
2:5, *129*
5:34–36, *129*
6:4–6, *129*
6:6, *56*
7:1–23, *103*
7:24–30, *20*
9:23, *129*
9:24, *56*
10:17–22, *103*
10:52, *129*
11:22–24, *129*
12:28–31, *102*

Luke
1:51–53, *177*
3:9, *26*
7:29, *43*
12:57–59, *59*
15:21, *42*
18:1–8, *178*
18:9–14, *178*
18:18–23, *103*

John
1:12, *129*
3:15–16, *129*
3:16, *178*
3:19, *178*
3:36, *129, 134*
5:24, *129*
5:24–29, *178*
6:29, *133, 178*
6:35, *129*
6:40, *178*
6:51, *178*
7:18, *178*
7:24, *178*
9:39–41, *131*
11:25, *178*
12:31, *178*
13:34–35, *178*
16:8–9, *178*
16:10, *178*

Acts
2:24–36, *130*
2:36, *29*
2:38, *134*
2:44, *134*
3:14, *31*
3:16, *129*
3:22–26, *29*
4:12, *29*
4:33, *130*
5:31, *130*

5:39, *32*
6:7, *134*
6:11, *29*
6:14, *29*
7:38, *56*
7:48–53, *29*
7:52, *30–31*
7:53, *108*
7:54 – 8:1, *30*
7:56, *30*
9:1, 30
9:1–2, *30*
9:1–19, *25*
9:8–19, *30*
9:17, *31*
11:17, *129*
13:37–39, *178*
13:39, *129*
13:48, *129*
14:22, *129*
15:9–11, *129*
15:16–18, *159*
16:31–34, *129*
16:31, *134*
17:5–10, *79*
18:12–17, *59*
18:18, *20*
21:15–26, *20*
22:1–21, *25*
22:4, *30*
22:5, *30*
22:11–13, *30*
22:12–16, *31*
22:14, *31*
22:17, *31*
23:12–16, *30*
26:1–23, *25*
26:9, 30, 32
26:10, *30*
26:14, *31*
26:18, *129*

Romans
1, *50– 51, 54, 58,
60*
1 – 3, *59, 111,
151, 165*
1:1–4, *47, 57,
160–161*
1:1–17, *36, 163,
165*
1:4, *172*
1:5, 37, *130, 135*
1:5–6, *36*
1:8, *130, 132,
151*
1:12, *130, 164–
165*
1:14–15, *36*
1:15, *126, 154,
157, 161*
1:16, *46, 51, 92,
100, 105, 151,
165*
1:16–17, *36–37,
48–49, 131*
1:17, *37, 45, 47–
48, 64–65, 71,
98, 147, 154,
160, 162, 172*
1:18, *48–49, 58,
61, 158, 161,
171*
1:18–32, *48, 50*
1:18 – 3:20, *48,
66, 119*
1:18 – 3:26, *48*
1:19, 50, *157*
1:19–25, *125*
1:20, *49–50*
1:20 – 3:20, *49*
1:21, *51*
1:22, *49–50*
1:23, *49, 64, 137*

Romans (cont.)
1:24, *118*
1:24–25, *49*
1:24–32, *82*
1:25, *58*
1:26, *118*
1:26–27, *49*
1:28, *118*
1:28–29, *49*
1:28–32, *54*
1:29, *171*
1:32, *49, 51, 96,*
97, 119, 171
1 – 3, *111*
1 – 8, *152*
2, *49, 60*
2:1, *49*
2:1–11, *51*
2:1–16, *51–52*
2:1 – 3:20, *127*
2:2, *52, 62*
2:4, *65*
2:5, *49, 52, 171*
2:5–6, *52*
2:6, *47, 52, 101*
2:6–16, *71*
2:7, *46*
2:7–8, *101, 149*
2:8, *52, 171*
2:8–11, *50*
2:9–10, *49, 151*
2:9–11, *51–52*
2:11, *53*
2:12, *52–53, 96*
2:12–13, *114*
2:12–16, *52, 61,*
149
2:13, *53, 171*
2:14, *51–53, 96*
2:14–16, *100,*
125
2:15, *51, 53–56*

2:15–16, *54*
2:16, *47, 50, 54,*
101, 148
2:17, *96*
2:17–19, *17*
2:17–24, *64, 100*
2:17–29, *27, 50,*
53–56, 60–61,
104, 135
2:17 – 3:20, *60*
2:18–20, *53*
2:22, *50*
2:24, *169*
2:25, *55*
2:25–28, *20*
2:25–29, *20*
2:26, *55, 97–98,*
125
2:26–28, *55*
2:27, *52, 54, 96,*
98, 101
2:27–29, *101*
2:28–29, *55, 99,*
105
2:29, *54, 133*
3, *49, 56, 67*
3:1–2, *56, 151*
3:1–18, *56*
3:2, *56–57*
3:3, *57–58, 142*
3:4, *56–60, 151*
3:4–7, *58*
3:5, *59, 65*
3:5–6, *47, 58*
3:5–8, *58, 118,*
154
3:6, *58, 84*
3:7, *58*
3:7–8, *58*
3:9, *17, 27, 59,*
65, 151
3:9–18, *125*

3:10–18, *56, 59*
3:11, *60*
3:13–18, *60*
3:19, *62, 96, 98,*
115
3:19–20, *60, 62,*
99, 108, 115
3:20, *100, 103,*
105, 115–116,
143
3:20–22, *99*
3:20–26, *21*
3:21, *37, 61, 63–*
64–65, 95,
120, 125, 135
3:21–16, *118*
3:21–22, *145,*
172
3:21–26, *31, 61,*
63, 133, 143
3:22, *63–64, 139,*
142–143, 145,
176
3:22–24, *64*
3:22b–25a, *64*
3:23, *45, 64, 137*
3:24, *64, 134,*
174
3:24–25a, *65*
3:24–25, *71*
3:24–26a, *64*
3:25, *64–66, 92,*
134, 145, 176
3:25–26a, *65*
3:26, *63–64, 66,*
139, 142–143,
145, 147
3:27, *97–98, 100,*
105, 135
3:27–28, *68, 100,*
103, 105, 133
3:27–30, *100*

Romans (cont.)

3:27–31, *21, 67–
68*

3:27 – 4:25, *105*

3:27 – 5:21, *114*

3:27 – 8:39, *61, 67*

3:28, *54, 100,
147–148*

3:28–29, *67*

3:29–30, *68*

3:30, *147*

3:31, *68, 95, 124*

4, *55, 67–69, 90,
100, 107*

4:1, *68*

4:1–8, *67, 70,
100, 137*

4:1–12, *67*

4:1 – 5:21, *74*

4:1–8, *68, 100*

4:2, *68, 100–101,
104*

4:3, *137, 174*

4:4, *92*

4:5, *68, 144–145,
147*

4:6, *100*

4:6–8, *68, 93,
100, 175*

4:9, *147*

4:9–12, *20, 68–
69, 79, 100*

4:10–12, *20*

4:11, *55, 147*

4:12, *68, 69, 80,
136*

4:12–25, *136*

4:13, *69, 147*

4:13–15, *64, 108,
156*

4:13–16, *100*

4:13–17, *68, 114*

4:13–25, *21, 67,
68*

4:14, *20–21*

4:15, *63, 115,
120, 122, 136*

4:16, *106, 147,
151*

4:16–17, *146*

4:17, *68, 137,
152*

4:17–19, *69*

4:19, *137*

4:20, *56, 137*

4:20–21, *130*

4:23, *137*

4:23–25, *69*

4:24, *146*

4:24–25, *152*

4:25, *31, 47, 144,
165, 174–175*

5, *50, 67, 70, 74,
79*

5:1, *131, 147*

5:1–2, *70*

5:1–11, *67, 104,
150, 172*

5:2, *45, 147, 153*

5:3, *70, 104*

5:4–5, *70*

5:5–8, *70*

5:8, *59*

5:8–9, *71*

5:9, *131, 134,
142, 148*

5:9–10, *70*

5:12b, *70*

5:12–21, *67, 70,
144, 151*

5:13, *70*

5:14, *63, 116*

5:15, *91, 116,
144*

5:16, *71, 97*

5:17, *21, 69, 71,
116, 174*

5:17–18, *71*

5:18, *46, 70, 71,
97, 174*

5:18–19, *142*

5:19, *63, 71, 142,
172*

5:20, *63, 114,
116, 118*

5:21, *46, 71*

6, *67, 72–74, 83,
115, 137, 173*

6:1–11, *131*

6:1–14, *72–73*

6:1 – 8:39, *74*

6:4, *45, 70, 72,
82, 153*

6:4–5, *72*

6:6, *72*

6:7, *72*

6:8, *72, 82*

6:10, *142*

6:11, *73–74, 125*

6:11–13, *137*

6:12, *74, 135*

6:12–13, *126*

6:13, *73–74*

6:14, *95, 115*

6:15–23, *72*

6:16, *74, 135*

6:17, *38, 134*

6:17–18, *73, 131*

6:17–23, *65*

6:18, *74*

6:19, *73–74*

6:20, *74*

6:21, *121*

6:22–23, *46*

6:23, *73*

6:23 – 7:1, *115*

Romans (cont.)

7, *67, 115, 119,
    136, 156, 173,
184, 118*
7:1–3, *96*
7:1–6, *95, 107*
7:1–25, *67, 115*
7:1 – 8:*11, 114*
7:2, *115*
7:3–4, *115*
7:5, *115–116*
7:6, *95, 98–99,
    115–116*
7:7, *62, 115–116*
7:7–13, *97, 101,
    116–118*
7:7–25, *25, 62–
    63, 115*
7:8, *116, 118*
7:8–13, *97*
7:9, *92, 119*
7:9–10, *96, 116*
7:9–13, *96*
7:10, *117–119*
7:11, *116–118*
7:12, *13, 119,
    121*
7:13, *115, 117*
7:14, *60, 62, 110,
    115–117*
7:14–16, *118*
7:14–25, *115–
    116, 150*
7:15, *117*
7:17, *118*
7:17–20, *118*
7:20, *118*
7:21–25, *118*
7:23, *17, 73, 97*
7:24, *118*
7:25, *97, 116–
    117, 124–125*

7:25a, *119*
7:25b, *119*
8, *74–75, 79,
    116, 119, 167*
8:1–2, *119*
8:1–11, *116*
8:2, *96–97*
8:3, *63, 71, 119,
    124, 144*
8:4, *97, 119*
8:6–9, *133*
8:9–11, *72*
8:10, *172, 185*
8:10–11, *119*
8:11, *172*
8:12–13, *72, 125*
8:12–39, *67*
8:13, *125–126,
    133*
8:15, *54*
8:15–23, *69*
8:16, *172*
8:17, *70, 76*
8:17–18, *75*
8:18, *45, 75, 153*
8:21, *70, 153*
8:22, *62*
8:23, *65, 75, 81,
    153*
8:28, *62, 180*
8:28–30, *75*
8:28–39, *76*
8:29, *75, 164*
8:30, *70, 75–76,
    176*
8:31–35, *75*
8:32, *17, 76*
8:34, *75*
8:36, *75*
9:1, *54, 152*
9:1–3, *152, 165*
9:1–5, *13, 166*

9:1–13, *152–153*
9 – 10, *26*
9 – 11, *25, 56–
    58, 67–69,
    151–152, 168*
9:3, *153, 167*
9:4, *45, 56, 96,
    122*
9:4–5, *153*
9:5, *71, 153–154*
9:6, *153*
9:6–9, *55, 165*
9:6–13, *157*
9:7, *154*
9:7–9, *153*
9:8, *153*
9:10–13, *153*
9:11–12, *28*
9:12–13, *154*
9:14–15, *154*
9:14 – 10:21,
    120, 152, 154
9:16, *123, 154–
    156*
9:17, *154–155*
9:18, *155*
9:19, *155*
9:20, *155*
9:20–21, *58*
9:21, *155, 158*
9:22, *65*
9:22–23, *155*
9:23, *45, 153*
9:24, *154, 165*
9:25–26, *57*
9:26, *157*
9:27, *158, 160,
    162, 165, 167,
    169*
9:27–28, *157,
    159*
9:27–29, *157–159*

Romans (cont.)
9:28, *158, 168*
9:29, *57, 157–
158, 160*
9:30, *120*
9:30–33, *21, 26,
56, 64, 156*
9:30 – 10:3, *101*
9:30 – 10:4, *17*
9:30 – 10:13, *120*
9:30 – 10:21, *127*
9:31, *120, 123,
156, 165*
9:32, *100, 120*
9:32–33, *156*
9:33, *121, 131,
147, 158, 168*
10:1, *167*
10:1–2, *152, 165*
10:1–3, *131*
10:2–3, *156*
10:2–4, *121*
10:3, *38, 121,
134*
10:3–4, *156*
10:3–10, *120*
10:4, *47, 121,
147*
10:5, *96–98, 105,
116, 120–122,
126, 156*
10:5–8, *98, 121,
123*
10:6, *122, 134,
147*
10:6–8, *121, 123,
153, 156*
10:9–10, *146–
147*
10:9–13, *121*
10:10, *147*
10:11, *121, 131*

10:14–17, *131,
176*
10:14–21, *156*
10:15–16, *157*
10:16, *134*
10:17, *146–147*
10:19, *157, 163,
165, 168*
10:20, *163*
10:20–21, *157*
10:21, *164–165*
11, *164, 167*
11:1, *168*
11:1–2, *13, 158,
164–165*
11:1–10, *164*
11:1–36, *152,
158*
11:3–4, *160*
11:3–6, *157*
11:4–5, *158–159*
11:5–6, *162*
11:7, *161*
11:7–8, *158*
11:7–9, *168*
11:9–10, *157,
161*
11:11, *163*
11:13, *164*
11:13–24, *167*
11:14, *153, 163,
166*
11:15, *20, 46,
165–166*
11:16, *165*
11:19, *163*
11:19–24, *167*
11:20, *56, 168*
11:20–22, *168*
11:21, *152, 165*
11:23, *56*
11:24, *165*

11:25, *165, 167*
11:25–26, *57*
11:25–36, *20*
11:26, *165–166*
11:27, *166*
11:28, *154, 164,
168*
11:31b, *167*
11:31–32, *167*
11:32, *57–58,
167*
11:33–36, *152*
11:36, *152, 167*
12:1–2, *51, 153*
12:1–3, *36*
12:16, *168*
13:8–10, *100,
125*
13:11, *147*
13:14, *138*
14:10–12, *59, 101*
14:10–13, *51*
14:17, *177*
14:23, *134, 149*
15:7–13, *163–
164*
15:7–21, *166*
15:8, *20, 58*
15:13–16, *36*
15:14–33, *36*
15:14–19, *126*
15:16, *153*
15:17–19, *135*
15:18, *132*
15:25–27, *36*
15:25–29, *164*
15:30–33, *162*
16:25–27, *37,
135*
16:26, *37*
16:27, *135*

1 Corinthians
1:9, *142*
1:18, *131*
1:19, *85, 168*
1:21, *130–132,*
  147
1:21–23, *146*
1:23, 29, *132*
1:24, *85*
1:26–29, *85*
1:26–31, *104*
1:30, *85, 88, 103,*
  174
1:30–31, *85*
1:31, *86, 131*
2:5, *92, 131*
2:6–16, *131*
3:1, *110*
3:5, *132*
3:11, *84*
3:13–15, *101*
3:16–17, *101*
4:2, *90, 142*
4:4–5, *149*
4:5, *52, 101*
4:7, *104*
4:8, *84*
5:7, *138*
6:2, *180*
6:2–3, *52*
6:5, *131*
6:9, *86*
6:11, *86, 88, 172,*
  177
7:18–19, *20*
7:19, *55, 98*
8:1, *62*
8:4, *62*
9:8–14, *98, 126*
9:9, *96*
9:20, *20, 95*
9:20–21, *97*

11:17–34, *110*
11:23–26, *91*
12:13, *132*
13, *125, 139*
13:2, *139*
13:6, *149*
13:13, *139*
14:21, *97*
14:34, *97, 126*
14:37, *98*
15:1–2, *131*
15:1–3, *130*
15:1–11, *131*
15:2, *147*
15:8, *28*
15:8–10, *25*
15:9, *27, 29*
15:10–11, *132*
15:11, *146*
15:14, *92*
15:15, *90*
15:17, *146*
15:45, *133*
15:45–49, *144*
15:56, *73*
16:13, *131*

2 Corinthians
1:20, *121*
1:24, *130–132*
2:12, *146*
2:14–17, *112*
3, *83, 109, 114,*
  121–122
3:1–18, *109, 153*
3:3, *110, 132*
3:6, *112, 126*
3:6–7, *98*
3:7, *112–114*
3:7–8, *113*
3:7–11, *112*
3:7–17, *124*

3:7–18, *123*
3:9, *112*
3:10, *113*
3:11, *113*
3:12–18, *28, 62*
3:13, *113*
3:14, *113–114*
3:14–18, *124*
3:17–18, *114*
3:18, 114
4, *114*
4:1–6, *18, 25*
4:3–6, *131*
4:4, *28*
4:4–6, *28, 114*
4:6, *28, 131*
4:7–18, *112*
4:9, *160*
4:13–14, *146*
5:1, *62*
5:3, *90*
5:4, *70*
5:10, *59, 101,*
  149
5:12, *104*
5:16, *62*
5:16–17, *18*
5:17, *112*
5:19, *144, 176*
5:20, *86*
5:21, *31, 62, 88,*
  174, 176
6:1, *168*
6:1–2, *136*
6:1–13, *112*
6:2, *87*
6:5, *131*
6:14, *87*
6:14 – 7:1, *168*
8:9, *144*
9:6, *88*
9:8, *87*

9:9, *87*
9:10, *87–88*
9:12, *88*
9:14, *88*
9:15, *88*
10:3, *138*
10:8–17, *104*
10:12–18, *104*
10:17, *103*
10:18, *150*
11:10, *146*
12:2, *106*
13:5, *131, 149*

Galatians
1, *25, 28*
1:4, *81, 91, 108,*
    142, 144
1:6–8, *144*
1:8, *108*
1:10 – 2:10, 22
1:12, *31*
1:13, 27
1:13–14, *26, 29*
1:14, *17–18, 27–*
    28, 61, 82,
    108, 117
1:15–16, *28, 31*
1:22, *29*
1:23, *130*
1:23–24, *29*
2, *82*
2:11–12, *79*
2:11–21, *17,* 22
2:15, *82, 107*
2:15–16, *31*
2:15–21, *21,*
    105–106
2:16, 20, *99–100,*
    106, 139,
    142–143,
    145–147

2:16–17, *82*
2:16–21, *130*
2:17, *90*
2:17–19, *106*
2:19, *79, 82, 95–*
    96, 107
2:19b–20, *82,*
    132
2:20, *33, 83, 91,*
    97, 107, 118,
    131, 138,
    143–144, 145,
    184
3:1 – 4:7, *105,*
    107, 121
3:1 – 4:21, *67*
3:1–5, *176*
3:1–14, *100*
3:1 – 4:31, *79*
3:2, *100, 132,*
    147
3:3, *132*
3:5, *100, 106,*
    132, 147
3:6, *80, 174*
3:6–8, *130*
3:6–9, *107*
3:7, *80*
3:8, *80–81, 131,*
    147
3:9, *80, 107*
3:10, *20, 80, 96,*
    100–101, 106,
    108
3:10–14, *21*
3:11, *96, 147*
3:11–12, *80*
3:12, *97–98, 105,*
    116, 120, 136
3:13, *72, 124*
3:13–14, *80*
3:14, *81, 92, 107,*

147
3:15, *81, 103*
3:15–29, *79*
3:16, *69, 81, 83,*
    107
3:17, *96*
3:17–18, *81*
3:18, *81*
3:19, *81, 96,*
    107–108
3:19–29, *82*
3:21, *83, 108*
3:22, *27, 81–82,*
    107–109, 139,
    142–143, 145,
    147
3:22–23, *146*
3:23, *108*
3:23–25, *131*
3:24, *83, 108,*
    147
3:25, *95, 146*
3:26, *134*
3:26–27, *131*
3:26–28, *107*
3:26–29, *81, 153*
3:27–29, *81*
3:28, *83*
3:29, *69, 83, 107*
4:3, *81, 96*
4:4, *71, 144*
4:4–5, *108–109*
4:4–7, *81*
4:5, *95*
4:5–7, *81, 153*
4:6, *132, 172*
4:8–11, *81*
4:19, *83, 97*
4:21, *95, 109*
4:21–31, 22, *81,*
    97, 109, 144,
    153

4:24, *112*
4:25–26, *81*
4:26, *81*
4:28, *165*
4:29, *133, 162*
5:1, *81*
5:2–6, *20*
5:3, *96*
5:4, *83, 174*
5:5, *82, 147, 172*
5:5–6, *185*
5:6, *20, 55, 97, 125, 134, 139*
5:7, *81*
5:13 – 6:10, *89*
5:14, *125, 185*
5:16–18, *125*
5:16–26, *125*
5:17, *126, 132, 184*
5:17–26, *99, 126*
5:18, *97*
5:23, *125*
5:24, *83, 97*
5:25, 22, *81*
6:2, *97, 146*
6:7–10, *81*
6:11–17, *162*
6:15, *20, 55, 81, 83*
6:15–16, *165*
6:16, 22
6:17, *81, 97*

Ephesians
1:6–7, *92*
1:7, *92*
1:13, *145*
1:14, *65, 92*
1:15, *134, 145*
1:19–23, *93*
2:1, *92*

2:2, *92–93*
2:3, *92*
2:6, *82*
2:8, *132, 147*
2:8–10, *91*
2:9, *92–93, 100*
2:10, *92*
2:11–13, *20*
2:11–22, *93*
2:14–18, *92*
2:15, *92, 97*
3:2, *92*
3:12, *139, 142–143, 145, 147*
3:17, *147*
4:30, *65*
4:32, *92*
5:29–33, *115*
5:31, *160*
6:1, *135*
6:1–3, *92*
6:2, *97*
6:5, *135*
6:10–17, *93*

Philippians
1:11, *172*
1:21, *89*
1:25, *130*
1:29, *132*
2:5–11, *89*
2:6–11, *90, 130*
2:7–8, *89*
2:8, *144*
2:8–11, *89*
2:9–11, *89*
2:17, *134*
3, 28, *79, 89*
3:1, *89*
3:1 – 4:1, *88*
3:2–6, *89*
3:3, *20, 90*

3:4–6, *15, 17–18, 26, 61*
3:6, *25, 27, 29, 89, 103, 117*
3:6–8, *89*
3:7–8, *27, 89*
3:8, *13, 89*
3:9, *90, 139, 142–143, 145, 147*
3:10, *90*
3:10–11, *89, 125*
3:10–12, *89*
3:12, *70*
3:13–14, *150*
3:17–19, *89*
3:20–21, *89*
4:10, *70*

Colossians
1:6, *92*
1:13–15, *92*
2:5, *145*
2:11, *20*
2:11–15, *93*
2:12, *82, 146*
2:13–15, *92*
2:14, *92*
2:15, *93*
2:16–23, *93*
3:1, *82*
3:4–6, *92*
3:11, *20*
3:13, *92*

1 Thessalonians
1:3, *78, 139*
1:4, *154*
1:5, *132*
1:8, *145*
1:8–10, *146*
1:9–10, *77, 130*

INDEX OF BIBLE REFERENCES

1:10, *48–49, 78*
1:15–16, *79*
2:13, *132*
2:14–16, *162*
3:1, *160*
3:1–10, *79*
3:5, *129*
3:6–8, *131*
4:1–6, *78*
4:3–8, *126*
4:4–5, *78*
4:9, *111*
4:13–18, *130*
4:14, *78*
5:4–5, *78*
5:5, *78*
5:8, *78*
5:10, *78*
5:24, *142*

2 Thessalonians
1:3, *79*
1:4–10, *77*
1:7, *49*
1:8, *134*
1:10–11, *79*
1:13–15, *79*
3:6–7, *78*

1 Timothy
1:8, *62, 92–93*
1:8–11, *91, 123*
1:12–16, *25*
1:13, *29*
1:14, *92*
3:16, *91, 172*
6:11, *91*
6:14, *98*

2 Timothy
1:9, *92, 100*
2:18, *82*

2:22, *91*
3:15–16, *92*
3:16, *91*
4:8, *91*
4:10, *160*
4:16, *160*

Titus
1:8, *91*
1:10, *93*
2:11, *92*
2:12, *91*
3:4–7, *91*
3:5, *92, 100, 133*

Philemon, *126*
5, *145*

Hebrews
1:1–2, *141*
2:1, *130*
2:2, *102*
2:5–9, *141*
2:10–18, *141*
2:17, *141*
3:1, *130, 141, 178*
3:2, *141*
3:12, *56, 130, 134*
3:14, *141*
3:19, *56, 134*
4:2–3, *134*
4:3, *129*
4:12–16, *141*
4:14–16, *130*
5:1–10, *141*
5:7–10, *130*
7:15–17, *130*
8:10, *97*
9:11 – 10:18, *141*
10:10, *178*

10:14, *178*
10:19, *178*
10:19–23, *179*
10:22, *129*
10:38–39, *134*
11:1, *129*
11:6, *134*
11:17–19, *181*
11:19, *182*
11:39–40, *141*
12:1, *141*
12:2, *134*
12:18–24, *179*
13:7, *134*

James
1:2–4, *180*
1:3, *130*
1:19–21, *182*
1:25, *180*
2:1, *130, 140, 179*
2:8, *180*
2:10–11, *102*
2:11, *180*
2:12, *180*
2:12–13, *180*
2:14, *179*
2:14–26, *129, 140, 179*
2:15–16, *180*
2:17, *179*
2:18–19, *148, 180*
2:19, *140, 179*
2:20, *179–180*
2:21, *180–181*
2:22, *180*
2:23, *180–182*
2:24, *180–181*
2:25, *180–181*
2:26, *179–181*

4:4, *181*
4:11–12, 52, *180*
5:1–6, *181*
5:9, *181*
5:10–11, *140,
182*

1 Peter, *66*
1:5–7, *130*
3:6, *135*
3:21, *178*
4:11, *56*

2 Peter
1:1, *130*
2:11, *52*

1 John, *130,
134, 178*
1:9, *178*
2:1, *178*
2:29, *178*
3:7, *178*
3:10, *178*
3:12, *178*
3:23, *134*

Jude
5, *130*
9, *52*

Revelation
1:2–3, *142*
1:5–6, *142*
2:10, *141*
2:13, *140–141*
2:15, *141*
2:19, *141*
3:14, *141*
5:1–14, *142*
11:7, *142*
12:10–12, *178*
12:17, *141*
13:10, *142*
14:12, *141–142*
15:5, *141*
17:14, *141*
19:10, *142*
19:11, *141*
22:16, *142*
22:18, *142*
22:20, *142*

Index of ancient writings

1 Enoch, *23*
2 Macc. 8:13, *56*
4 Ezra, *23*
  7:24, *136*

'Abot R. Natan B 10, *16*
Aelius Aristides, *Pros Platōna*
  peri rhētorikēs, line 230, *32*
Aeschylus, *Agamemnon* line
  1624, 32
Aristophanes Gramm.
  Historiae animalum
  epitome 2.431.3, *32*

b. 'Abod. Zar.
  10b, *16*
  18a, *66*
Baruch
  3:7, *23*
  4:36, *23*
  5:5–9, *23*

Euripides, *Bacchanalia* 795,
  32

Josephus, *Antiquities*
  18:57, *59*
  4:314, *24*
  10:112–113, *24*
  10:247–277, *24*
  11:1–4, *24*
Josephus, *Vita* 74, *61*
Josephus, *War* 2:301, *59*
Judith
  4:1–5, *23*

  5:17–19, *23*

Lev. Rab.
  1:11, *16*
  27:3, *16*
  30:12, *16*

m. 'Aboth
  1:11, *24*
  4:18, *24*
Midr. Deut. 33:2, *16*
m. Pesaḥ.
  10:4, *24*
  10:5, *24*
  10:6, *24*

Philo, *De Praemiis et Poenis*,
  162–172, *23*
Philo, *Quis Rerum Divinarum*
  Heres, 26–27, *23*
Philo*, Spec. Leg.* 2.249, *61*
Pindar (Maehler edition), 2:94,
  32
Prayer of Azariah 18, *23*
Psalms of Solomon, *23*

Qumran
  Cairo Damascus Document
    1:1–17, *23*
    3:10–21, *23*
  Temple Scroll 64:7–12, *30*

Sirach
  32:24, *136*
  33:3, *136*

28:6–7, *102*

Tobit
  14:1–9, *23*
14:7–9, *23*
t. Sanh. 13:2, *16*

Wis. Sol.
  1:2, *57*

10:7, *57*
12:17, *57*
14:25, *57*
15:7, *155*
18:13, *57*
13 – 14, *50*

y. Pe'a 1:1, *16*